Bounce

Bounce

Mozart, Federer,
Picasso, Beckham, and
the Science of Success

Matthew Syed

HARPER

An Imprint of HarperCollins*Publishers*
www.harpercollins.com

HarperCollins books may be purchased for educational, business, or sales promotional use. For information, please write: Special Markets Department, HarperCollins Publishers, 10 East 53rd Street, New York, NY 10022.

Grateful acknowledgment for permission to reproduce illustrations is made to the following: *Richard Gregory*, page 218; *John Cassidy*, page 223; *Jon Entine*, page 259.

FIRST EDITION

Designed by Eric Butler

Library of Congress Cataloging-in-Publication Data

Syed, Matthew.
    Bounce : Mozart, Federer, Picasso, Beckham, and the science of success / Matthew Syed. — 1st ed.
        p.   cm.
    ISBN: 978-0-06-172375-9 (Hardcover)
    ISBN: 978-0-06-200474-1 (International Edition)
    1. Success. 2. Ability. 3. Expertise. 4. Gifted persons. 5. Excellence.
I. Title.
    BF637.S8S867   2010
    650.1—dc22   2009048135

10   11   12   13   14   ID/RRD   10   9   8   7   6   5   4   3   2   1

For Dilys

Contents

PART I: The Talent Myth

CHAPTER 1

The Hidden Logic of Success

3

CHAPTER 2

Miraculous Children?

55

CHAPTER 3

The Path to Excellence

77

CHAPTER 4

Mysterious Sparks and Life-Changing Mind-Sets

113

PART II: Paradoxes of the Mind

CHAPTER 5

The Placebo Effect

149

Contents

CHAPTER 6

The Curse of Choking and How to Avoid It

181

CHAPTER 7

Baseball Rituals, Pigeons, and Why Great Sportsmen
Feel Miserable After Winning

201

PART III: Deep Reflections

CHAPTER 8

Optical Illusions and X-Ray Vision

217

CHAPTER 9

Drugs in Sport, Schwarzenegger Mice,
and the Future of Mankind

233

CHAPTER 10

Are Blacks Superior Runners?

255

Acknowledgments   *287*
Notes   *289*
Index   *303*

PART I

The Talent Myth

CHAPTER 1

The Hidden Logic of Success

The Autobiographical Bias

In January 1995, I became the British number-one table tennis player for the very first time, which, I am sure you will agree, is a heck of an achievement. At twenty-four years of age, I suddenly found myself on the receiving end of regular invitations to speak to school audiences about my rise to international glory, and would often take my gold medals along to dazzle the youngsters.

Table tennis is a pretty big sport in the UK, with 2.4 million participants, 30,000 paid-up members of the governing body, thousands of teams, and serious riches for those who excel. But what made me special? What had marked me out for sporting greatness? I came up with a number of attributes: speed, guile, gutsiness, mental strength, adaptability, agility, reflexes.

Sometimes I would marvel at the fact that I had these skills in such abundance that they were capable of elevating me— little me!—beyond hundreds of thousands of others aspiring for that precious top spot. And all this was doubly amazing, considering I had been born into a family in an ordinary suburb of an ordinary town in southeast England. There was no silver spoon. No advantages. No nepotism. Mine was a triumph of individuality; a personal odyssey of success; a triumph against the odds.

This, of course, is the way that many who have reached the top in sport, or indeed in any other field, choose to tell their stories. We live in a culture that encourages this kind of soaring individualism. Hollywood is full of such narratives, often sugarcoated in American Dream sentimentality. But while these stories are inspirational, rousing, and compulsively entertaining, are they true? Here is my story in table tennis, retold with the bits that I chose to ignore the first time around, as they diminished the romance and the individuality of my triumph.

1. Table

In 1978 my parents, for a reason they are still unable to explain (neither of them play table tennis), decided to buy a table tennis table—a super deluxe 1000 with gold lettering, since you ask—and to put it in our large garage. I do not know the exact percentage, but you can imagine that there were not many youngsters of my age in my hometown who possessed a full-size, tournament-specification table. Fewer still had a garage in which it could be housed full-time. This was my first bit of good fortune.

2. My Brother

My second piece of good fortune was having an older brother named Andrew who came to love table tennis as much as I. We would play for hours in the garage after school: dueling, battling, testing each other's reflexes, experimenting with new spins, investigating new paddles, inviting friends over, who, although often more accomplished in other sports, were bemused to see just how far we had advanced in table tennis. Without knowing it, we were blissfully accumulating thousands of hours of practice.

3. Peter Charters

Mr. Charters was a teacher at the local primary school, a tall man with mustache, a twinkle in his eye, a disdain for conventional teaching methods, and a passion for sports that bordered on the fanatical. He was the coach of almost all of the after-school sporting clubs, the manager of the school soccer team, the organizer of school sports day, custodian of the badminton equipment, and inventor of a game called "Bucket Ball," a kind of improvised basketball.

But Charters cared about one thing above all: table tennis. He was the nation's top coach and a senior figure in the English Table Tennis Association. The other sports were just a front; an opportunity to scout sporting talent wherever it emerged so he could focus it—ruthlessly and exclusively—upon table tennis. No child who passed through Aldryngton School in Reading was not given a tryout by Charters. And such was his zeal, energy, and dedication to table tennis that anybody who showed potential was persuaded to take their skills forward at the local club, Omega.

Charters invited me and my brother Andy to join Omega in 1980, at the very moment we were beginning to outgrow the garage.

4. Omega

Omega was not a luxurious club—it was a one-table hut in a gravel enclosure a couple of miles from where we lived in suburban Reading: cold in winter, ferociously hot in summer, with plants growing through the roof and floor. But it had one advantage that made it almost unique anywhere in the county: it was open twenty-four hours a day, for the exclusive use of its tiny group of members, each of whom had a set of keys.

My brother and I took full advantage, training after school, before school, on weekends, and during the holidays. We were also joined by other Aldryngton alumni who had been spotted and snapped up by Charters, so that by 1981 Omega was becoming something of a sensation. One street alone (Silverdale Road, on which the school was situated) contained an astonishing number of the nation's top players.

At number 119 were the Syeds. Andrew, my brother, went on to become one of the most successful junior players in the history of the UK, winning three national titles before retiring due to injury in 1986. He was later described by Charters as the best young player to emerge from England for a quarter of a century. Matthew (that's me) also lived at 119 and became a long-serving England senior number one, a three-time Commonwealth champion, and a two-time Olympian.

At number 274, just opposite Aldryngton, lived Karen Witt.

She was one of the most brilliant female players of her generation. She won countless junior titles, the national senior title,
the hugely prestigious Commonwealth championship, and
dozens of other competitions in a sparkling career. When she
retired with back trouble at the age of twenty-five, she had
changed the face of women's table tennis in England.

At number 149, equidistant between the Syeds and the Witts,
lived Andy Wellman. He was a powerful player who would go
on to win a series of titles, mainly in doubles, and was widely
feared, particularly after defeating one of the top English players in the prestigious Top 12 event.

At the bottom of Silverdale Road was Paul Trott, another
leading junior, and Keith Hodder, an outstanding county
player. Around the corner were Jimmy Stokes (England junior
champion), Paul Savins (junior international), Alison Gordon
(four times English senior champion), Paul Andrews (top national player), and Sue Collier (England schools champion). I
could go on.

For a period in the 1980s, this one street, and the surrounding vicinity, produced more outstanding table tennis players
than the rest of the nation combined. One road among tens
of thousands of roads; one tiny cohort of schoolkids against
millions up and down the country. Silverdale Road was the
wellspring of English table tennis: a Ping-Pong mecca that
seemed to defy explanation or belief.

Had some genetic mutation spread throughout the local
vicinity without touching the surrounding roads or villages?
Of course not: the success of Silverdale Road was about the
coming together of factors of a beguilingly similar kind to
those that have, from time to time, elevated other tiny areas
on our planet into the sporting ascendancy (Spartak, an
impoverished tennis club in Moscow, for example, created

more top-twenty women players between 2005 and 2007 than the whole of the United States).

In particular, all of the sporting talent was focused ruthlessly on table tennis, and all of the aspiring players were nurtured by an outstanding coach. And as for me, with a table in the garage and a brother as passionate about Ping-Pong as myself, I had a head start before I even got to Aldryngton.

The Myth of Meritocracy

My parents—bless them—continue to describe my success in table tennis as an inspirational triumph against the odds. That is kind indeed, and I thank them for it. When I showed them a draft of this chapter, they disputed its entire thesis. Yes, but what about Michael O'Driscoll (a rival from Yorkshire)? He had all your advantages, but he didn't make it. What about Bradley Billington (another rival from Derbyshire)? He had parents who were international table tennis players, but he did not become England's number one.

This is merely a slightly different twist on what I call the autobiographical bias. My point is not that I was a bad table tennis player; rather, it is that I had powerful advantages not available to hundreds of thousands of youngsters. I was, in effect, the best of a very small bunch. Or, to put it another way, I was the best of a very big bunch, only a tiny fraction of whom had my opportunities.

What is certain is that if a big enough group of youngsters had been given a table at eight, had a brilliant older brother to practice with, had been trained by one of the top coaches in the country, had joined the only twenty-four-hour club in the county, and had practiced for thousands of hours by their early teens, I would not have been number one in England. I might not have even been number one thousand and one in England. Any other conclusion is a crime against statistics (it is of course *possible* that I would have been number one, but the possibility is strictly theoretical).

We like to think that sport is a meritocracy—where achievement is driven by ability and hard work—but it is nothing of the sort. Think of the thousands of potential table tennis champions not fortunate enough to live on Silverdale Road, with its peculiar set of advantages. Think of the thousands of potential Wimbledon champions who have never been fortunate enough to own a tennis racket or receive specialized coaching. Think of the millions of potential major-winning golfers who have never had access to a golf club.

Practically every man or woman who triumphs against the odds is, on closer inspection, a beneficiary of unusual circumstances. The delusion lies in focusing on the individuality of their triumph without perceiving—or bothering to look for—the powerful opportunities stacked in their favor.

This is one of the central points made by Malcolm Gladwell in his marvelous book *Outliers*. Gladwell shows how the success of Bill Gates, the Beatles, and other outstanding performers is not so much to do with "what they are like" but rather "where they come from." "The people who stand before kings may look like they did it all by themselves," Gladwell writes. "But in fact they are invariably the beneficiaries of hidden advantages and extraordinary opportunities and cultural legacies that allow them to learn and work hard and make sense of the world in ways others cannot."

Whenever I am inclined to think I am unique and special, I remind myself that had I lived one door farther down the road, I would have been in a different school district, which would have meant that I would not have attended Aldryngton, would never have met Peter Charters, and would never have joined Omega. It is often said that in elite sport the margins of victory and defeat are measured in milliseconds: the reality is that they are measured in variables that are far more elusive.

But it is worth pausing here for a moment to consider an objection. You may agree with the thrust of the argument that opportunity is *necessary* for success, but is it *sufficient*? What about the natural gifts that mark out the very best from the rest? Are these skills not necessary to get to a Wimbledon final or the top of an Olympic podium? Are they not vital to becoming a chess grandmaster or the CEO of a multinational? Is it not delusional to suppose that you (or your children) can achieve great success without also possessing rare talent?

This has been the abiding presumption of modern society ever since Francis Galton, an English Victorian polymath, published his book *Hereditary Genius*. In the book, Galton wields the insights of his half cousin Charles Darwin to come up with a theory of human achievement that remains in the ascendancy to this day.

"I propose to show," Galton wrote, "that a man's natural abilities are derived by inheritance, under exactly the same limitations as are the form and physical features of the whole organic world. . . . I have no patience with the hypothesis . . . that babies are born pretty much alike and the sole agencies in creating differences . . . are steady application and moral effort."

The idea that natural talent determines success and failure is, today, so powerful that it is accepted without demur. It *seems* indisputable. When we watch Roger Federer caressing a cross-court forehand winner or a chess grandmaster playing twenty games simultaneously while blindfolded or Tiger Woods launching a 350-yard fade, we are irresistibly drawn to the conclusion that they possess special gifts not shared by the rest of us.

The skills are so qualitatively different, so detached from our own lives and experience, that the very idea that we could achieve similar results if given the same opportunities seems nothing less than ridiculous.

The metaphors we use to describe outstanding achievers encourage this way of thinking. Roger Federer, for example, has been said to have "tennis encoded in his DNA." Tiger Woods is said to have been "born to play golf." Top performers subscribe to this way of thinking, too. Diego Maradona once claimed he was born with "soccer skill in my feet."

But is talent what we think it is?

What Is Talent?

In 1991 Anders Ericsson, a psychologist at Florida State University, and two colleagues conducted the most extensive investigation ever undertaken into the causes of outstanding performance.

Their subjects—violinists at the renowned Music Academy of West Berlin in Germany—were divided into three groups. The first group comprised the outstanding students: the boys and girls expected to become international soloists, the pinnacle of musical performance. These were the kids who would normally be described as supertalented, the youngsters supposedly lucky enough to have been born with special musical genes.

The second group of students was extremely good, but not as accomplished as the top performers. These students were expected to end up playing in the world's top orchestras, but not as star soloists. In the final group were the least able students: teenagers studying to become music teachers, a course with far less stringent admission standards.

The ability levels of the three groups were based on the assessment of the professors and corroborated by objective measures such as success in open competitions.

After a painstaking set of interviews, Ericsson found that the biographical histories of the three groups were remarkably similar and showed no systematic differences. The age when the students began practice was around eight years old, which was the same time when they began formal lessons. The average age when they first decided to become musicians was just before they turned fifteen. The average number of music teachers who had taught them was 4.1, and the average number of musical instruments that they had studied beyond the violin was 1.8.

But there was one difference between the groups that was both dramatic and unexpected; indeed, it was so stark that it almost jumped out at Ericsson and his colleagues—the number of hours devoted to serious practice.

By the age of twenty, the best violinists had practiced an average of ten thousand hours, *more than two thousand hours more than the good violinists* and *more than six thousand hours more than the violinists hoping to become music teachers*. These differences are not just statistically significant; they are extraordinary. Top performers had devoted thousands of additional hours to the task of becoming master performers.

But that's not all. Ericsson also found that there were no

exceptions to this pattern: nobody who had reached the elite group without copious practice, and nobody who had worked their socks off but failed to excel. Purposeful practice was the only factor distinguishing the best from the rest.

Ericsson and his colleagues were astounded by these findings, sensing that they heralded a paradigm shift in the way excellence is understood—that it is practice, not talent, that ultimately matters. "We deny that these differences [in skill level] are immutable; that is, due to innate talent," they wrote. "Instead we argue that the differences between expert performers and normal adults reflect a life-long persistence of deliberate effort to improve performance."

The aim of the first part of this book is to convince you that Ericsson is right; that talent is not what you think it is; that you can accomplish all manner of things that seem so far beyond your current capabilities as to occupy a different universe. But this will not be a wishy-washy exercise in the power of positive thinking. Rather, the arguments will be grounded in recent findings in cognitive neuroscience that attest to the way the body and mind can be transformed with specialized practice.

After all, what *is* talent? Many people feel sure they know it when they see it; that they can look at a group of kids and discern from the way they move, the way they interact, the way they adapt, which of them contain the hidden genes necessary for success. As the managing director of a prestigious violin school puts it: "Talent is something a top violin coach can spot in young musicians that marks them out as destined for greatness."

But how does the teacher know that this accomplished young performer, who looks so gifted, has not had many hours of special training behind the scenes? How does she know that the initial differences in ability between this young-ster and the rest will persist over many years of practice? In fact, she doesn't, as a number of studies have demonstrated.

An investigation of British musicians, for example, found that the top performers had learned no faster than those who reached lower levels of attainment: hour for hour, the various groups had improved at almost identical rates. The differ-ence was simply that top performers had practiced *for more hours*. Further research has shown that when top performers seem to possess an early gift for music it is often because they have been given extra tuition at home by their parents.

But what about child prodigies—kids who reach world class while still in adolescence? Have they not learned at a super-fast rate? Well, no. As we shall see in the next chapter, child prodigies may look as if they have reached the top in double-quick time, but the reality is that they have compressed astronomical quantities of practice into the short period be-tween birth and adolescence.

As John Sloboda, professor of psychology at Keele Uni-versity, puts it: "There is absolutely no evidence of a 'fast track' for high achievers." Jack Nicklaus, the most successful golfer of all time, has made the same point: "Nobody—but *nobody*—has ever become really proficient at golf without practice, without doing a lot of thinking and then hitting a lot of shots. It isn't so much a lack of talent; it's a lack of being able to repeat good shots consistently that frustrates most players. And the only answer to that is practice."

The same conclusion—about the primacy of practice—is arrived at by widening the perspective, as Ericsson has shown. Just consider the way in which standards have risen dramatically in just about every area of human endeavor. Take music: When Franz Liszt composed "Feux Follets" in

1826, it was said to be virtually unplayable; today it is performed by every top pianist.

The same is true in sports. When the winner of the men's 100 meters in the 1900 Olympics clocked 11.0 seconds, it was considered a miracle; today that time would not be sufficient to qualify for the final of the high school national trials. In diving, the double somersault was almost prohibited in the 1924 Olympics because it was considered dangerous; now it is routine. The fastest time for the marathon in the 1896 Olympics was just a few minutes faster than the entry time for the Boston Marathon, which is met by thousands of amateurs.

In academia, too, standards are spiraling ever upward. Thirteenth-century English scholar Roger Bacon argued that it was impossible to master mathematics in less than thirty to forty years; today calculus is taught to almost every college student. And so it goes on.

But the key point is that these improvements have not occurred because people are getting more talented: Darwinian evolution operates over a much longer time span. They must have occurred, therefore, because people are practicing longer, harder (due to professionalism), and smarter. It is the quality and quantity of practice, not genes, that is driving progress. And if that is true of society, why not accept that it is also true of individuals?

So the question is: How long do you need to practice in order to achieve excellence? Extensive research, it turns out, has come up with a very specific answer to that question: from art to science and from board games to tennis, it has been found that a minimum of ten years is required to reach world-class status in any complex task.

In chess, for example, Herbert Simon and William Chase, two American psychologists, found that nobody had attained the level of an international grandmaster "with less than a decade's intense preparation with the game." In music composition, John Hayes also found that ten years of dedication is required to achieve excellence, a verdict that features centrally in his book *The Complete Problem Solver*.

An analysis of the top nine golfers of the twentieth century showed that they won their first international competition at around twenty-five years of age, which was, on average, more than ten years after they started golfing. The same finding has been discovered in fields as diverse as mathematics, tennis, swimming, and long-distance running.

The same is even true in academia. In a study of the 120 most important scientists and 123 most famous poets and authors of the nineteenth century, it was found that ten years elapsed between their first work and their best work. Ten years, then, is the magic number for the attainment of excellence.

In *Outliers*, Malcolm Gladwell points out that most top performers practice for around one thousand hours per year (it is difficult to sustain the quality of practice if you go beyond this), so he redescribes the ten-year rule as the ten-thousand-hour rule. This is the minimum time necessary for the acquisition of expertise in any complex task. It is also, of course, the number of hours that the top violinists had practiced in the Ericsson experiment.*

Now think about how often you have heard people dismiss their own potential with statements like "I am not a natural linguist" or "I don't have the brain for numbers" or "I lack the coordination for sports." Where is the evidence for such

---

* One rather obvious proviso: in activities where there are not many participants, world-class status can be achieved in somewhat less than ten thousand hours. After all, it is not difficult to be among the best in the world in a sport—or, indeed, anything else—that few others play seriously.

pessimism? Often it is based upon nothing more than a few weeks or a few months of halfhearted effort. What the science is telling us is that *many thousands of hours of practice* are necessary to break into the realm of excellence.

Before going on, it's worth emphasizing something about the upcoming chapters: the truth of the arguments will have urgent implications for the way we choose to live our lives. If we believe that attaining excellence hinges on talent, we are likely to give up if we show insufficient early promise. And this will be perfectly rational, given the premise.

If, on the other hand, we believe that talent is not (or is only marginally) implicated in our future achievements, we are likely to persevere. Moreover, we will be inclined to move heaven and earth to get the right opportunities for ourselves and our families: the right teacher, access to decent facilities; the entire coalition of factors that leads to the top. And, if we are right, we *will eventually excel*. What we decide about the nature of talent, then, could scarcely be more important.

To conclude this section, here's an example from *Outliers* that evokes the twin insights of modern research on excellence: namely, the importance of *opportunity* on the one hand and *practice* on the other.

In the mid-1980s, Roger Barnsley, a Canadian psychologist, was with his family at a Lethbridge Broncos ice hockey game when he was alerted by his wife—who was leafing through the program—to what looked like an extraordinary coincidence: many of the players had birthdays in the early months of the calendar.

"I thought she was crazy," Barnsley told Gladwell. "But I looked through it, and what she was saying just jumped out at me. For some reason, there were an incredible number of January, February, and March birth dates."

What was going on? Had a genetic mutation affected only those Canadian hockey players born in the early part of the year? Was it something to do with the alignment of the stars in the early part of the calendar?

In fact the explanation was simple: the eligibility cutoff date for all age-based hockey in Canada is January 1. That means that a ten-year-old boy born in January could be playing alongside another boy born almost twelve months later. This difference in age can represent a huge difference in terms of physical development at that time of life.

As Gladwell puts it:

> This being Canada, the most hockey-crazed country on earth, coaches start to select players for the traveling "rep" squad—the all-star teams—at the age of nine or ten, and of course they are more likely to view as talented the bigger and more coordinated players, who have had the benefit of critical extra months of maturity.
>
> And what happens when a player gets chosen for a rep squad? He gets better coaching, and his teammates are better, and he plays fifty or seventy-five games a season instead of twenty games a season. . . . [By] the age of thirteen or fourteen, with the benefit of better coaching and all that extra practice under his belt, he really *is* better, so he's the one more likely to make it to the Major Junior A league, and from there into the big leagues.

The skewed distribution of birth dates is not limited to the Canadian junior hockey league. It is also seen in European youth soccer and U.S. youth baseball; indeed, most sports where age-based selection and streaming are part of the process of molding the stars of the future.

This punctures many of the myths that cling to elite performers. It shows that those who make it to the top, at least in certain sports, are not necessarily more talented or dedicated than those left behind: it may just be that they are a little older. An arbitrary difference in birth date sets in train a cascade of consequences that, within a matter of a few years, has created an unbridgeable chasm between those who, in the beginning, were equally well equipped for sporting stardom.

Month of birth is, of course, just one of the many hidden forces shaping patterns of success and failure in this world. But what most of these forces have in common—at least when it comes to attaining excellence—is the extent to which they confer (or deny) opportunities for serious practice. Once the opportunity for practice is in place, the prospects of high achievement take off. And if practice is denied or diminished, no amount of talent is going to get you there.

This speaks directly to my experiences in table tennis. With a table tennis table in the garage at home and a brother to practice with, I had a head start on my classmates. It was only a slight head start, but it was sufficient to create a *trajectory of development* with powerful long-term consequences. My superior ability was taken for evidence of talent (rather than lots of hidden practice), and I was selected for the school team, leading to yet more practice sessions. Then I joined Omega, the local club, then the regional team, then the national team.

By the time—a few years later—I was given a chance to perform in an exhibition match in front of the whole school, I possessed skills of an entirely different kind from those of my classmates. They stomped their feet and cheered as I whipped the ball back from all parts of the court. They marveled at my finesse and coordination and the other "natural gifts" that marked me out as an outstanding sportsman. But these skills were not genetic; they were, in large part, *circumstantial*.

In the same vein, it is not difficult to imagine a spectator in the stands of a major league hockey match watching in awe as a former classmate scores a winning goal of spellbinding brilliance. You can imagine him standing and applauding and, later, congregating with friends for an after-match drink to eulogize his hero and to reminisce about how he once played hockey alongside him at school.

But now suppose you suggested to the hockey fan that his hero—a player whose talent seems so irrepressible—might now be working in the local hardware store had his birthday been a few days earlier; that the star player could have strained every sinew to reach the top, but his ambition would have been swept away by forces too powerful to resist and too elusive to alter.

And now imagine suggesting to the fan that it is just possible that he may himself have become an all-star ice hockey player had his mother given birth just a few hours later: on January 1 instead of December 31.

He would probably think you were crazy.

Talent Is Overrated

If I were to utter random consonants one after the other with, say, a one-second pause between each one, how many do you think you could you repeat back to me? Let's try the experiment with the letters on the next page. Read along the line, pausing for a second or two at each letter; then, when you get to the end, close the book and see how many you can recall.

J E L C G X O R T N K L S

I'm guessing you managed around six or seven. If so, you are proving the basic tenet of one of the most renowned papers in cognitive psychology: "The Magical Number Seven, Plus or Minus Two," by George A. Miller of Princeton University, published in 1956. In that paper, Miller showed that the memory span of most adults extends to around seven items, and that greater recall requires intense concentration and sustained repetition.

Now consider the following feat of memory achieved by a person known in the literature as "SF" in a psychology lab at Carnegie Mellon University in Pittsburgh on July 11, 1978. The experiment was conducted by William Chase, a leading psychologist, and Anders Ericsson (the man who would later undertake the study of the violinists in Berlin).

They were testing SF on the digit span task. In this test, a researcher reads a list of random numbers, one per second, before asking the subject to repeat back as many digits, in order, as she can remember. On this day SF is being asked to recall an amazing twenty-two digits. Here is how SF got on, as described by Geoff Colvin in his wonderful book *Talent Is Overrated*:

> "All right, all right, all right," he muttered after Ericsson read him the list. "All right! All right. Oh . . . geez!" He clapped his hands loudly three times, then grew quiet and seemed to focus further. "Okay. Okay. . . . Four-thirteen-point-one!" he yelled. He was breathing heavily. *"Seventy-seven eighty-four!"* He was nearly screaming. *"Oh six oh three!"* Now he was screaming. *"Four-*

nine-four, eight-seven-oh!" Pause. *"Nine-forty-six!"*
Screeching now. Only one digit left. But it isn't there.
"Nine-forty-six-point . . . Oh, nine-forty-six-point . . ."
He was screaming and sounding desperate. Finally,
hoarse and strangled: *"TWO!"*

He had done it. As Ericsson and Chase checked the
results, there came a knock on the door. It was the
campus police. They'd had a report of someone screaming in the lab area.

Pretty amazing and rather dramatic, is it not? But this
memory performance by SF was just the beginning. A little
time later SF managed forty numbers, then fifty. Eventually,
after 230 hours of training over a period of almost two years,
SF managed to recall eighty-two digits, a feat that, if we were
to watch it unfold before our eyes, would lead us to the conclusion that it was the product of special "memory genes,"
"superhuman powers," or some other phrase from the vocabulary of expert performance.

This is what Ericsson calls the iceberg illusion. When we
witness extraordinary feats of memory (or of sporting or artistic prowess), we are witnessing the *end product of a process
measured in years*. What is invisible to us—the submerged
evidence, as it were—is the countless hours of practice that
have gone into the making of the virtuoso performance: the
relentless drills, the mastery of technique and form, the solitary concentration that have, literally, altered the anatomical
and neurological structures of the master performer. What we
do not see is what we might call the hidden logic of success.

This is the ten-thousand-hour rule revisited, except that
now we are going to dig down into its meaning, its scientific
provenance, and its application in real lives.

SF was selected by the researchers with one criterion in mind: his memory was no better than average. When he embarked on his training, he was able to remember only six or seven digits, just like you and me. So the amazing feats he eventually achieved must have been due not to innate talent, but to practice. Later, a friend of SF's reached 102 digits, with no indication that he had reached his ceiling. As Ericsson puts it, "There are apparently no limits to improvements in memory skill with practice."

Think about that for a moment or two, for it is a revolutionary statement. Its subversive element is not its specific claim about memory but its promise that *anybody* can achieve the same results with opportunity and dedication. Ericsson has spent the last thirty years uncovering the same groundbreaking logic in fields as diverse as sports, chess, music, education, and business.

"What we see again and again is the remarkable potential of 'ordinary' adults and their amazing capacity for change with practice," says Ericsson. This is tantamount to a revolution in our understanding of expert performance. The tragedy is that most of us are still living with flawed assumptions: in particular, we are laboring under the illusion that expertise is reserved for special people with special talents, inaccessible to the rest of us.

So, how did SF do it? Let's look again at the letter-remembering exercise. We saw that, under normal circumstances, remembering more than six or seven letters is pretty difficult without a great deal of concentration and without constantly repeating the letters to oneself. Now try remembering the thirteen letters on the next page. I suspect you will be able to do so without any difficulty whatsoever; indeed, without even bothering to read through the letters one by one.

ABNORMALITIES

Piece of cake, wasn't it? Why? For the simple reason that the letters were arranged in a sequence, or pattern, that was instantly familiar. You were able to recall the entire series of letters by, as it were, encoding them in a higher-order construct (i.e., a word). This is what psychologists call "chunking."

Now, suppose I was to write down a list of random words. We know from our previous exercise that you would probably be able to remember six or seven of them. That is the number of items that can be comfortably stored in short-term memory. But, at thirteen letters per word, you would, by implication, be remembering around eighty letters. By a process of "chunking," you have been able to remember as many letters as SF remembered numbers.

Think back to SF's battle with the digit span task. He kept saying things like "Three-forty-nine-point-two." Why? Geoff Colvin explains: "[W]hen he heard the digits 9 4 6 2, he thought of it as 9 minutes, 46.2 seconds, an excellent time for running two miles. Similarly, 4 1 3 1 became 4:13.1, a mile time."

SF's "words" were, in effect, mnemonics based on his experience as a club runner. This is what psychologists call a retrieval structure.

Now, let's take a detour into the world of chess. You'll be aware that chess grandmasters have astonishing powers of recall and are able to play a mind-boggling number of games at the same time, without even looking at the boards. Alexander Alekhine, a Russian grandmaster, once played twenty-eight games simultaneously while blindfolded in Paris in 1925, winning twenty-two, drawing three, and losing three.

Surely these feats speak of psychological powers that extend beyond the wit of "ordinary" people like you and me. Or do they?

In 1973, William Chase and Herbert Simon, two American psychologists, constructed a devastatingly simple experiment to find out (Chase is the researcher who would later conduct the experiment with SF). They took two groups of people—one consisting of chess masters, the other composed of novices—and showed them chessboards with twenty to twenty-five pieces set up as they would be in normal games. The subjects were shown the boards briefly and then asked to recall the positions of the pieces.

Just as expected, the chess masters were able to recall the position of every piece on the board, while the nonplayers were able to place only four or five pieces. But the genius of the experiment was about to be revealed. In the next set of tests, the procedure was repeated, except this time the pieces were set up not as in real games, but randomly. The novices, once again, were unable to recall more than five or so pieces. But the astonishing thing is that the experts, who had spent years playing chess, *were no better*: they were also stumped when trying to place more than five or six pieces. Once again, what looked like special powers of memory were in fact nothing of the kind.

What was going on? In a nutshell, when chess masters look at the positions of the pieces on a board, they see the equivalent of a word. Their long experience of playing chess enables them to chunk the pattern with a limited number of visual fixations in the same way that our familiarity with language enables us to chunk the letters constituting a familiar word. It is a skill derived from years of familiarity with the relevant "language," not from talent. As soon as the language of chess is disrupted by the random positioning of pieces, chess masters find themselves looking at a jumble of letters, just like the rest of us.

The same findings extend to other games like bridge, and much else besides. Time and again, the amazing abilities of experts turn out to be not innate gifts but skills drawn from years of dedication that disappear as soon as they are transported beyond their specific realm of expertise. Take SF. Even after he had built up the capacity to remember an astonishing eighty-two numbers, he was unable to recall more than six or seven random consonants.

Now let's shift up a gear by taking these insights into the realm of sports.

The Mind's Eye

In December 2004 I played a game of tennis with Michael Stich, the former Wimbledon tennis champion from Germany, at the Harbour Club, a plush sports facility in west London. The match was part of a promotional day pitting journalists against top tennis players to publicize an upcoming competition at the Royal Albert Hall in London. Most of the matches were lighthearted affairs, with Stich hamming it up and giving the journalists the runaround, much to the amusement of onlookers. But when I came up against Stich, I wanted to conduct a little experiment.

I asked Stich to serve at maximum pace. He has one of the fastest serves in the history of the sport—his personal best is 134 mph—and I was curious to see whether my reactions, forged over twenty years of international table tennis, would enable me to return it. Stich smiled at the request, graciously assented to it, and then spent a good ten minutes warming up, loosening his shoulders and torso to gain maximum leverage on the ball. The onlookers—around thirty or so club members—suddenly became very curious, and the atmosphere a little tense.

Stich came back onto court sporting a light sweat, bounced the ball, and glanced across the net, as was his routine. I crouched down and focused hard, coiled like a spring. I was confident I would return the serve, although I was not certain it would be much more than a soft mid-court lob. Stich tossed the ball high into the air, arched his back, and then, in what seemed like a whirl of hyperactivity, launched into his service action. Even as I witnessed the ball connecting with his racquet, it whirred past my right ear with a speed that produced what seemed like a clap of wind. I had barely rotated my neck by the time it thudded against the soft green curtains behind me.

I stood up straight, bemused, much to Stich's merriment and that of the onlookers, many of whom were squealing with laughter. I couldn't fathom how the ball had traveled so effortlessly fast from his racquet onto the court, and then pinged past my head. I asked him to send down another, then another. He served four straight aces before approaching the net with a shrug of the shoulder and a slap of my back. He told me that he had slowed down the last two serves to give me a fighting chance. I hadn't even noticed.

Most people would conclude from this rather humbling experience that the ability to connect with, let alone return, a serve delivered at more than 130 mph must belong exclusively to those with innate reaction speeds—what are sometimes called instincts—at the outer limits of human capability. It is an inference that almost jumps up and bites you when the ball has just rocketed so fast past your nose that you're relieved at having avoided injury.

But I was forbidden from reaching any such conclusion. Why? Because in different circumstances, *I have those extraordinary reaction speeds*. When I stand behind a table tennis table, I am able to react to, and return, smash-kills in the blink of an eye. The time available to return a serve in tennis is approximately 450 milliseconds; but there are fewer than 250 milliseconds in which to return a smash-kill in table tennis. So, why could I return the latter and not the former?

In 1984 Desmond Douglas, the greatest ever UK table tennis player, was placed in front of a screen containing a series of touch-sensitive pads at the University of Brighton. He was told that the pads would light up in a random sequence and that his task was to touch the relevant pad with the index finger of his favored hand as soon as he could, before waiting for the next pad to light up. Douglas was highly motivated, as all the other members of the team had already undergone the test and were ribbing him in the familiar manner of team rivalry.

First one pad, then another, lit up. Each time Douglas jabbed his finger toward the pad, his eyes scanning the screen for the next target. After a minute, the task ended and Douglas's teammates (I was one of them: at thirteen years of age, I was at my first senior training camp) gave him a round of applause. Douglas grinned as the researcher left the room to collate the results. After five minutes, the researcher returned. He announced that Douglas's reactions were the slowest in the entire England team: he was slower than the juniors and the cadets; slower even than the team manager.

I remember the intake of breath to this day. This wasn't supposed to happen. Douglas was universally considered to have the fastest reactions in world table tennis, a reputation he continues to command more than ten years after his retirement. His style was based on standing with his stomach a couple of inches from the edge of the table, allowing the ball to ricochet from his paddle using lightning reflexes that astounded audiences around the world. He was so sharp that even the leading Chinese players—who had a reputation for extreme speed—were forced to retreat when they came up against him. But here was a scientist telling us that he had the most sluggish reactions in the whole of the England team.

It is not surprising that, after the initial shock, the researcher was laughed out of the room. He was told that the machine must be faulty or that he was measuring the wrong data. Later, the England team manager informed the science staff at Brighton that their services would no longer be required. Sports science was a new discipline back then, and the England manager had shown unusual innovation in seeing if his team could benefit from its insights, but this experiment seemed to prove that it had little to teach table tennis.

What nobody considered—not even the unfortunate researcher—was that Douglas really *did* have the slowest reactions in the team, and that his speed on a table tennis court was the consequence of something entirely different. But what?

I am standing in a room at Liverpool John Moores University in the northwest of England. In front of me is a screen containing a life-size projection of a tennis player standing at the other end of a virtual court. An eye-tracking system is trained on my eyes, and my feet are placed on sensors. The whole thing has been put together by Mark Williams, professor of motor behavior at Liverpool John Moores and arguably the world's leading expert on perceptual expertise in sport.

Mark hits the play button and I watch as my "opponent" tosses the ball to serve and arches his back. I am concentrating hard and watching intently, but I have already demonstrated why I was unable to return the serve of Stich.

"You were looking in the wrong place," says Mark. "Top tennis players look at the trunk and hips of their opponents on return in order to pick up the visual clues governing where they are going to serve. If I was to stop the picture in advance of the ball being hit, they would still have a pretty good idea about where it was going to go. You were looking variously at his racquet and the arm, which give very little information about the future path of the ball. You could have had the fastest reactions in history, and you still would not have made contact with the ball."

I ask Mark to replay the tape and adjust my focus to look at the places rich in information, but it makes me even more sluggish. Mark laughs. "It is not as simple as just knowing about where to look; it is also about grasping the meaning of what you are looking at. It is about looking at the subtle patterns of movement and postural clues and extracting information. Top tennis players make a small number of visual fixations and 'chunk' the key information."

Think back to the master chess players. You'll remember that when they looked at a board, they saw words: that is to say, they were able to chunk the position of the pieces as a consequence of their long experience of trying to find the best moves in chess games. Now we can see that the very same thing is happening in tennis.

When Roger Federer returns a service, he is not demonstrating sharper reactions than you and I; what he is showing is that he can extract more information from the service action of his opponent and other visual clues, enabling him to move into position earlier and more efficiently than the rest of us, which in turn allows him to make the return—in his case a forehand cross-court winner rather than a queen to checkmate.

This revolutionary analysis extends across the sporting domain, from badminton to baseball and from fencing to football. Top performers are not born with sharper instincts (in the same way that chess masters do not possess superior memories); instead, they possess enhanced awareness and anticipation. In cricket, for example, a first-class batsman has already figured out whether to play off the back foot or front foot more than 100 milliseconds before a bowler has even released the ball.

As Janet Starkes, professor emerita of kinesiology at McMaster University, has put it, "The exploitation of advance information results in the time paradox where skilled performers seem to have all the time in the world. Recognition of familiar scenarios and the chunking of perceptual information into meaningful wholes and patterns speeds up processes."

The key thing to note is that these cannot possibly be innate skills: Federer did not come into this mortal world with knowledge of where to look or how to efficiently extract information on a service return any more than SF was born with special memory skills (he wasn't: that is precisely why he was selected by Ericsson) or chess players have innate board-game memory skills (remember that their advantage is eliminated when the pieces are randomly placed).

No, Federer's advantage has been gathered from experience: more precisely, it has been gained from a painstaking process of encoding the meaning of subtle patterns of movement drawn from more than ten thousand hours of practice and competition. He is able to see the patterns in his opponent's movements in the same way that chess players are able to discern the patterns in the arrangement of pieces on a chessboard. It is his regular practice that has given him this expertise, not his genes.

You might suppose that Federer's speed is transferable to all sports and games (rather as one is inclined to assume that SF's memory skill is transferable), but you would be wrong. I played a match of real tennis—an ancient form of tennis played indoors with sloping roofs called penthouses, a hard ball, and entirely different techniques—with Federer at Hampton Court Palace in southwest London in the summer of 2005 (part of a promotional day for his watch sponsor). I found that, for all his grace and elegance, Federer could scarcely make contact with the ball when it was played at any serious speed (neither, for that matter, could I).

Some of the onlookers were surprised by this, but this is precisely what is predicted by the new science of expertise. Speed in sport is not based on innate reaction speed, but derived from highly specific practice. I have regularly played table tennis with world-renowned soccer players, tennis players, golfers, boxers, badminton players, rowers, squash players, and track and field athletes and discovered that they are all dramatically slower in their table-tennis-specific response times than even elderly players who have had the benefit of regular practice.

Recently I went to the Birmingham home of Desmond Douglas, the Speedy Gonzales of English table tennis, to try to figure out how someone with such unimpressive innate reactions could have become the fastest man in the history of one of the world's fastest sports. Douglas welcomed me through the door with a friendly grin: he is now in his fifties, but remains as lean and fit as when he was terrorizing players around the world with speed that seemed to defy logic.

Douglas offered the suggestion that he has a "great eye for the ball," which is the way quick reactions are often "explained" in high-level sport. The problem is that researchers have never been able to find any connection between sporting ability and the special powers of vision supposedly possessed by top performers. In 2000 the visual function of elite and non-elite soccer players was tested using standardized measures of visual acuity, stereoscopic depth, and peripheral awareness. The elite players were no better than their less accomplished counterparts, and neither group recorded above-average levels of visual function.

It had to be something else. I asked Douglas to tell me about his early education in table tennis, and the mystery was instantly solved. It turns out that Douglas had perhaps the most unusual grounding of any international table tennis player of the last half century. Brought up in working-class Birmingham, struggling and unmotivated in his academic work, Douglas happened upon a table tennis club at school. The tables were old and decrepit, but functional.

The problem was that they were housed in the tiniest of classrooms. "Looking back, it was pretty unbelievable," Douglas said, shaking his head. "There were three tables going along the length of the room to accommodate all the players who wanted to take part, but there was so little space behind the tables that we had to stand right up against the edge of the tables to play, with our backs almost touching the blackboard."

I managed to track down a few of the others who played in that era. "It was an amazing time," one said. "The claustrophobia of the room forced us to play a form of 'speed table tennis' where everyone had to be super-sharp. Spin and strategy hardly came into it; the only thing that mattered was speed."

Douglas did not spend a few weeks or months honing his skills in that classroom, but *the first five years of his development*. "We all loved playing table tennis, but Des was different," another classmate told me. "While the rest of us had other hobbies and interests, he spent all his time in that classroom practicing his skills and playing matches. I have never seen anyone with such dedication."

Douglas was sometimes called the "lightning man," because he seemed to be so fast he could duck a bolt from the blue. His speed baffled opponents and teammates for decades. Even Douglas was perplexed by it. "Maybe I have a sixth sense," he said. But we can now see that the solution to the riddle is simple. In essence, Douglas spent more hours than any other player in the history of the sport encoding the characteristics of a highly specific type of table tennis: the kind played at maximum pace, close to the table. By the time he arrived in international table tennis, he was able to perceive where the ball was going before his opponents had even hit it. That is how a man with sluggish reactions became the fastest player on the planet.

It is worth pausing here to anticipate an objection or two. You might agree with the thrust of the argument that expertise in table tennis, tennis, soccer, or anything else requires the performer to have built up a powerful knowledge base drawn from experience. But you might still sense that something in this account is missing.

In particular you may feel that recognizing the patterns in an opponent's movement and framing the optimal response (a cross-court forehand, say) is a very different thing from actually *executing the stroke*. The former is a mental skill drawn from experience, but the latter seems to be more of a *physical talent* requiring coordination, control, and feel. But is this schism between the mental and the physical quite what it seems?

It is often said that Federer and other top sportsmen have "amazing hands," which neatly emphasizes the supposed physical dimension of hitting a winning smash or dabbing a delicate drop shot. But is there really something in Federer's fingers or palm that sets him apart from other tennis players?

Or would it not be more accurate to say that his advantage consists in the sophistication with which he is able to control the motor system (the part of the peripheral nervous system responsible for movement) such that his racket impacts the ball with precisely the right angle, force, speed, direction, and finesse? Or, to use computer parlance, is not the genius of Federer's shot execution reflected in a supremacy in software rather than hardware?

This is not to deny that any tennis player needs an arm and a hand (and a racquet!) to make a return, but simply to emphasize that the limiting factor in making a world-class stroke is not strength or brute force, but the executive control of fine motor movement to create *perfect timing*.

The key point, for our purposes, is that this is not something top sportsmen are born with. If you were to go back to the time when Roger Federer was learning technique, you would find that he was ponderous and sluggish. His movements would have been characterized by conscious control of the skill, lacking smoothness or unity. Only later, after countless of hours of practice, were his skills integrated into an intricate set of procedures capable of flexible execution.

Today Federer's motor programs are so deeply ingrained that if you were to ask him how he is able to play an immaculately timed forehand, he wouldn't be able to tell you. He might be able to talk about what he was thinking at the time or the strategic importance of the shot, but he wouldn't be able to provide any insight into the mechanics of the movements that made the stroke possible. Why? Because Federer has practiced for so long that the movement has been encoded in implicit rather than explicit memory. This is what psychologists call expert-induced amnesia.

It is also worth noting that the development of motor expertise (skilled movement) is inseparable from the development of perceptual expertise (chunking patterns). After all, perfect technique is hardly useful if you fail to hit the ball—think of a totally blind person trying to play tennis. Highly refined, instantly chunked perceptual information is necessary to integrate the movement of the body with the movement of the ball (hand-eye coordination). Without this information the motor program would be nothing more than a stab in the dark.

Great shot-making, then, is not about developing "muscle memory"; rather, the memory is encoded in the brain and central nervous system.

The ascendency of the *mental and the acquired* over the *physical and the innate* has been confirmed again and again. As Anders Ericsson, now widely acknowledged as the world's leading authority on expert performance, puts it: "The most important differences are not at the lowest levels of cells or muscle groups, but at the athletes' superior control over the integrated and coordinated actions of their bodies. Expert performance is mediated by acquired mental representations that allow the experts to anticipate, plan and reason alternative courses of action. These mental representations provide experts with increased control of the aspects that are relevant to generating their superior performance."

In other words, it is practice, not talent, that holds the key to success.

Knowledge Is Power

At 3:00 p.m. on February 10, 1996, Garry Kasparov strode into a small room in the Pennsylvania Convention Center to contest one of the most anticipated chess matches in history. He was smartly dressed in a dark suit and white shirt and wore a look of intense concentration. As he sat down at the match table, he glanced across the board to the man on the other side: Dr. Feng-Hsuing Hsu, a bespectacled Taiwanese American with a quizzical expression.

In the room, besides Kasparov and Hsu, were three cameramen, one match official, three members of Kasparov's entourage, and a technical adviser. A strict silence was enforced, with the five hundred spectators packed into a nearby lecture hall to witness the event on screens fed from three TV cameras and live commentary from grandmaster Yasser Seirawan. The atmosphere was, by common consent, quite unlike that of any other chess match in living memory.

Kasparov is almost universally considered to be the greatest player in the history of the sport. His ELO rating—an official score measuring relative skill—remains the highest ever recorded: 71 points higher than that of Russian grandmaster Anatoly Karpov, and 66 higher than that of the great American player Bobby Fischer. Kasparov, at the time of the contest, had been the world number one for ten straight years, and his mere presence before a chessboard was enough to intimidate some of the world's most revered grandmasters.

But his opponent on this day was susceptible neither to intimidation nor the other mind games for which Kasparov was famous. His opponent was oblivious to Kasparov's status and reputation for guile and audacity. Indeed, his opponent was not even in the room, but many miles away in a large, dimly lit building in Yorktown Heights, New York. His opponent was a computer. Its name was Deep Blue.

The media, rather predictably, hyped the match as an historic showdown between man and machine. "The future of humanity is on the line," declared one newscaster. "The match goes further than mere chess, presenting a challenge to mankind's sovereignty," intoned *USA Today*. Even Kasparov seemed to be seduced by the apocalyptic tenor of the prematch hype, saying, "This is a mission to defend human dignity. . . . It is species-defining."

Kasparov's opening move, pawn to C5, was typed into a computer adjacent to the match table by Mr. Hsu (the brains behind the development of Deep Blue, on behalf of electronics giant IBM) and then transmitted across to the IBM Center in New York by a relatively new technology called the Internet.

At this point Deep Blue sprang into action. Powered by 256 specially developed chess processors operating in parallel, 32 concentrated on each eight-square section of the board, it was able to compute more than 100 million positions per second. A few moments later, Deep Blue's response came winging its way across the ether, and Mr. Hsu dutifully executed the instruction: pawn to C3.

For six games over eight days, the thrust and counterthrust between man and machine was beamed to a captivated world. Kasparov, an eccentric and hot-tempered Azerbaijani, was famous for his histrionics, often growling and shaking his head vigorously. Many had criticized Kasparov's antics, accusing him of deliberately trying to disturb adversaries. But Kasparov was no less animated against his machine opponent, often rising from his chair to pace the room.

Just before the fortieth move in the final game on February 17, Kasparov took his watch from the table and put it on his wrist. This was a familiar sign that the world champion believed the match was nearing its conclusion. The audience in the lecture room held its breath. Three moves later Dr. Hsu rose slowly to his feet and offered his hand to his opponent. The audience burst into wild applause.

Kasparov had triumphed.

The question is: How? How could a man unable to search more than three moves per second (this represents the current limit of human capacity) defeat a machine whose computing speed was measured in the tens of millions? The answer, as we shall see, will help us to unlock some of the deepest mysteries of expert performance, both within sport and in the wider world.

In the 1990s Gary Klein, a New York psychologist, embarked on a major study funded by the U.S. military to examine decision making in the real world. He was looking to test the theory that expert decision makers wield logical methods, examining the various alternatives before selecting the optimal choice. Klein's problem was that the longer the study went on, the less the theory bore any relation to the way decisions are made in practice.

The curious thing was not that top decision makers—medical professionals, firefighters, military commanders, and so on—were making choices based on unexpected factors; it was that they *did not seem to be making choices at all*. They were contemplating the situation for a few moments and then just deciding, without considering the alternatives. Some were unable even to explain how they happened upon the course of action they actually took.

Here is an example of a fire lieutenant making a lifesaving decision, as recounted in Klein's book *Sources of Power: How People Make Decisions*:

There is a simple house fire in a one-story house in a residential neighborhood. The fire is in the back, in the kitchen area. The lieutenant leads his hose crew into the building, to the back, to spray water on the fire, but the fire just roars back at them.

"Odd," he thinks. The water should have more of an impact. They try dousing it again, and get the same results. They retreat a few steps to regroup.

Then the lieutenant starts to feel as if something is not right. He doesn't have any clues; he just doesn't feel right about being in that house, so he orders his men out of the building—a perfectly standard building with nothing out of the ordinary.

As soon as his men leave the building, the floor where they had been standing collapses. Had they still been inside, they would have plunged into the fire below.

Later, when Klein asked the commander how he knew something was about to go terribly wrong, the commander put it down to "extrasensory perception." That was the only thing he could come up with to explain a lifesaving decision, and others like it, that seemed to emerge from nowhere. Klein was too much of a rationalist to accept the idea of ESP, but by now he had begun to notice equally perplexing abilities among other expert decision makers. They seemed to know what to do, often without knowing why.

One of Klein's coworkers, who had spent many weeks studying the neonatal unit of a large hospital, had found that experienced nurses were able to diagnose an infection in babies even when, to outsiders, there seemed to be no visible clues. This was not merely remarkable, but often lifesaving: infants at an early stage of life can quickly succumb to infections if they are not detected early.

Perhaps the most curious thing of all was that the hospital would perform tests to check the accuracy of the nurse's diagnosis, and occasionally these would come back negative. But sure enough, by the next day, the tests would come back positive—the nurse had been right all along. To the researcher this seemed almost magical, and even the nurses were baffled by it, attributing it to "intuition" or a "special sense."

What was going on? Can the insights gleaned from sport help to unlock the mystery?

Think back to Desmond Douglas, the Speedy Gonzales of English table tennis, who could anticipate the movement of a table tennis ball by chunking the pattern of his opponent's movement before the ball was even hit. Think, also, of how other top performers in sport seem to know what to do in advance of everyone else, creating the so-called time paradox where they are able to play in an unhurried way even under severe time constraints.

Klein came to realize that expert firefighters are relying on precisely the same mental processes. They are able to confront a burning building and almost instantly place it within the context of a rich, detailed, and elaborate conceptual scheme derived from years of experience. They can chunk the visual properties of the scene and comprehend its complex dynamics, often without understanding how. The fire commander called it "extrasensory perception"; Douglas, you will remember, cited his "sixth sense."

We can get an idea of what is going on by digging down into the mind of the fire commander who pulled his men out moments before the floor caved in. He did not suspect that the seat of the fire was in the basement, because he did not even know the house had a basement. But he was already curious, based upon his extensive experience, as to why the fire was not reacting as expected. The living room was hotter than it should have been for such a small fire, and it was altogether too quiet. His expectations were breached, but in ways so subtle he was not consciously aware of why.

Only with hindsight—and after hours of conversation with Klein—was it possible to piece together the sequence of events. The reason the fire was not quenched by his crew's attack was because its base was underneath them, and not in the kitchen; the reason it was hotter than expected was because it was rising from many feet below; the reason it was quiet is because the floor was muffling the noise. All this—

and many more interconnecting variables of indescribable complexity—was responsible for the fire commander taking the lifesaving decision to pull his men.

As Klein puts it, "The commander's experience had provided him with a firm set of patterns. He was accustomed to sizing up the situation by having it match one of these patterns. He may not have been able to articulate the patterns or describe their features, but he was relying on the pattern-matching process to let him feel comfortable that he had the situation scoped out."

A set of painstaking interviews with the nurses in the neonatal unit provided the same insights. In essence, the nurses were relying on their deep knowledge of perceptual cues, each one subtle, but which together signaled an infant in distress. The same mental process is used by pilots, military generals, detectives, you name it. It is also true, as we have seen, of top athletes. What they all have in common is long experience and deep knowledge.

For years knowledge was considered relatively unimportant in decision making. In experiments, researchers would choose participants with no prior experience of the area under examination in order to study the "cognitive processes of learning, reasoning and problem solving in their purest forms." The idea was that talent—superb general reasoning abilities and logical prowess—rather than knowledge makes for good decision makers.

This was the presumption of top business schools and many leading companies, too, as author Geoff Colvin has noted. They believed they could churn out excellent managers who could be parachuted into virtually any organization and transform it through superior reasoning. Experience was irrelevant, it was said, so long as you possessed a brilliant mind and the ability to wield the power of logic to solve problems. This approach was seriously misguided. When Jeff Immelt became the chief executive of General Electric in 2001, he commissioned a study of the best-performing companies in the world. What did they have in common? According to Colvin in *Talent Is Overrated*, "One key trait the study found was that these companies valued 'domain expertise' in managers—extensive knowledge of the company's field. Immelt has now specified 'deep domain expertise' as a trait required for getting ahead at GE."

These insights have not just become central to modern business strategy; they also form the basis of artificial intelligence. In 1957 two computer experts created a program they called the General Problem Solver, which they billed as a universal problem-solving machine. It did not have any specific knowledge, but possessed a "generic solver engine" (essentially a set of abstract inference procedures) that could, it was believed, tackle just about any problem.

But it was soon realized that knowledge-free computing—however sophisticated—is impotent. As Bruce Buchanan, Randall Davis, and Edward Feigenbaum, three leading researchers in artificial intelligence, put it: "The most important ingredient in any expert system is knowledge. Programs that are rich in general inference methods—some of which may even have some of the power of mathematical logic—but poor in domain-specific knowledge can behave expertly on almost no tasks."

Think back to the firefighters. Many young men are drawn to the profession because they think they're good at making decisions under pressure, but they quickly discover they just can't cut it. When they look at a raging fire, they are drawn to the color and height of the flames and other perceptually salient features, just like the rest of us. Only after a decade or more of on-the-job training can they place what they are seeing within the context of an interwoven understanding of the patterns of fires.

The essential problem regarding the attainment of excellence is that expert knowledge simply cannot be taught in the classroom over the course of a rainy afternoon, or indeed a thousand rainy afternoons (the firefighters studied by Klein had an average of twenty-three years of experience). Sure, you can offer pointers on what to look for and what to avoid, and these can be helpful. But relating the entirety of the information is impossible because the cues being processed by experts—in sport or elsewhere—are so subtle and relate to each other in such complex ways that it would take forever to codify them in their mind-boggling totality. This is known as *combinatorial explosion*, a concept that will help to nail down many of the insights of this chapter.

The best way to get a sense of the strange power of combinatorial explosion is to imagine folding a piece of paper in two, making the paper twice as thick. Now repeat the process a hundred times. How thick is the paper now? Most people tend to guess in the range of a few inches to a few yards. In fact the thickness would stretch eight hundred thousand billion times the distance from Earth to the sun.

It is the rapid escalation in the number of variables in many real-life situations—including sports—that makes it impossible to sift the evidence before making a decision: *it would take too long.* Good decision making is about compressing the informational load by decoding the meaning of patterns derived from experience. This cannot be taught in a classroom; it is not something you are born with; it must be lived and learned. To put it another way, it emerges through practice.

As Paul Feltovich, a researcher at the Institute for Human and Machine Cognition at the University of West Florida, has put it: "Although it is tempting to believe that upon knowing how the expert does something, one might be able to teach this to novices directly, this has not been the case. Expertise is a long-term developmental process, resulting from rich instrumental experiences in the world and extensive practice. These cannot simply be handed to someone."

All of which hints at the decisive advantage held by Kasparov over his machine opponent. Deep Blue had all the "talent": the ability to search moves at a rate measured in tens of millions per second. But Kasparov, although limited to a derisory three moves per second, had the knowledge—a deep, fertile, and endlessly elaborate knowledge of chess: the configurations of real games, how they can be translated into successful outcomes, the structure of defensive and offensive positions, and the overall construction of competitive chess. Kasparov could look at the board and see what to do in the same way an experienced firefighter can confront a blazing building and see what to do. Deep Blue can't.

It is worth noting something else here. You'll remember that SF, the person who performed so well on the digit span task, was able to remember more than eighty numbers by relating them to his experiences as a competitive runner. The numbers 9 4 6 2, for example, became 9 minutes, 46.2 seconds, a very good time for running two miles. SF's retrieval structure was, in effect, an ad hoc device derived from his life beyond the test.

Kasparov's memory of chess positions, on the other hand, is embedded in the living, breathing reality of playing chess. When he sees a chessboard, he does not chunk the pattern by relating it to an altogether different experience but by perceiving it immediately as the Sicilian Defense or the Latvian Gambit. His retrieval structure is rooted within the fabric of the game. This is the most powerful type of knowledge, and is precisely the kind possessed by firefighters, top athletes, and other experts.

By now it should be obvious why Deep Blue's gigantic advantage in processing speed was not sufficient to win—combinatorial explosion. Even in a game as simple as chess, the variables rapidly escalate beyond the capacity of any machine to compute. There are around thirty ways to move toward the beginning of a game, and thirty ways in which to respond. That amounts to around 800,000 possible positions after two moves each. A few moves after that, and the number of positions are measured in trillions. Eventually, there are more possible positions than there are atoms in the known universe.

To be successful, a player must cut down on the computational load by ignoring moves unlikely to result in a favorable outcome and concentrating on those with greater promise. Kasparov is able to do this by understanding the meaning of game situations. Deep Blue is not.

As Kasparov put it after winning game two of the six-game match: "Had I been playing the same game against a very strong human I would have had to settle for a draw. But I simply understood the essence of the end game in a way the computer did not. Its computational power was not enough to overcome my experience and intuitive appreciation of where the pieces should go."

Gary Klein, the psychologist who studied the firefighters, wanted to double-check whether chess players really do make rapid decisions based on the perceptual chunking of patterns (as opposed to conducting brute-force searches, like computers).

He reasoned that if the chunking theory is correct, top chess players would make similar decisions even if the available time was dramatically reduced. So he tested chess masters under "blitz" conditions, where each player has only five minutes on the clock, with around six seconds per move (in standard conditions there are forty moves in a ninety-minute period, allowing around two minutes, fifteen seconds per move).

Klein found that, for chess experts, the move quality hardly changed at all in blitz conditions, even though there was barely enough time to take the piece, move it, release it, and hit the timer.

Klein then tested the pattern-recognition theory of decision making directly. He asked chess experts to think aloud as they studied midgame positions. He asked them to tell him everything they were thinking, every move considered, including the poor ones, and especially the very first move considered. *He found that the first move considered was not only playable but also in many cases the best possible move from all the alternatives.*

This obliterates the presumption that chess is exclusively about computational force and processing speed. Like firefighters and tennis players, chess masters generate usable options as *the first ones they think of.* This looks magical when you first see it (particularly when chess masters are playing lots of games simultaneously), but that is because we have not seen the ten thousand hours of practice that have made it possible.

It is a bit like learning a language. At the beginning, the task of remembering thousands of words and fitting them together using abstract rules of grammar seems impossible. But after many years of experience, we can look at a random sentence and instantly comprehend its meaning. It is estimated that most English language users have a vocabulary of around 20,000 words. American psychologist Herbert Simon has estimated that chess masters command a comparable vocabulary of patterns, or chunks.

Now consider the scope of combinatorial explosion in games like ice hockey, American football, rugby, tennis, soccer, and the like. Even when scientists have invented simplified representations of these sports, they have quickly been overwhelmed by complexity. In robot soccer, for example, positions on the pitch are represented by 1680 × 1088 pixels. When you consider that a chessboard has eight by eight squares and that the pieces move in well-defined ways—unlike a soccer ball, which can fly anywhere at any time—you get some idea of the fiendish difficulty of designing a machine to compete without falling victim to information overload.

Now here's a description of Wayne Gretzky, arguably the greatest player in the history of ice hockey, taken from an article in the *New York Times Magazine* in 1997:

> Gretzky doesn't look like a hockey player. . . . Gretzky's gift, his genius even, is for seeing.
>
> To most fans, and sometimes even to the players on the ice, hockey frequently looks like chaos: sticks flailing, bodies falling, the puck ricocheting just out of reach. But amid the mayhem, Gretzky can discern the game's underlying pattern and flow, and anticipate what's going to happen faster and in more detail than anyone else in the building. . . .

Several times during a game you'll see him making what seem to be aimless circles on the other side of the rink from the traffic, and then, as if answering a signal, he'll dart ahead to a spot where, an instant later, the puck turns up.

This is a perfect example of expert decision making in practice: circumventing combinatorial explosion via advanced pattern recognition. It is precisely the same skill wielded by Kasparov, but on an ice hockey pitch rather than a chessboard. How was Gretzky able to do this? Let's hear from the man himself: "I wasn't naturally gifted in terms of size and speed; everything I did in hockey I worked for." And later: "The highest compliment that you can pay me is to say that I worked hard every day. . . . That's how I came to know where the puck was going before it even got there."

All of which helps to explain a qualification that was made earlier in the chapter: you will remember that the ten-thousand-hour rule was said to apply to any *complex* task. What is meant by complexity? In effect, it describes those tasks characterized by combinatorial explosion; tasks where success is determined, first and foremost, by superiority in software (pattern recognition and sophisticated motor programs) rather than hardware (simple speed or strength).

Most sports are characterized by combinatorial explosion: tennis, table tennis, soccer, hockey, and so on. Just try to imagine, for a moment, designing a robot capable of solving the real-time spatial, motor, and perceptual challenges necessary to defeat Roger Federer on a tennis court. The complexities are almost impossible to define, let alone solve. It is only in sports like running and lifting—simple activities testing a single dimension such as speed or strength—that the design possibilities become manageable.

Of course, not all expert decision making is rapid and intuitive. In some situations, chess players are required to conduct deep searches of possible moves, and firefighters are required to think logically about the consequences of actions. So are top athletes and military commanders.

But even in the most abstract decisions, experience and knowledge play a central role. In an experiment carried out by David Rumelhart, a psychologist at Stanford University, five times as many participants were able to figure out the implications of a logical expression when it was stated in a real setting ("every purchase over thirty dollars must be approved by the manager") than when stated in a less meaningful way ("every card with a vowel on the front must have an integer on the back").

Earlier in this chapter we saw that the talent myth is disempowering because it causes individuals to give up if they fail to make rapid early progress. But we can now see that it is also damaging to institutions that insist on placing inexperienced individuals—albeit with strong reasoning skills—in positions of power.

Think, for example, of the damage done to the governance of Britain by the tradition of moving ministers—the most powerful men and women in the country—from department to department without giving them the opportunity to develop an adequate knowledge base in any of them. It is estimated that the average tenure of a ministerial post in recent years in Britain has been 1.7 years. John Reid, a long-serving member of Tony Blair's government, was moved from department to department no less than seven times in seven years.

This is no less absurd than rotating Tiger Woods from golf to baseball to football to hockey and expecting him to perform expertly in every arena.

What we decide about the relative importance of practice and knowledge on the one hand and talent on the other has major implications not just for ourselves and our families, but for corporations, sports, governments, and, indeed, the future of artificial intelligence.*

On May 3, 1997, Kasparov and Deep Blue went head-to-head for a second time. The hype was no less intense and the stakes no less high. IBM put up over a million dollars in prize money, and the world's media descended upon the venue—this time the thirty-fifth floor of the Equitable Center on Seventh Avenue in New York—in even greater numbers (IBM would later estimate that the company gained more than $500 million in free publicity).

But this time, Deep Blue was triumphant, defeating the world champion by two games to one, with three draws. It was a crushing blow for Kasparov, who stormed out of the venue. He would later allege that IBM had created playing conditions advantageous to Deep Blue and that they had

---

* One rather obvious proviso regarding the importance of practice in sports: In activities like basketball and sumo wrestling, height and basic body size are clearly significant factors determining success and failure—but they cannot be improved with any amount of practice. They are, to a very large extent, set in genetic stone.

So, in these kinds of sports, we can think of height (or basic body size) operating as a kind of threshold. Too short, and you are not going to make it. But if you are lucky enough to be sufficiently tall to play in, say, the NBA, success and failure will once again hinge on your perceptual and motor skill—things that can be developed only through practice.

refused to provide computer printouts which would have helped his preparation. He also made entirely unsubstantiated claims that IBM had cheated. He was not a good loser.

What had happened over the course of the preceding fifteen months? How had Deep Blue managed to convert defeat into a famous victory? Firstly, the machine had been provided with double the processing power (it was now able to compute more than 200 million moves per second). But its victory would have been impossible without another key innovation.

As the American Physical Society put it, "Deep Blue's general knowledge of chess was significantly enhanced through the efforts of IBM consultant and international grandmaster Joel Benjamin, so that it could draw on vast resources of stored information, such as a database of opening games played by grandmasters over the last 100 years."

Deep Blue's programmers—like Gary Klein, Jim Immelt, and Wayne Gretzky—had realized that knowledge is power.

CHAPTER 2

Miraculous Children?

The Myth of the Child Prodigy

Wolfgang Amadeus Mozart was a sensation in the courts of Europe of the eighteenth century. At the age of just six, he was enchanting members of the aristocracy with his skills on the piano, often with his sister Maria Anna playing alongside him. He began composing pieces for the violin and piano at the age of five, going on to produce many works before his tenth birthday. Pretty impressive stuff for a boy in short trousers.

How do you solve a conundrum like Mozart? Even those sympathetic to the idea that excellence emerges over the course of ten thousand hours of practice are stumped when attempting to explain the timeless genius of one of history's greatest composers, a man who has changed lives with his artistic insight and intricate creativity.

Surely this is an example of a man who was born with his sublime abilities intact, a man who came into the world stamped with the mark of genius? After all, Mozart had scarcely even *lived* ten thousand hours by the time he was getting to grips with the piano and his early compositions.

But is that the whole story? Here is Mozart's early life, told in a little more detail by the journalist and author Geoff Colvin:

> Mozart's father was of course Leopold Mozart, a famous composer and performer in his own right. He was also a domineering parent who started his son on a program of intensive training in composition and performing at age three. Leopold was well qualified for his role as little Wolfgang's teacher by more than just his own eminence; he was deeply interested in how music was taught to children.
>
> While Leopold was only so-so as a musician, he was highly accomplished as a pedagogue. His authoritative book on violin instruction, published the same year Wolfgang was born, remained influential for decades. So, from the earliest age, Wolfgang was receiving heavy instruction from an expert teacher who lived with him. . . .
>
> Mozart's first work regarded today as a masterpiece, with its status confirmed by the number of recordings available, is his Piano Concerto No. 9, composed when he was twenty-one. That's certainly an early age, but we must remember that by then Wolfgang had been through eighteen years of extremely hard, expert training.

The extraordinary dedication of the young Mozart, under the guidance of his father, is perhaps most powerfully articulated by Michael Howe, a psychologist at the University of Exeter, in his book *Genius Explained*. He estimates that Mozart had clocked up an eye-watering 3,500 hours of practice even before his sixth birthday.

Seen in this context, Mozart's achievements seem suddenly rather different. He no longer looks like a musician zapped with special powers that enabled him to circumvent practice; rather, he looks like somebody who *embodies* the rigors of practice. He set out on the road to excellence very early in life, but now we can see why.

It is only by starting at an unusually young age and by practicing with such ferocious devotion that it is possible to accumulate ten thousand hours while still in adolescence. Far from being an exception to the ten-thousand-hour rule, Mozart is a shining testament to it.

Child prodigies amaze us because we compare them not with other performers who have practiced for the same length of time, but with children of the same age who have not dedicated their lives in the same way. We delude ourselves into thinking they possess miraculous talents because we assess their skills in a context that misses the essential point. We see their little bodies and cute faces and forget that, hidden within their skulls, their brains have been sculpted—and their knowledge deepened—by practice that few people accumulate until well into adulthood, if then. Had the six-year-old Mozart been compared with musicians who had clocked up 3,500 hours of practice, rather than with other children of the same age, he would not have seemed exceptional at all.

What about Mozart the child composer rather than Mozart the child performer? The facts follow the same logic. Sure, he wrote compositions as a young boy, but they had nothing in common with the sublime creations of his later years. His first four piano concertos, written at the age of eleven, and his next three, written at sixteen, contain no original music: they are simply rearrangements of the music of other composers.

"There is nothing distinctively 'Mozartian' about them," writes Robert Weisberg, a psychologist specializing in creativity and problem solving. In this context, it is not surprising that music insiders rarely describe Mozart as a prodigy. Indeed, the critic Harold Schonberg argues that Mozart "developed late," as his greatest works did not emerge until he had been composing for two decades.

Of course, none of this explains why Mozart eventually managed to produce compositions that are considered among the greatest artistic creations in human history, but it ought to dispel the myth that they emerged from on high, like gifts from the gods. Mozart was one of the hardest-working composers in history, and without that deep and sustained application he would have got nowhere.

The same essential truth is revealed when looking at child prodigies in sport.

When Tiger Woods became the youngest-ever winner of the U.S. Masters golf championship in 1997, he was hailed by many experts as the most naturally gifted golfer to play the game. This was understandable given his audacious stroke-making around the hallowed Augusta course. But dig down into his past, and an entirely different explanation reveals itself. And, once again, it starts with a highly motivated father. Here is a flavor of Tiger's early years:

Earl Woods was a former baseball player and Green Beret who was obsessed with the idea that practice creates greatness. He started his son at what he himself describes as "unthinkably early age," before he could even walk or talk. "Early practice is vital so that performances became totally ingrained and flow from the subconscious," Woods senior would later say.

Placed in his high chair in the garage at home, so he could watch as Earl hit balls into the net, little Tiger was given a golf club at Christmas—five days before his first birthday—and at eighteen months had his first golf outing. He couldn't yet count to five, but little Tiger already knew a par 5 from a par 4.

By the age of two years and eight months Woods was familiar with bunker play, and by his third year he had developed his preshot routine. Soon his practice sessions were taking place on the driving range and putting green, where he would hone his skills for hours at a time.

At the age of two Woods entered his first pitch-and-putt tournament at the Navy Golf Course in Cypress, California. He could already hit the ball eighty yards with his 2.5 wood and pitch accurately from forty yards. When Tiger was four, Earl hired the services of a professional to accelerate his development. Tiger won his first national major tournament at thirteen.

Practice sessions would typically end with a competitive drill, like placing the ball three feet from the hole to see how many consecutive putts Tiger could make. After seventy in a row, Earl would still be standing there.

By his mid-teens, Woods had clocked ten thousand hours of dedicated practice, just like Mozart.

The Williams sisters, both multiple grand slam winners in tennis, are also held up as testaments to the talent theory of excellence (they are also, rightly, regarded as having achieved amazing things in the teeth of formidably tough circumstances). But the really striking thing about the sisters' story is neither their talent nor their humble beginnings but their almost fanatical devotion. Here's a summary of their early days on the courts:

Two years before Venus Williams was born, her father Richard was flipping television channels when he saw the winner of a tennis match receive a check for $40,000. Impressed with the money top players could earn, he and his new wife, Oracene, decided to create a tennis champion. Venus was born on June 17, 1980, and Serena a year later, on September 26, 1981.

To learn how to coach, Richard watched videotapes of famous tennis stars, read tennis magazines at the library, and spoke to psychiatrists and tennis coaches. He also taught himself and his wife to play tennis so they could hit with their daughters.

After Serena was born, the family moved from the Watts area of Los Angeles to Compton. An economically depressed area, Compton was rough and violent, and the family occasionally witnessed gunfire. Richard became the owner of a small company that hired out security guards, and Oracene a nurse.

Tennis training began in earnest when Venus was "four years, six months and one day old" and Serena three years old, and while the only courts available for practice were riddled with potholes and surrounded by gangs, Richard carved out remarkable opportunities for his daughters.

Training would often involve Richard standing on one side of the net, feeding five hundred and fifty balls he kept in a shopping cart. When they were finished, they would pick up the balls and start again.

As part of their training, the girls trained with baseball bats and were encouraged to serve at traffic cones until their arms ached. The two once had a practice session during the school holidays that began at 8:00 a.m. and lasted until 3:00 p.m. As Venus put it: "When you're little, you just keep hitting and hitting." Oracene said, "They were always in the courts early, even before their father or I would get there." Serena entered her first competition at the age of four and a half.

"My dad worked hard to build our technique," Venus has said. "He's really a great coach. He's very innovative. He always has a new technique, new ideas, new strategies to put in place. I don't really think of those things, but he does."

When the sisters were twelve and eleven, Richard invited teaching pro Rick Macci—who had earlier coached such tennis stars as Mary Pierce and Jennifer Capriati—to come to Compton and watch his daughters play. He was impressed by the sisters' skill and athleticism and invited them to study with him at his Florida academy, and soon after, the family relocated to the Sunshine State.

By then, both sisters had already clocked up thousands of hours of practice.

Examine any sporting life where success has arrived early and the same story just keeps repeating itself. David Beckham, for example, would take a soccer ball to the local park in East London as a young child and kick it from precisely the same spot for hour upon hour. "His dedication was breathtaking," his father has said. "It sometimes seemed that he lived on the local field."

Beckham concurs. "My secret is practice," he said. "I have always believed that if you want to achieve anything special in life you have to work, work, and then work some more." By the time he was fourteen, Beckham's dedication paid off: he was spotted and signed by the youth team of Manchester United, one of the most prestigious soccer clubs in the world.

Matt Carre, director of the sports engineering group at the University of Sheffield, has conducted a research project on the mechanics of Beckham's trademark free kick. "It may look completely natural, but it is, in fact, a very deliberate technique," Carre said. "He kicks to one side of the ball to create the bend and is also able to effectively wrap his foot around the ball to give it topspin to make it dip. He practiced this over and over when he was a young footballer, the same way Tiger Woods practiced putting backspin on a golf ball."

The arduous logic of sporting success has perhaps been most eloquently articulated by Andre Agassi. Reliving his early years in tennis in his autobiography *Open*, he wrote: "My father says that if I hit 2,500 balls each day, I'll hit 17,500 balls each week, and at the end of one year I'll have hit nearly one million balls. He believes in math. Numbers, he says, don't lie. A child who hits one million balls each year will be unbeatable."

What does all this tell us? It tells us that if you want to bend it like Beckham or fade it like Tiger, you have to work like crazy, regardless of your genes, background, creed, or color. There is no shortcut, even if child prodigies bewitch us into thinking there is.

Extensive research has shown that there is scarcely a single top performer in any complex task who has circumvented the ten years of hard work necessary to reach the top. Well, that's not quite true. Chess master Bobby Fischer is said to have reached grandmaster status in nine years, although even that is disputed by some of his biographers.

A different question concerns the optimal route to the top. Given that thousands of hours must be clocked up on the road to excellence, does it make sense to start children at a very early age, before they have even reached their fifth birthday, like Mozart, Woods, and the Williams sisters? The advantages are obvious: the young performer has a sizable head start on anybody who commences their training, as is more common, a few years later.

Yet there are also very real dangers. It is only possible to clock up meaningful practice if an individual has made an *independent decision* to devote himself to whatever field of expertise. He has to care about what he is doing, not because a parent or a teacher says so, but for its own sake. Psychologists call this "internal motivation," and it is often lacking in children who start too young and are pushed too hard. They are, therefore, on the road not to excellence but to burnout.

"Starting kids off too young carries high risk," Peter Keen, a leading sports scientist and architect of Great Britain's success at the 2008 Olympic Games, has said. "The only circumstances in which very early development seems to work is where the children themselves are motivated to clock up the hours, rather than doing so because of parents or a coach. The key is to be sensitive to the way the child is thinking and feeling, encouraging training without exerting undue pressure."

But where the motivation *is* internalized, children tend to regard practice not as grueling but as fun. Here is Monica Seles, the tennis prodigy: "I just love to practice and drill and all that stuff." Here is Serena Williams: "It felt like a blessing to practice because we had so much fun." Here is Tiger Woods: "My dad never asked me to go play golf. I asked him. It's the child's desire to play that matters, not the parent's desire to have the child play."

We will look more closely at the nature of motivation in chapter 4, but it is worth noting that only a minority of top performers start off in early childhood, and even fewer reach exalted levels of performance while still in early adolescence. This would seem to indicate—taking the widest possible perspective and recognizing that individual cases vary greatly—that the dangers of starting out too hard, too young often outweigh the benefits. One of the skills of a good coach is to tailor a training program to the mind-set of the individual.

But, on the wider point, do child prodigies prove the talent theory of excellence? The truth is precisely the reverse. Child prodigies do not have unusual genes; they have unusual upbringings. They have compressed thousands of hours of practice into the small period between birth and adolescence. That is why they have become world-class.

A Tale of Three Sisters

On April 19, 1967, Laszlo Polgar and his girlfriend Klara married at a registry office in the small Hungarian town of Gyöngyös. The guests showered the newlyweds with confetti as they left the building for their three-day honeymoon (Polgar had to get back to the army, where he was midway through his national service) and commented on how happy they looked together.

What none of the guests realized was that they were witnessing the start of one of the most audacious human experiments of recent times.

Polgar, an educational psychologist, was one of the earliest advocates of the practice theory of expertise. He had written papers outlining his ideas and talked about them to his colleagues at the school where he worked as a math teacher; he had even lobbied local government officials, arguing that an emphasis on hard work rather than talent could transform the education system if given half a chance.

"Children have extraordinary potential, and it is up to society to unlock it," he says when I meet him and his wife at the family apartment in Budapest, overlooking the Danube. "The problem is that people, for some reason, do not want to believe it. They seem to think that excellence is only open to others, not themselves."

Polgar is an extraordinary person to meet in the flesh. His face is etched with the wary enthusiasm of a man who has spent a lifetime trying to convince a skeptical world of his theories. His eyes sparkle with appeal, his hands work as he elaborates his thoughts, and his face undergoes a triumphant transformation when one so much as nods in agreement.

But back in the 1960s, when Polgar was contemplating his experiment, his ideas were considered so outlandish that a local government official told him to see a psychiatrist to "heal him of his delusions." This was Hungary at the height of the Cold War, where radicalism of any kind was considered not merely eccentric but subversive.

But Polgar was not deterred. Realizing that the only way to vindicate his theory was to test it on his own future children, he started corresponding with a number of young ladies, in search of a wife. This was a time when having pen pals was not uncommon among Eastern Europeans, as young men and women living under state oppression sought to broaden their horizons.

A young Ukrainian named Klara was one of those women. "His letters fizzed with passion as he explained his theories of how to produce children with world-class abilities," Klara, a warm and gentle lady, a perfect counterpoint to her husband, tells me. "Like many at the time, I thought he was crazy. But we agreed to meet."

Face to face, she found the force of his arguments (not to mention his charm) irresistible and agreed to take part in his bold experiment. On April 19, 1969, she gave birth to their first daughter, Susan.

Polgar spent hours trying to decide on the specific area in which Susan would be groomed for excellence. "I needed Susan's achievements to be dramatic, so that nobody could question their authenticity," he says. "That was the only way to convince people that their ideas about excellence were all wrong. And then it hit me: chess."

Why chess? "Because it is objective," Polgar says. "If my child had been trained as an artist or novelist, people could have argued about whether she was genuinely world-class or not. But chess has an objective rating based on performance, so there is no possibility of argument."

Although Polgar was only a hobby player (and Klara not a player at all), he read as much as he could on the pedagogy of chess. He schooled Susan at home, devoting many hours a day to chess even before her fourth birthday. He did so jovially, making great play of the drama of the game, and over time Susan became hooked. By her fifth birthday she had accumulated hundreds of hours of dedicated practice.

A few months later, Polgar entered Susan in a local competition. She was so small she could barely see over the table on which the boards were placed, and her competitors and their parents looked on in amusement as she took her place to play her games, her eyes scanning the board and her tiny hands moving the pieces.

"Almost all the girls qualified for my section were twice my age or older," Susan, an attractive and confident forty-year-old now living in New York, recounts. "At that point I did not realize the importance of that event in my life. I just looked at it as one chess game at a time. I was having fun. I won game after game, and my final score was 10–0. The fact that such a young girl won the championship was already a sensation in itself, but winning all my games added to people's amazement."

On November 2, 1974, Klara gave birth to a second daughter, Sofia; then, on July 23, 1976, to a third daughter, Judit. As soon as they were old enough to crawl, little Judit and Sofia would make their way across to the door of the chess room in the family apartment and peer through the tiny window, watching Susan being put through her paces by their father.

They longed to get involved, but Polgar did not want them to start too early. Instead he put the chess pieces in their tiny hands, encouraging them to take pleasure in their texture and shapes. Only when they turned five did he embark on their training.

The girls trained devotedly throughout their childhoods, but they also enjoyed it enormously. Why? Because they had internalized the motivation. "We spent a lot of hours on the chessboard, but it did not seem like a chore because we loved it," says Judit. "We were not pushed; chess fascinated us," says Sofia.

Susan concurs: "I loved playing chess. It expanded my horizons and gave me wonderful experiences."

By the time they had reached adolescence, all three sisters had accumulated well over ten thousand hours of specialized practice, arguably more than any other women in chess history.

This is how they fared:

Susan

In August 1981, at the age of twelve, Susan won the world title for girls under sixteen. Less than two years later, in July 1984, she became the top-rated female player in the world.

In January 1991 she became the first woman player in history to reach the status of grandmaster. By the end of her career she had won the world championship for women on four occasions and five chess Olympiads and remains the only person in history, male or female, to win the chess Triple Crown (the rapid, blitz, and classical world championships).

Susan was also a pioneer. Despite huge obstacles placed in her way by the chess authorities—she was barred from playing the 1986 World Championships (for men), even though she had qualified—she eventually paved the way for women to compete in the world's most prestigious events.

She now runs a chess center in New York.

Sofia

In 1980, at the age of five, Sofia won the under-eleven Hungarian championship for girls. She went on to win the gold medal for girls at the world under-fourteen championships in 1986 and numerous gold medals in chess Olympiads and other prestigious championships.

But her most extraordinary achievement was the "Miracle in Rome," where she won eight straight games in the Magistrale di Roma against many of the greatest male players, including the grandmasters Alexander Chernin, Semon Palatnik, and Yuri Razuvaev. One chess expert wrote, "The odds against such an occurrence must be billions to one." Kevin O'Connell, an Irish chess player, rated the performance as the fifth greatest, by man or woman, in history:

Player	Event	Performance Rating
Bobby Fischer	U.S. Championships, 1963	3000
Anatoly Karpov	Linares, 1984	2977
Garry Kasparov	Tilburg, 1989	2913
Alexander Alekhine	San Remo, 1930	2906
Sofia Polgar	Rome, 1989	2879

Sofia married fellow chess player Yona Kosashvili in 1999 and moved to Israel, where they live with their two children. She now helps to run a chess Web site and is an acclaimed painter.

Judit

After a succession of record-breaking victories in her early teens, Judit won the world under-twelve championships in Romania in 1988. It was the first time in history a girl had won an overall (open to both men and women) world championship.

Three years later, in 1991, at the age of fifteen years and four months, she became the youngest-ever grandmaster—

male or female—in history. In the same year she also won the Hungarian championships, defeating grandmaster Tibor Tolnai in the final.

She has now been the number-one female chess player in the world for well over a decade, excluding a brief period when she was taken off the list due to inactivity when she gave birth to her first son in 2004 (to be replaced at the top of the list by her older sister Susan).

Over the course of her career, she has had victories over almost every top player in the world, including Garry Kasparov, Anatoly Karpov, and Viswanathan Anand.

She is universally considered to be the greatest female player of all time.

The tale of the Polgar sisters provides scintillating evidence for the practice theory of excellence. Polgar had publicly declared that his yet-to-be-born children would become world-beaters—setting himself up for a fall in the time-honored tradition of science—and had been proved right. His girls had lived up to the prebirth hype and then some.

Note, also, the public reaction to the girls' success. When Susan stormed to victory in a local competition at the age of five, everyone present was convinced that this was the consequence of unique talent. She was described by the local newspaper as a prodigy, and Polgar remembers being congratulated by another parent on having a daughter with such amazing talent. "That is not something my little Olga could do," the parent said.

But this is the iceberg illusion: onlookers took the performance to be the consequence of special abilities because they had witnessed only a tiny percentage of the activity that had gone into its making. As Polgar puts it: "If they had seen the painfully slow progress, the inch-by-inch improvements, they would not have been so quick to call Susan a prodigy."

Human Calculators

How good are you at mental arithmetic? I'm guessing that you have a pretty clear answer to this question. Math is one of those things you either can do or can't. Either you have a brain for numbers or you don't. And if you don't, you may as well give up.

The idea that calculating ability is predetermined at birth is perhaps even more deeply ingrained than the idea that sporting ability is predetermined at birth. It represents the ultimate expression of the talent theory of expertise. For that reason, it is worth taking a closer look to see if things are quite as they seem.

Often, the talent theory of calculating skill finds its most eloquent testimony in the abilities of child prodigies: young boys and girls who perform mental arithmetic at speeds approaching that of computers. Like the six-year-old Mozart, these kids are so remarkable that they often perform to enraptured audiences.

Shakuntala Devi, born in Bangalore in 1939, for example, stunned university academics in India by performing three-digit multiplications at the age of eight. She is now in the *Guinness World Records* for being able to multiply two thirteen-digit numbers (for example, 8574930485948 times 9394506947284) in twenty-eight seconds.

Rüdiger Gamm from Germany, another world-famous "human calculator," is able to calculate ninth powers and fifth roots with incredible accuracy, and to find the quotient of two primes to sixty decimal places. It is remarkable to watch Gamm in action. When asked a question, he closes his eyes and furrows his brow, his eyelids flickering intensely as he grapples with the calculation. A few moments later he opens his eyes, and the numbers spew out at astonishing speed.

Surely these feats speak of natural gifts beyond those bestowed on the rest of us. Or do they?

In 1896, Alfred Binet, a French psychologist, carried out a simple experiment to find out. He compared the performance of two calculating prodigies with that of cashiers from the Bon Marché department store in Paris. The cashiers had an average of fourteen years experience in the store but *had shown no early gift for mathematics*. Binet gave the prodigies and the cashiers identical three- and four-digit multiplication problems and compared the time taken to solve them.

What happened? You guessed it: *the best cashier was faster than either prodigy for both problems*. In other words, fourteen years of calculating experience had been sufficient, on its own, to bring perfectly "normal" people up to and beyond the remarkable speed of prodigies. Binet concluded that calculating ability is more about practice than talent— which means that you and I could perform lightning-quick multi-digit calculations if we had the proper training.

So, how is it done? As with most "miraculous" feats, there is a trick. Suppose, for example, that you had to multiply 358 and 464. Now, most of us can multiply 300 and 400 to get 120,000. The trick is to commit that number to memory while solving the next component of the problem, say, 400 times 50. This is 20,000, which you add to the running total to get 140,000. Now multiply 400 by 8 to get 320, and add that to the running total, to get 140,320.

Eventually, by adding the remaining components of the calculation (there are eighteen separate steps), you get the answer: 166,122. This is still a formidable feat, of course, but it is no longer the *calculation* that is daunting; it is remembering the running total while performing the various steps.

But now consider how much more difficult it is to keep track of a narrative while reading a book. There are tens of thousands of words in the English language, and they are used in new and unforeseen combinations in every sentence of every page. To understand a new sentence, the reader must not only understand its specific meaning; he must also be able to integrate it with all sentences previously read. He must, for example, remember previously mentioned objects and people in order to resolve references to pronouns.

This is a memory task of almost unimaginable dimensions. And yet most of us are able to get to the last word of the book—comprising hundreds of pages and tens of thousands of words—without once losing the thread of the narrative. The experience we have clocked up as "language users" enables us to do this in just the same way that the hours clocked up as "number users" enables mathematicians to get to the end of a multi-digit multiplication by keeping track of the "narrative" of the calculation.

The difference between calculators and the rest of us, then, is that calculators have spent lives immersed in the vocabulary of numbers, while the rest of us have wimped out by using electronic calculators.

Mathematical genius Srinivasa Ramanujan, for example, often stayed up all night working on problems, while Rüdiger Gamm trains for four hours a day, studiously learning number facts and calculation procedures. Sarah Flannery, who won the 1999 Esat Young Scientist Exhibition at the age of sixteen for her pioneering work in the mathematics of code-breaking, spent her entire childhood absorbed in numbers. The opening page of her wonderful book *In Code* begins: "There is a blackboard in our kitchen. It might be said that my mathematical journey began there."

It was on that board that her father, a lecturer in mathematics, chalked up problems when Sarah was as young as five, leaving his daughter to gaze at them, ponder them, and eventually solve them. Math puzzles were the staple of dinnertime conversation and formed the basis of countless discussions and debates.

Is it any wonder that, after a while, numbers begin to have "meaning" for mathematicians in the same way that words have meaning for us? As Brian Butterworth, professor of cognitive neuropsychology at University College London and widely acknowledged as the world's foremost expert on mathematical ability, observes:

Calculators from an early age develop a kind of intimacy with numbers. When Bidder [a math prodigy] was learning to count to 100, the numbers became "as it were, my friends, and I knew all their friends and acquaintances." Klein [another prodigy] once said, "Numbers are friends for me, more or less. It doesn't mean the same for you, does it, 3,844? For you it's just a three and an eight and a four and a four. But I say, 'Hi, 62 squared.' " In a famous story, Hardy [a researcher] visited Ramanujan [a prodigy] in hospital and mentioned that the taxi in which he had come was number 1729, "A rather dull number." "No, Hardy! It is a very interesting number. It is the smallest number expressible as the sum of cubes in two different ways."

Put simply, calculating prodigies are made, not born. As Butterworth has said, "There is *no evidence* at the moment for differences in innate specific capacities for mathematics" (my italics). Flannery agrees: "I am not a genius," she has written. "I simply had the benefit of a childhood steeped in numbers."

Two years after Susan Polgar had become the world's first female grandmaster, her father, Laszlo, was offered a fresh challenge. Joop van Oosterom, a Dutch billionaire and chess sponsor, tried to persuade him to adopt three boys from a developing country to see if he could replicate the results he had achieved with his three daughters.

Polgar jumped at the idea but was overruled, unexpectedly, by Klara, his usually laid-back wife. It was not that she was pessimistic about the chances of success, but that she just did not have the energy to conduct another experiment. "I thought the first time around would be enough to prove the theory!" she says with a warm smile as we enjoy a lunch of fish and vegetables in their apartment overlooking the Danube.

Sitting alongside her, her husband is unusually quiet. His eyes are still sparkling, but he is deep in thought. "People tell me the success of my daughters was pure luck," he says finally. "They say it was a coincidence that a man who set about proving the practice theory of excellence using chess just happened to beget the three most talented female chess players in history.

"Maybe some people just do not want to believe in the power of practice."

CHAPTER 3

The Path to Excellence

The Power (and Impotence) of Practice

How many hours have you spent driving your car? I spent a little time working this out recently and figured that I have averaged 12,000 miles a year since passing my driving test more than twenty-two years ago, adding up to 264,000 miles in total. At an average speed of around thirty miles an hour, that means I have spent almost precisely ten thousand hours at the wheel.

But I am not a world-class driver. In fact, I probably have more bad habits now, and less knowledge of the rules of the road, than when I passed my test. I know what you are thinking: Doesn't this undermine the entire thesis of the book so far? Haven't I attempted to explain expertise in terms of the number of hours practiced? Well, not quite.

What happens when I drive my car? I am certainly clocking up countless hours at the wheel, but does this constitute the acquisition of knowledge? It is not as if I am straining to improve. Rather, my mind is on other things: I am figuring out what to make for dinner; I am speaking to my passenger; I am listening to the radio and strumming my fingers against the steering wheel. I am, in effect, driving on autopilot.

This may sound like an extreme example, but it applies (to only a slightly lesser extent) to a surprising number of us. We do our jobs, but often with our minds absent—partially or wholly—from what we are doing. We go through the motions. This is why (as dozens of studies have shown) length of time in many occupations is only weakly related to performance. Mere experience, if it is not matched by deep concentration, does not translate into excellence.

Of course, some jobs *demand* deep application. As we saw in chapter 1, firefighters and nurses are constantly challenged to operate at the upper limit of their powers: if they don't, people die. Ambling along on autopilot is not an option, which is why number of years in the job is strongly correlated with expertise. Those who have been on the front line for ten years plus are, invariably, world-class in their field.

The same was true of the cashiers in the last chapter. The constant requirement to make accurate calculations, and the fact that errors are immediately revealed by the company accounts, mean that cashiers are continually challenged to build accuracy and speed.

But in many jobs, and in most sports, it is possible to clock up endless hours without improving at all. I play tennis every Sunday—an amiable game with a friend before heading over to the club canteen for a hot sandwich. It is fun and sociable, but it has nothing to do with the kind of practice undertaken by aspiring Grand Slam champions. I have not improved in five years. Why? Because I have been cruising along on auto-pilot.

Take a look at the anagrams in List A below and try to solve them. Then do the same for List B.

List A	List B
FAHTER	HERFAT
FOOTBLAL	LBOFTOAL
DCOTOR	RTOCOD
OUTCOEM	ECMUTOO
TEACHRE	EERTACH

If you solved the anagrams from both lists you will have noticed that they actually refer to precisely the same words: FATHER, FOOTBALL, DOCTOR, OUTCOME, TEACHER. The only difference is that in List A, the anagrams were easy, requiring only a single movement of adjacent letters. In List B, however, the letters were completely jumbled up, making the solution far more difficult.

But here's the curious thing. When researchers had participants work on lists of anagrams like those in List A, they found that, when later questioned, the participants were not very good at remembering the words. Even though they had successfully solved the anagrams, their recall was poor. When participants worked on more difficult anagrams, however, their recall soared.

Why such a dramatic difference? With difficult anagrams the jumble of letters forces you to do something other than breeze through. You have to stop for a few moments and think; you have to deepen your concentration and engage with the anagram to figure out what it is. In short, you are forced to click out of autopilot. In those few seconds of striving, the word is imprinted on your memory.

This example, taken from the work of psychologist S. W. Tyler, neatly emphasizes the power of practice when it is challenging rather than nice and easy. "When most people practice, they focus on the things they can do effortlessly," Ericsson has said. "Expert practice is different. It entails considerable, specific, and sustained efforts to do something you can't do well—or even at all. Research across domains shows that it is only by working at what you can't do that you turn into the expert you want to become."

So far the focus in this book has been on the *quantity* of practice required to reach the top, and we've seen that it's a staggering amount of time, stretching for a period of at least ten years. But now we are going to dig down into an even more vital facet of expertise, the *quality* of practice: the specialized learning used by top performers to attain master status and the deep concentration that is needed during each of those ten thousand hours to make them count.

Ericsson calls it "deliberate practice," to distinguish it from what most of the rest of us get up to. I am going to call it *purposeful* practice. Why? Because the practice sessions of aspiring champions have a specific and never-changing purpose: progress. Every second of every minute of every hour, the goal is to extend one's mind and body, to push oneself beyond the outer limits of one's capacities, to engage so deeply in the task that one leaves the training session, literally, a changed person.

Think back to the violinists at the music academy in Berlin. The top performers had not practiced for more hours per se than the lesser violinists. Rather, the difference was in the number of hours devoted to *purposeful* practice—the kind of practice that the violinists themselves said was the most conducive to improvement. The top performers had pushed themselves harder for longer. The others had not. That was the crucial difference.

We will get to the heart of purposeful practice—what it means, what it takes, and how it should be designed and structured—over the next couple of sections in the company of some of the most brilliant performers in sports and elsewhere, but we can get a good sense about where we are going by taking an example from my own experience in table tennis.

From the age of fifteen to nineteen I practiced for many hours, using the routines conventional in England at that time: regular movement patterns where my opponent would play one shot to my forehand, then one shot to my backhand, and then back again, over and over. It was physically arduous, in its way, but only because of its repetitiveness, rather than by placing special demands on my mind and body.

But a few weeks after I turned nineteen, a quirk of fate occurred. Chen Xinhua of China, one of the greatest players in the history of the sport, married a lovely Yorkshire woman and moved to England. It was rumored that he wanted to retire from table tennis, but after a long conversation he agreed to coach me. Within minutes of getting together at a small training hall on the outskirts of Reading, it became apparent that his concept of practice bore no relation to anything I had yet seen or imagined.

Instead of playing against each other with a single ball, he took a bucket of a hundred balls (rather like Richard Williams, father of Venus and Serena, in tennis), placed them beside the table, and then proceeded to fire them at me from different angles, at different speeds, with different spins, but always (and this was the ultimate revelation of his genius for coaching) calibrated so as to be constantly nudging the outer limits of my speed, movement, technique, anticipation, timing, and agility.

My body and mind were forced to leap into a new gear to keep up with this "multi-ball" training, and in response Chen upped the ante again and again, finally widening the table at my end (adding half a table in width) so that my footwork patterns were now straining to cope with extraordinary demands. Over a period of five years, my movement, speed, and positional awareness were transformed, and my world ranking rocketed.

In a flash, the riddle of why China is so successful at table tennis was solved. For years, their success had been put down to faster reaction speeds, secret diet, and any number of mysterious factors. Others suggested that it was because they were training longer hours. But they were not training longer; they were training smarter. They were training more purposefully. They were, in effect, training on turbo drive.

And now I was training the same way. It wasn't that I *felt* like a changed player; it was that I *was* a changed player. My body and mind had been transformed though a sustained process of being pushed beyond existing limitations; by grappling with tasks that, to use the words of Ericsson, were "outside the current realm of reliable performance, but which could be mastered within hours of practice by gradually refining performance through repetitions."

That is worth stating again: world-class performance comes by striving for a target just out of reach, but with a vivid awareness of how the gap might be breached. Over time, through constant repetition and deep concentration, the gap will disappear, only for a new target to be created, just out of reach once again.

Accelerated Learning

Falling Down

I am standing at the edge of the rink at the Guildford Spectrum, one of the largest and most prestigious ice-skating facilities in England. Around two dozen youngsters are circling the ice, warming up and occasionally breaking into swirls executed at dizzying speed. It is 7:00 a.m.

The most brilliant skater on the rink today is a slight, slim sixteen-year-old with a long brown ponytail. Kirsty has just taken part in her first international competition in Italy, but she is not resting on her laurels. Her eyes are set on the top of podium at the Winter Olympics in 2014.

For the last couple of months Kirsty has been trying to master the triple salchow, a formidably difficult jump where the skater takes off from one foot and rotates three times in the air before landing on the other foot with the smoothness and grace demanded of top-class performers. Kirsty has already spent many hours practicing the movement on the carpet at home, painstakingly elaborating her inner comprehension of the skill.

Today she is hoping to perform her first successful triple on the ice itself. As she skates around the rink, she occasionally leaps into the air to perform a double salchow. This she does with ease and remarkable assurance, landing fluently and elegantly. But this is just the warm-up. After a few minutes, Stewart, her coach, fits Kirsty into a harness attached by a wire to what looks like a fishing rod. He then skates just a few feet behind her, rod in hand.

After a few moments Kirsty readies herself for her first attempt of the morning at the triple salchow. Her face bathed in concentration, she finds her takeoff spot, then leaps high into the air. As she does so, Stewart tugs ever so slightly on the rod, cushioning the effects of gravity, permitting Kirsty a few precious extra milliseconds in the air. Kirsty completes the three rotations and lands on her right foot with panache. Again and again she nails the jump, with Stewart gradually lessening his tug on the rod.

Then the harness comes off. Kirsty is on her own.

She circles the ice gingerly as Stewart looks on. After a few moments, she resolves to go for it, hitting her takeoff spot with a detonation of energy and soaring high into the air. But her rotation lacks bite, and she is only two and half revolutions through the jump when she lands, loses her balance, and—bang!—lands hard on her behind.

I wince. But Kirsty is already off again. She jumps again and again, regularly falling onto the cold, hard surface. Only with her seventh attempt does she sail through two and three-quarters rotations, landing perfectly, and allowing herself a grim smile of satisfaction. Stewart gives her a pat on the back. She has not quite completed a full triple, but it is only a matter of time.

"It is remarkable how quickly youngsters can master these seemingly impossible jumps if they are willing to keep pushing themselves to the limit and beyond," Stewart tells me when we sit down after the session. I ask Kirsty if it is painful falling over again and again. "To be honest, yes," she says. "But I just get on with it. It'll be worth it when I nail that jump."

Figure skating provides a vivid illustration of the accelerated learning permitted by purposeful practice, but it also tells us something more. Consider how, when watching Olympic skaters, we wonder at their athleticism, agility, elegance, and finesse. Consider how we marvel at their ability to sustain their balance in the midst of dizzying rotations and audacious leaps. And now consider how many bruises, how many crash landings, went into the making.

In the 1990s researchers conducted a revelatory study into figure skating. They found that the major difference between elite skaters and their less elite counterparts is not to be found in genetics, personality, or family background. Rather, it is to be found in the *type of practice*. Elite skaters regularly attempt jumps beyond their current capabilities; less elite skaters do not.

Note that elite skaters do not merely undertake more difficult jumps—after all, that is what you would expect from better performers. No, the point is that elite skaters attempt jumps that are more difficult *even when measured relative to their superior abilities*. The conclusion is as counterintuitive as it is revealing: top skaters fall more often during their training sessions.

Purposeful practice is about striving for what is just out of reach and not quite making it; it is about grappling with tasks beyond current limitations and falling short again and again. Excellence is about stepping outside the comfort zone, training with a spirit of endeavor, and accepting the inevitability of trials and tribulations. Progress is built, in effect, upon the foundations of necessary failure. That is the essential paradox of expert performance.

Author Geoff Colvin has estimated that Shizuka Arakawa of Japan, one of the greatest skaters of all time, tumbled over more than twenty thousand times in her progression from five-year-old wannabe to 2006 Olympic champion. "Araka-wa's story is invaluable as a metaphor," Colvin has written. "Landing on your butt twenty thousand times is where great performance comes from."

Calypso Magic and Hoop Lessons

I am standing in a sports hall in Leeds in the north of England. Ten youngsters are in the middle of the hall, playing a game, but it is a game unlike any I have seen before. It is a bit like soccer, except distilled into concentrated form. The ball is smaller and heavier; the theater of space is shrunken relative to the wide-open expanses of a conventional pitch. It is as if all the complex dynamics, competitive intensity, and ferocious interaction of soccer have been packed into a nutshell. The game is called *futebol de salão* or, more commonly, futsal.

For many years the extraordinary success of Brazil in soccer, the planet's most popular sport, was a mystery. The world looked on in a state of something close to amazement at the silky skills, the creative audacity, and the sublime poetry of the Brazilian national team and its litany of icons such as Pelé, Rivelino, Zico, Juninho, Ronaldo, and Rivaldo. How do they do it? Where do they find such fluid tempo? How do they create so effortlessly the intricate threads of pass and move?

Some speculated that there is something inherently creative in the blood of the Brazilian players, something magical in their souls. Others were rather less mystical in their explanation, citing the poverty in the favelas (slums) and the economic imperative of reaching the top in soccer. But this left them at a rather obvious loss to explain why it is that dozens of other poor countries are so unsuccessful at soccer.

Simon Clifford, a tall and charismatic English primary school teacher and soccer coach, arrived at a radically different conclusion. In the summer of 1997, he took out a £5,000 loan and spent his school holiday on a trip to Brazil. It changed his life. Armed with a backpack, a camera, and a notepad, he stayed in grubby dorms, filmed children playing in the favelas, and trained with a number of top players. And everywhere he went, Clifford saw futsal.

"It is played across Brazil," Clifford says. "It is the way they learn their skills and the way they build their speed. People have this idea of Brazilian football being played on beaches and of the players being relaxed and just naturally good at it. What I found was that they worked ferociously hard. The image of Brazilians kicking around on the beach all day comes because what you see when you first get to the country is all the beach football. But if you really look at the areas where great Brazilian footballers come from, there are no beaches around."

Here is Daniel Coyle, whose analysis of futsal in his book *The Talent Code* alerted many to its extraordinary effectiveness:

One reason [for the success of futsal] lies in the math. Futsal players touch the ball far more often than soccer players—six times more often per minute, according to a Liverpool University study. The smaller, heavier ball demands and rewards more precise handling— as coaches point out, you can't get out of a tight spot simply by booting the ball downfield.

Sharp passing is paramount: the game is all about looking for angles and spaces and working quick combinations with other players. Ball control and vision are crucial, so that when futsal players play the full-size game, they feel as if they have acres of space in which to operate. . . . As Dr. Miranda [professor of soccer at the University of São Paolo] summed up, "No time plus no space equals better skills. Futsal is our national laboratory of improvisation."

Almost all of the most revered Brazilian players were schooled in futsal. Here is Pelé, widely regarded as the greatest player of all time: "Futsal was important in helping to develop my ball control, quick thinking, and passing." Here is Zico, a brilliant striker who scored fifty-two goals in seventy-two international matches for Brazil: "I played only futsal as a youngster. It's the best start for kids."

Here is Ronaldo, the highest goal scorer in the history of the World Cup and one of only two men to have been named FIFA World Player of the Year three times: "Futsal is how I really got started. This is my love, the thing that I enjoyed the most." Here is Ronaldinho, one of the most creative players of his generation and twice World Player of the Year: "When you come to play normal soccer, it's easy if you've come from futsal."

After returning from Brazil, Clifford set up a number of Brazilian-style soccer skills academies around the world, including the one in Leeds. His results have been remarkable. As manager of Garforth Town (a team in the lower reaches of English soccer), Clifford has won two promotions in just three seasons. "Garforth will really take off when the team is fully populated by youngsters who have come through my soccer schools," he says.

Futsal is a perfect example of how well-designed training can accelerate learning; how the knowledge that mediates any complex skill can be expanded and deepened at breathtaking speed with the right kind of practice. The finesse and intricacy of the game, together with its ferocious speed, mean that players make plenty of mistakes as they seek to master the skills. But this does not imply that futsal is ineffective; rather, it is proof that it *is* effective.

The difference between Brazil and the rest of the world in soccer, then, is not to be found in economics or any other grand theory, and certainly not in genetics, but in the thousands of futsal pitches that pepper the nation like gold dust. It is to be found in turbo-charged learning. It is to be found in the deep truths of purposeful practice.*

John Amaechi is a former center for the Cleveland Cavaliers, the Orlando Magic, and the Utah Jazz. He is also one of the most fascinating characters in modern sport: a doctor in psychology, a political activist, and the founder and mastermind of one of the most crusading sporting charities in the United Kingdom. He was also, incidentally, the first NBA player to come out as gay.

---

* Simon Kuper and Stefan Szymanski, two leading authorities on soccer, conducted a major examination of international soccer performance. They found that Brazil outperformed other major nations by a huge margin even after controlling for influences such as population size and history of playing international soccer. They describe Brazil's capacity to consistently exceed expectations as "phenomenal."

I went to his South London apartment recently to explore how the world's top basketball players train and improve, and the principles of purposeful practice kept cropping up again and again. Here is what he had to say:

When I started at Penn State University, nobody on the team was a match for me. So my coach recruited a "walk-on," someone who joined the practice as a volunteer. He was six foot eight.

Every time my team went on offense, the "walk-on" would jump onto the court and play defense so we were playing five on six. This meant two things: firstly, I was marked by a double team. Normally, this would create a weakness on a defensive team by pulling a man from his one-to-one guarding responsibilities. But with six men on defense, it meant our opposing team could stick two men on me, plus a man for each of my teammates.

In order for a teammate to be open, he would have to get free, and I would have to make a pass that was perfectly on time and perfectly on target for the split second he was open. Even when you execute a play perfectly you are only open in a spatial pocket in a specific time and a specific place. But I had two people marking me, making the play far more difficult. It forced me to up my game, to engage with greater awareness.

I had to create time and space that scarcely seemed to exist. It pushed me past my limits, forcing me to think faster, sharper, deeper and with far greater creativity. In turn, my limits just kept expanding.

It's easy when traveling across the terrain of elite sport to be overwhelmed by the seemingly endless diversity of training methods. But scratch beneath the surface, and you will find that all the successful systems have one thing in common: they *institutionalize the principles of purposeful practice*. China, the greatest table-tennis-playing nation, wields multi-ball training; Brazil, the most successful soccer nation, has futsal; top basketball teams use "walk-ons," and so it goes on.

Sometimes learning can be accelerated by something as simple as training with superior players. As Mia Hamm, one of the greatest female soccer players, has said: "All my life I've been playing up, meaning I've challenged myself with players older, bigger, more skillful, more experienced— in short, better than me." First she played with her older brother, then with the top U.S. college team. "Each day I attempted to play up to their level . . . and I was improving faster than I ever dreamed possible."

But often the training systems that most powerfully evoke the tenets of purposeful practice are highly sophisticated. The Great Britain Cycling Team, which has a stranglehold over the sport at the highest levels, is extremely secretive about the training methods used at their citadel of excellence in Manchester. For understandable reasons, they are fearful that if their methods leak out, their competitive advantage will be diluted just as surely as if a patent had expired.

In this context, sport no longer looks like the pure, untainted, objective battle between two individuals or teams; instead it is revealed, at least in part, as a battle of ideas; a battle between the men and women who, behind the scenes, design and construct the training systems. And if, by whatever dint of circumstance, an individual does not have access to the most enlightened system of training, no amount of hard work is likely to get him there.

As we saw in the opening chapter, circumstance and opportunity are deeply and inevitably implicated in the success of every high achiever.

Brain Transformation

The ten-thousand-hour rule, then, is inadequate as a predictor of excellence. What is required is ten thousand hours of *purposeful* practice. And for practice to be truly purposeful, concentration and dedication, although important, are not sufficient. You also need to have access to the right training system, and that sometimes means living in the right town or having the right coach.

For the early years of my table tennis career, I worked with Peter Charters, the top coach in the United Kingdom. When I reached late adolescence, I had Chen Xinhua, who brought with him the secrets of multi-ball training from China. These were formidable advantages not available to thousands of others of youngsters.

In effect, my practice was guided by the tenets of purposeful practice almost from day one. When these conditions are in place, learning takes off, knowledge escalates, and performance soars. You are on the path to excellence.

You are also on the path to personal transformation. Literally. One of the most striking things about modern research on expertise is how the body and mind can be radically altered with the right kind of practice. "When the human body is put under exceptional strain, a range of dormant genes in the DNA are expressed and extraordinary physiological processes are activated," Anders Ericsson has written. "Over time the cells of the body reorganize in response to the metabolic demands of the activity by, for example, increases in the number of capillaries supplying blood to the muscles."

Long-distance runners have larger hearts than average, not because they were born with them, but as the consequence of training. Table tennis players have more supple wrists, typists have more flexible fingers, and ballet dancers are able to rotate their feet through more degrees.

But while the adaptability of the human body is impressive, it is the plasticity of the brain that has astonished researchers. In an experiment led by Thomas Elbert of the University of Konstanz, Germany, for example, it was found that the region of the brain responsible for controlling fingers in young musicians grew in direct proportion to the number of years of training.

Further studies have uncovered similar transformations. In a study of London taxi drivers—who must pass a famously stringent set of examinations to gain a license—it was discovered that the region of the brain governing spatial navigation was substantially larger than for non–taxi drivers and that this region continued to grow with additional time on the job.

A key aspect of brain transformation is myelin, a substance that wraps around the nerve fibers and that can dramatically increase the speed with which signals pass through the brain. A 2005 experiment that scanned the brains of concert pianists found a direct relationship between the numbers of hours practiced and the quantity of myelin.

But myelin is not the only theme in the brain change story. Purposeful practice also builds new neural connections, increases the size of specific sections of the brain, and enables the expert to co-opt new areas of gray matter in the quest to improve.

All this speaks directly to the hardware-software distinction touched upon in chapter 1, but takes it a step further. We have seen that in any complex task, it is knowledge, above all, that determines excellence; the kind of knowledge built through deep experience and encoded in the brain and central nervous system.

But we can now see that *the very process of building knowledge transforms the hardware in which the knowledge is stored and operated*. It is as if in the process of downloading some ultrasophisticated piece of software, the inner circuitry of your PC is miraculously upgraded from Pentium 1 to Pentium 4.

Is it any wonder, then, that when we look at experts, they seem so far beyond the rest of us as to appear superhuman? They have, in a literal sense, different onboard computers, each individually manufactured for a specific domain of expertise.

Think back to Rudiger Gamm, the mathematical "prodigy." In a neuroimaging study, it was found that he not only used conventional neural networks when making calculations, he also used a system of brain areas implicated in episodic memory (this is the immensely powerful memory used to store autobiographical experiences).

Needless to say, your skull also contains this system, and you too can corral it into action when performing multi-digit calculations. But there is a catch: you can purchase access to this prime neural real estate only by building up a bank deposit of thousands of hours of purposeful practice.

That, if you like, is the price of excellence.

Think of how most of us go about our lives. My mother was a secretary for many years and, before embarking on her career, went on a course to learn how to type. After a few months of training she reached seventy words a minute, but then hit a plateau that lasted for the rest of her career. The reason is simple: this was the level required to gain employment, and once she had started work, it hardly seemed important to get any better. When she typed, she had her mind on other things.

That is the way most of us operate. When we learn a new task, like driving a car, we concentrate hard to master the skills. At first we are slow and awkward, and our movements are characterized by conscious control, but as we get more familiar, the skills are absorbed in implicit memory, and we no longer give much thought to them. We cruise along, attending to other things while at the wheel. This is what psychologists call "automaticity."

This is the way many of us play sports, too. We go to the driving range, buy a bucket of balls, rip a few drives, and then trundle off to the first tee, supposing that we have done something that will reduce our handicap. It is easy, fun, and enjoyable—and almost completely worthless. As golfing expert Bill Kroen puts it, "Many players confuse hitting balls with practice. If you watch golfers at a crowded driving range you will see many that are hitting the ball with the same club (usually a driver) without ever checking their grip, stance or alignment."

Top performers have an entirely different approach, taking active steps to stretch their limitations in every session. Tiger Woods, for example, treads his balls into the sand on bunker shots to maximize the difficulty, and then hits them over and over. Table tennis player Marty Reisman spent hours whacking balls at a solitary standing cigarette on the other side of the net to hone his directional accuracy and fine motor skills.

Purposeful practice may not be easy, but it is breathtakingly effective. As Sam Snead, the legendary golfer, put it, "It is only human nature to want to practice what you can already do well, since it's a hell of a lot less work and a hell of a lot more fun. Sad to say, though, that it doesn't do a lot to lower your handicap. . . . I know it's a lot more fun to stand on the practice tee and rip drivers than it is to chip and pitch, and to practice sand shots with sand flying back in your face, but it all comes back to the question of how much you're willing to pay for success."

Think back to my mother's typing, which remained constant at seventy words per minute for thirty years. Now consider an experiment in which a group of typists were provided with many hours of purposeful practice.

After a while, they began to make remarkable and unforeseen adaptations, improving finger flexibility, developing novel finger movements, and looking farther and farther ahead in the text. Some eventually got up to 140 words per minute, a staggering number that few could have foreseen before they started on the course.

That is the thing about purposeful practice: *it is transformative.* And that is true whether you're into table tennis, tennis, soccer, basketball, football, typing, medicine, mathematics, music, journalism, public speaking, you name it.

The Structure of Innovation

It is often said that human achievement will eventually run its course; that we will, sooner or later, bump our collective head up against the ceiling of possibilities. The basic laws of mathematics—let alone physics and anatomy—dictate that we cannot keep on running faster and faster forever: if the record for the 100 meters kept falling by a tenth of a second every year, a sprinter would eventually have to cross the finishing line before the starting gun had fired.

But while this may be true of some very simple tasks, it is certainly not true of activities characterized by complexity. In complex tasks, human achievement has many more centuries, possibly millennia, to run before it hits any kind of immovable ceiling. This is not just because the principles of purposeful practice are constantly being elaborated and improved, but also because of what we might call paradigm shifts—completely unforeseen innovations—in technique and application.

Take music. There was a time when it was believed that the world record for holding a note had just about reached its limit when a musician managed to get up to a pretty impressive sixty seconds. Then a musician called Kenny G, a saxophonist, invented an innovative method of circular breathing, inhaling through the nose while exhaling through the mouth in a constant stream, thus managing to hold a note for a staggering forty-five minutes.

This kind of creative innovation is also seen in sports. Dick Fosbury broke the world record for the high jump with a new style where he took off from his outside foot before sailing over the bar headfirst and with his back facing downward. Jan-Ove Waldner transformed the service action in table tennis by holding the paddle between thumb and forefinger, dramatically increasing flexibility and spin. Parry O'Brien broke the world shot put record seventeen times by rotating his body through 180 degrees rather than rocking back and forth before releasing the shot.

The question is: Where do these paradigm shifts come

from? How do these creative leaps, which transform performance by circumventing seemingly immovable constraints, emerge? It is easy to suppose, following the apocryphal story of Isaac Newton, who was said to have invented the theory of gravity after being hit on the head by an apple, that they are like bolts from the blue: random, capricious, and entirely inexplicable. And when you think about it, there is something deeply mysterious about eureka moments.

But careful study has shown that creative innovation follows a very precise pattern: like excellence itself, it emerges from the rigors of purposeful practice. It is the consequence of experts absorbing themselves for so long in their chosen field that they become, as it were, pregnant with creative energy. To put it another way, eureka moments are not lightning bolts from the blue, but tidal waves that erupt following deep immersion in an area of expertise.

Take Pablo Picasso, an artist who is often held up as a perfect example of the lightning bolt theory of creativity. How else to explain how a man born in relative anonymity in the Spanish region of Andalusia came to produce some of the most innovative and influential artistic works of the twentieth century? Surely this speaks of a jolt from above, or at the very least, a very special genetic inheritance?

Robert Weisberg, a psychologist at Temple University, has undertaken an extensive study of Picasso and arrived at a very different view. Weisberg discovered that the young Picasso spent his early years painstakingly carefully drawing eyes and the human body in difficult poses: not just a few hours or a few weeks, but countless hours studiously learning his craft.

But Picasso's creative genius was *not at all evident in his early career*. His early paintings were of no greater merit than those of his peers. Yet these "failures" were not in conflict with his later genius; they were part and parcel of it. It was only by trying—and often failing—that Picasso was able to build the knowledge necessary for the eruption of creativity. (Precisely the same story reveals itself when looking at Mozart, whose early works were imitative and whose masterpieces emerged only after eighteen years of practice.)

The incremental nature of Picasso's creativity can be most vividly seen by examining *Guernica*, the painting inspired by the bombing in 1937 of the Basque town of Guernica during the Spanish Civil War, widely regarded as one of the most innovative works of art in history. We know a lot about how the painting was created, because all forty-five preliminary sketches are numbered and dated.

And guess what? *Guernica* was nothing like a bolt from above. Rather, the sketches show how Picasso wielded the knowledge built up over thirty years to construct the multiple layers: the first sketch, underpinning the overall structure, is based on Picasso's earlier work; others are drawn from his knowledge of Goya; and so on. Each stratum of the masterwork is drawn from experience. What seems like pure, untainted, mystical creativity is, in fact, the consequence of a lifetime of devotion.

The ten-year rule for creativity has been found across the spectrum of human endeavor. In a study of 66 poets by N. Wishbow of Carnegie Mellon University, more than 80 percent needed ten years or more of sustained preparation before they started writing their most creative pieces. In an exhaustive study of eminent scientists, Anne Roe, a psychologist at the University of Arizona, concluded that scientific creativity is "a function of how hard you work at it."

Even the Beatles needed ten years of intensive collaboration before entering what has been called their middle period. It was in this era that they produced *Rubber Soul, Revolver,* and *Sgt. Pepper's Lonely Hearts Club Band*, arguably among the most innovative popular music albums of the twentieth century. As Michelangelo, another artist often taken to exemplify the lightning bolt theory of creativity, put it: "If people knew how hard I had to work to gain my mastery, it would not seem so wonderful at all."

When creativity manifests itself not in artistic expression but in technical innovation, a subtle but immensely powerful interaction is created: purposeful practice changing individuals, and also changing *the means* of changing individuals. In stage one, experts engage in purposeful practice and, as a consequence, develop new techniques. In stage two, other individuals corral these innovations to increase the efficacy of practice, leading to new innovations in stage three, and so on.

This explains one of the key observations of the opening chapter. In the thirteenth century, it was believed that it would take thirty years for anyone to master mathematics; today calculus is mastered by almost every college student. But this is not because we are getting smarter; it is because mathematical technique and education is getting smarter. Similarly, soccer and table tennis standards are rising, at least in part, because technique is improving. So are the training systems, as we have seen.

It all adds up to one inexorable conclusion: human performance in complex tasks will continue on an upward trajectory into the distant future, punctuated by innovations that are not merely unforeseen but unforeseeable.

Feedback Loops

In 1992 Chen Xinhua—the Chinese player-turned-coach who transformed my speed and movement with multi-ball training—proposed another career-changing innovation: he asked me to alter the technique of my forehand slice.

At the time, my stroke was highly variable, sometimes played with a high arc, sometimes with a bit of sidespin, often from below the level of the table. I prided myself on the variability of the shot, supposing it to be an aspect of my inventiveness.

Chen took a different view, instructing me to develop a stroke that was identical in every respect on each and every shot. We spent two months repeating the stroke—played with long, sweeping arc, starting from my right ear and finishing a few inches above my ankle and taken at precisely the same height of the net with exactly 80 degrees of knee bend—until it had been ruthlessly encoded and could be played without deviation.

It was a grueling task, and as we clocked up the hours, I began to question whether it was worth the sweat and toil. Only at the end of the process did I come to comprehend the curious power of this adjustment. It was not that the new technique was better or more effective on any given shot, but that it *provided the perfect conditions for feedback*.

What does that mean? Consider the situation when my technique was variable: it was virtually impossible to identify what had gone wrong when I made an error. Was it because of the backswing, my opponent's spin, the height of the ball? My stroke varied so much from shot to shot, it was impossible to pin down what had gone awry on any one of them.

Feedback, to use the jargon, was corrupted by "biomechanical noise."

By creating a perfectly reproducible stroke, I was able to instantly identify what had gone wrong when I made a mistake, leading to automatic refinement and readjustment. Within months the accuracy and consistency of my forehand had been transformed, with the number of strokes I could hit in a row escalating from fifteen to more than two hundred. That is the power of feedback. As Chen says: "If you don't know what you are doing wrong, you can never know what you are doing right."

The importance of feedback will be familiar to anyone involved in science. Scientific knowledge progresses when the defects of a theory are revealed through testing, which in turn paves the way for a new theory. A theory that is not testable (i.e., a theory that is immune from feedback) can never be improved upon.

With many activities, like steering a car, feedback is integral to the activity (every time you oversteer, the car moves toward the side of the road, forcing you to adjust), but there are dozens of other areas—including sports and many jobs— where feedback must be actively sought. We need to know where we are going wrong if we are going to improve.

Take chess. A player receives feedback after every move, but it is neither instant nor obvious. After all, a player may go on to win a match, but it is very difficult to know, twenty moves down the line, whether a particular move was optimal given that you can never be sure how an opponent might have reacted to an alternative move, and how you would have responded in turn, and so on (this is combinatorial explosion, to use the jargon of chapter 1).

So, how to gain useful feedback? Quite early in the development of chess it was realized that a very simple device was to study historic games between acknowledged grandmasters. A player sets up a board in precisely the same situation as a previous match and then makes his move. He then checks his decision against the move made by the grandmaster.

This kind of feedback is strangely powerful. The aspiring player must ask himself why his choice of move was different from (or perhaps the same as) that of the grandmaster: What were the implications of the grandmaster's move in the match? What reasoning might the grandmaster have used when selecting that move? And how does all this fit into the wider analysis of, say, midgame theory? This is precisely the kind of practice that Laszlo Polgar used in the development of his three daughters.

Feedback is, in effect, the rocket fuel that propels the acquisition of knowledge, and without it no amount of practice is going to get you there.

Lessons from Golf

Most sports have feedback built in: when we play a bad stroke, the ball goes in the net (tennis) or out of bounds (golf). But is that all there is to it?

Think about an amateur golfer on the driving range, hitting toward a flag in the middle distance. He is hitting long irons and trying to get the ball to land near the flag, but he is not altogether sure how far away the flag is, he is not altogether focused on the trajectory of the ball, and when his stroke goes astray, he is not altogether sure whether it is because of an error of grip, alignment, club head speed, or whatever. He certainly has feedback, but it is far from complete.

Now think about a professional golfer hitting toward a flag. He will know precisely how far away the flag is, so that any overhit or underhit is immediately readjusted when he plays his next stroke. More important, because his technique is reproducible, he is aware of how each facet of his stroke—stance, alignment, backswing—is implicated in the outcome, enabling him to identify what went wrong on any given shot.

He also has a coach standing behind him, providing an extra dimension of feedback. His coach is not merely offering encouragement and assessing his levels of concentration, he is also on the lookout for small technical glitches that may have escaped the attention of his charge. The advantage of a coach is that he has a perspective—being able to look from the outside in—that the player lacks.

Only when the player goes inside and watches a video of his practice session does he gain access to a third-person perspective, enabling him to discuss the session with his coach, providing yet another layer of feedback.

Now consider how the amateur and the professional go about playing a practice round of golf. The amateur plays eighteen holes, striking his ball from the fairways or from the edges of the greens, and leaves the course happy with his work for the day. He has concentrated hard and learned from his experience, but has he maximized feedback?

The professional's round could scarcely be more different. On each shot he hits not one ball but multiple balls from each lie, carefully monitoring how each shot compares with the intended outcome. When he finds a difficult or unusual shot, he hits up to half a dozen balls, providing feedback that will prove invaluable when he finds himself in a similar situation in a competition.

The amateur, when playing just one ball from a difficult

lie, has no feedback with which to recalibrate his shot, so when he finds himself in a competition in a similar predicament, he is effectively playing blind.

Jack Nicklaus—a master in the art of purposeful practice— always created a clear idea of precisely what he wanted to achieve on every shot. "I never hit a shot, even in practice, without having a very sharp, in-focus picture of it in my head," he said. "It's like a color movie. First I 'see' the ball where I want it to finish, nice and white and sitting up high on the bright green grass. Then the scene quickly changes and I 'see' the ball going there; its path, trajectory, and shape, even its behavior on landing."

Nicklaus did not create this vivid mental representation for the fun of it, but so that he could gain access to the most detailed feedback possible. By comparing the outcome of the shot with the "color movie" of his intention, he was able to learn and adapt in the most efficient way on every single stroke he ever played. It is difficult to exaggerate the power of the forces unleashed by this kind of learning.

Only when my forehand slice was perfectly reproducible did Chen allow me to make variations to introduce new spins and speeds. But guess what? Every variation—each of which looked to the outsider creative and spontaneous—was also honed through hours of practice so as to be perfectly reproducible, providing noiseless feedback.

This is worth remembering the next time you see a top sportsman doing something out of the ordinary, such as Tiger Woods hitting a zinger from beneath overhanging trees to an elevated lie. This may look like a manifestation of pure genius, but the reality is that he has practiced this type of shot more times, and with more rigorous feedback, than you have practiced your entire golf game.

Seen in this context, it is easy to see why aspiring athletes are so keen to work with top coaches. It is not just that they receive expert advice during training sessions; far more important is that great coaches are able to design practice so that feedback is embedded in the drill, leading to automatic readjustment, which in turn improves the quality of feedback, generating further improvements, and so on.

If you can position yourself in this kind of feedback loop, improvements will escalate in ways that will astonish you. This is the reason why mankind has progressed—and will continue to progress—in almost every area of human endeavor. It is why science has continued, unabated, on a steep upward trajectory toward greater power and accuracy.

It is also, incidentally, why the evolutionary process is so strangely powerful. An evolutionary mutation is "tested" against the "feedback" of survival and reproduction, which in turn permits new mutations, which are then tested once again, and so on. After a few hundred million years in this feedback loop, single-cell organisms have evolved into modern humans and the other wondrous species we see around us.

The difference, of course, is that evolution operates on an intergenerational time scale. We, on the other hand, can evolve into master performers in a matter of a few thousand hours.

Applying the Lessons

Imagine you are a junior doctor eagerly learning how to diagnose cancer from low-dose X-rays known as mammograms. You have been placed alongside an experienced doctor in a working clinic and are following him around diligently to pick up the skills necessary to become an expert. It seems like a pretty sensible way to learn the tools of the trade. But is it?

In this section we'll take some of the insights gained from the principles of purposeful practice in sport and see how they might be applied in the world beyond. We'll stick to the field of medicine, because the gains of improved performance (i.e., saved lives) are rather more dramatic than in other walks of life. But the examples should also offer hints and pointers to the ways that purposeful practice could be applied elsewhere.

So, back to our junior doctor. As he spends time in the clinic, he notices that malignancies are diagnosed pretty infrequently, so although he is working alongside an acknowledged expert, only on a few occasions each week does he get a chance to discuss positive cases and discover what patterns in the mammograms alerted his teacher to possible danger. To put it another way, his practice is sporadic.

But there's worse. When the senior doctor *does* diagnose a malignancy, what's to say he is correct in his judgment? Neither the doctor nor the junior will gain confirmation until many weeks later, when explorative surgery has been undertaken. But by then both the senior and junior doctor will have largely forgotten the reasons for the original diagnosis and will have become preoccupied with new cases.

Feedback, to use the jargon of the previous section, is noisy: corrupted by delay and the pressure of new concerns.

Seen in this context, is learning alongside an experienced practitioner in clinic quite as efficient as it seems? Does it evoke the principles of purposeful practice? The answer, very clearly, is no. And is it any surprise, therefore, that junior doctors learn so painfully slowly, gradually approaching the 70 percent diagnostic accuracy of their teachers but rarely exceeding it?

Now imagine a radically different training system, proposed by Anders Ericsson, where students have access to a library of digitized mammograms for which the correct diagnosis and the location of any tumors *have already been confirmed*. Students would be able to make diagnoses on an hour-by-hour basis and would receive instant feedback about the accuracy of their judgment, transforming diagnostic precision. "The library of mammograms could also be indexed to encourage the student to examine a series of related cases to facilitate detection of some critical feature or type of tumor," Ericsson has said.

This kind of training is strikingly similar to futsal and multiball training. It institutionalizes the principles of purposeful practice, partly through its mathematics—packing countless more diagnoses into the available time—and partly through the guiding power of feedback. Given the vast potential of this kind of training, it is deeply disappointing that, despite persistent lobbying from Ericsson, the medical world has yet to embrace it.

"The medical system is large and relatively conservative," Ericsson said. "There may also be some disincentives. As long as hospitals fail to measure many clinical performances objectively, there will not be sufficient pressure on change and improvement of training. But I am still hopeful that some organized effort will be initiated soon."

Let's take another medical example. In 1960 researcher Jeffrey Butterworth examined whether the ability to make diagnoses using heart sounds and murmurs improved with time on the job. He found that while accuracy increases with experience as a person progresses from student to certified cardiologist, he also found that accuracy actually diminishes over time for doctors in general practice.

That's to say, general practitioners with many years of clinical experience are actually worse at diagnosing heart complaints than doctors fresh out of med school. This sounds strange—not to say a little frightening—but it is not difficult to see why: while cardiac specialists are continually deepening their knowledge of specific cases, GPs encounter cardiac cases relatively infrequently.

In effect, GPs are like amateur golfers encountering a tricky lie and hitting only one ball: they have insufficient feedback to challenge and refine their judgment. The specialists, on the other hand, are like pro golfers hitting multiple balls from a difficult lie: they deepen and expand their knowledge over time, getting better and better.

So, how to improve the game of GPs? How to ensure they spot the warning signs? How about giving GPs a precious opportunity to "hit lot of balls"? How about a well-designed booster course handing GPs an opportunity to make as many diagnoses in one weekend as they would normally make in a year? Sure enough, when GPs were put through this kind of course, their diagnostic accuracy soared.

Zero-Sum Games

Sport is, to use the jargon of economics, a *zero-sum game*: if I win, you, by definition, lose. This may seem rather obvious, but it has weighty ramifications.

Suppose that I am a top sprinter, and I go away and adopt

the principles of purposeful practice and, as a result, reduce my time by 10 percent. When I come to run my next race, I will zoom past many of my competitors. This is great news for me, but it is very bad for them. My relative position has improved as a result of my new training regime, *but at their expense*. The net "benefit" across the group is zero.

Now suppose I adopt the principles of purposeful practice not in sport but in the workplace, and as a consequence, increase my productivity and salary by 10 percent. I have personally benefited from my new work ethic, but now I can also spend 10 percent more on groceries, running shoes, haircuts, and so on, benefiting all those with whom I do business.

I have improved my life, but I have also improved the lives of those around me. Economics, to use the jargon, is a *win-win* game.

Precisely the same insight applies if we widen the perspective. Suppose I am a runner, and that all my competitors join me in adopting the principles of purposeful practice, and that we *all* improve our times by 10 percent. Our *relative* positions in the next race will be precisely the same as they ever were. The net benefit, once again, is zero.

But if everyone applies purposeful practice in the workplace, improving all-around productivity by 10 percent, the gains to society are huge and, over time, cumulative. Economics is a game where everyone can win simultaneously: productivity gains allied to trade generate further productivity gains and more trade, and so on. Win-win-win.

This analysis goes to the heart of this chapter, and reveals its central irony. It is only in sport that the benefits of purposeful practice are accrued by individuals at the expense of other individuals, and never by society as a whole. But this is precisely the area in which purposeful practice is pursued with a vengeance, *while it is all but neglected in the areas where we all stand to benefit.*

As one business expert has put it, "Very few businesses have introduced the principles of [purposeful] practice into the workplace. Sure, the hours may be long in some jobs, but the tasks are often repetitive and boring and fail to push employees to their creative limits and beyond. There is very little mentoring or coaching . . . and objective feedback is virtually nonexistent, often comprising little more than a halfhearted annual review."

This was the point Laszlo Polgar was making in the days before he conducted his great experiment. He urged his colleagues at school and in local government to adopt his ideas, arguing that they could transform performance across society. He could see the ways in which the wider benefits would accumulate, how they could be magnified over time, and yet he spent years frustrated by an inability to get anyone to take him seriously.

He was not, of course, suggesting that all children should be put through ten thousand hours of rigorous, highly specific training before their sixteenth birthday; rather, he was saying that the application of purposeful practice, even in a modest way, can enable countless individuals to realize untapped potential. He was suggesting that everyone has the capacity for excellence, with the right opportunities and training.

His problem was that nobody believed him—and, to a very large extent, they still don't. Almost twenty years after his eldest daughter became the first female grandmaster in chess, Polgar's insights are repudiated by most academics and ignored by society, despite a growing avalanche of evidence in support. To put it simply: The talent theory of expertise continues to reign supreme.

This strangely resilient paradigm has had, and is having, devastating consequences. Why would any individual or parent spend time and energy seeking opportunities to improve if success is ultimately about talent rather than practice? Why would we make sacrifices if the gains are, at best, uncertain? Why would we leave the comfort zone for the rigors of the learning zone if the benefits accrue only to people with the right genes?

The talent theory of expertise is not merely flawed in theory; it is insidious in practice, robbing individuals and institutions of the motivation to change themselves and society. Even if we can't bring ourselves to embrace the idea that expertise is ultimately about the quality and quantity of practice, can't we accept that practice is far more significant than previously thought? That talent is a largely defunct concept? That each and every one of us has the potential to tread the path to excellence?

CHAPTER 4

Mysterious Sparks and Life-Changing Mind-Sets

Mysterious Sparks

Shaquille O'Neal was seventeen years old when he heard the words that would change his life. He had just spent his summer at basketball camp, and for the first time had begun to doubt whether he had what it takes to become an NBA player.

"Camp was real competitive," he would later tell Marlo Thomas for her book *The Right Words at the Right Time*. "You've got all the best high school players from everywhere in the country. At Cole High, I was always ranked first, but at camp I saw other guys ahead of me."

When he got home, O'Neal told his mother that he was having doubts about his future in the sport. She responded by encouraging him to try harder, but O'Neal was not having it: "I can't do that right now. Maybe later." Then his mother said the words that would change everything: "Later doesn't always come to everybody."

"That got to me," O'Neal told Thomas. "Those words snapped me into reality and gave me a plan. You work hard now. You don't wait. If you're lazy or you sit back and you don't want to excel, you'll get nothing. If you work hard enough, you'll be given what you deserve. Everything got easier for me after that."

For the actor Martin Sheen, that moment of transformation came when he was reading a newspaper report about Daniel Berrigan, a Jesuit priest in New York who organized nonviolent protests against Vietnam. Berrigan was challenged by a reporter with the question: "It's fine for you to go to prison, Father Berrigan. After all, you have no children. What's going to happen to our children if we go to prison?" To which Berrigan calmly responded: "What's going to happen to them if you don't?"

"When I read that statement in the newspaper it hit me like a thunderbolt," Sheen told Thomas. "His one comment forced me to re-evaluate everything about myself and the world in which I lived. Eventually it forced me to look at social justice in an entirely different light, and that light illuminated every political and social stand I would take for the rest of my life."

Carly Simon's pivotal moment came in high school, when her boyfriend referred to her stammer as "charming." It was a turning point for her self-esteem and her career. For Venus Williams, it was a pep talk given by her sister, Serena, during a doubles match early in their career. For Mia Hamm, the American soccer player, it was a team meeting with her coach when he dramatically turned the light off in the room before asking if she really wanted to make the grade.

Have you ever experienced a transformational moment— what psychologist Michael Rousell calls a spontaneous influence event? I have. It happened while I was sitting at home at the age of eighteen, watching the television news. The newscaster was going on about how the government was struggling to control inflation. This was nothing new, nothing unusual, nothing of any great importance. But for some strange, inexplicable reason, it lodged inside my head.

It suddenly seemed deeply fascinating that the government— which could put men on the moon—could not control the prices stapled on the products I bought at my local store. It seemed strange, almost surreal; certainly worthy of further investigation. And so I bought an economics textbook. This was pretty astonishing in itself—I had left school a year earlier with few qualifications and even fewer educational aspirations. Even though I had tried hard in class, the material had never really sunk in.

Until now. Armed with my textbook and a sudden, voracious appetite to understand this weird phenomenon called inflation, I discovered something that shocked me. As I read, it felt as if the author was speaking directly to me, that the information was fresh and vital, that it was metabolized and synthesized instantly in my brain, that I could recognize deep and intricate connections between the disparate parts of the book as I plunged through it, that learning was not laborious but liberating.

The book was no different than any of the others I had read at school. But *I* was different. My attitude was different. My motivational stance was different. I was no longer studying because my parents wanted me to or because my teacher had threatened to keep me behind after school, but because *I wanted to*. Because the material was relevant, urgent, even exciting. I would actually get home from training at my table tennis club and rush upstairs to absorb yet more insights.

As I dug ever deeper into cutting-edge economic models, the concepts would sometimes be complex and intricate, and I had to read through the material a few times before it made sense. Sometimes I failed to understand even after a week of striving. But that did not seem to matter. I kept going. Difficulties did not deter me, because the final destination— gaining a deeper understanding of economics—was where I wanted to be.

And I realized, while studying deep into the nights, that a key factor driving success and failure is to be found within the realm of motivation. Sure, clocking up thousands of hours of purposeful practice ultimately determines how far we make it along the path to excellence: but it is only those who *care* about the destination, whose motivation (to use the phrase in chapter 2) is "internalized," who are ever going to get there.

This had never fully occurred to me before, because my drive in table tennis seemed as much a part of the fabric of my being as my lack of motivation at school. But now I could see that one's attitudes could change, adapt, expand. And it seemed deeply significant.

So where do these sparks, these sudden detonations of psychic energy that fire us off in new and unforeseen directions, come from? The problem is that if you look through the various stories above, the disparate moments that triggered such vivid responses, it is impossible to find a unifying theme or cause.

That is partly why the stories are so compelling: they are individual, inimitable, highly specific to a given person at a given point in time. The sparks are, in a very real sense, mysterious, sometimes even to the people ignited by them. So how, then, to arrive at a *theory* of motivation?

This is the problem that has faced psychologists for decades. It is the reason why disagreements on the subject still abound among top mind coaches. It is why you see as many different approaches to motivation as there are self-help tomes on bookshelves. But before we become overly pessimistic (demotivated, even), it's worth broadening the perspective in search for some wider contours, some deeper patterns, within which to conduct the discussion.

Motivational Jolts

In 2003, Greg Walton and Geoffrey Cohen, two American psychologists, devised an intriguing experiment. They took a group of Yale undergraduates and gave them an insoluble math puzzle to work on—but with a small catch. Beforehand, the students were asked to read a report written by former Yale math student Nathan Jackson. This was ostensibly to provide the students with a bit of background information on the math department, but was actually a ruse put together by the two researchers.

Jackson was, in fact, a fictional student, and the article was written by Walton and Cohen. In the report, "Jackson" tells of how he had arrived at college unaware of what career to pursue, how he had got interested in math, and how he was now teaching math in a university department. In the middle of the report was a panel with a bit of biographical information about Jackson: his age, hometown, education, and birthday.

Now, here's the clever part. For half the students, Jackson's birthday was altered to match that of each individual student; for the other half it was not. "We wanted to examine whether something as arbitrary as having a shared birthday with someone who was good at math would ignite a motivational response," Walton said. Having read the report, the students were asked to solve the math puzzle.

To the astonishment of Walton and Cohen, the motivation level for the students in the shared-birthday group did not just nudge up, or even jump up: *it soared*. The matched students persevered on the insoluble puzzle a full 65 *percent longer* than those in the nonmatched group. They also reported significantly more positive attitudes toward math and greater optimism about their abilities. To be clear: These were students who shared the same attitudes toward math before they read Jackson's story.

"They were in a room by themselves taking the test," Walton said in an interview with the author Daniel Coyle. "The door was shut; they were socially isolated; and yet [the birthday connection] had meaning for them. They weren't alone. The love and interest in math became part of them. They had no idea why. Suddenly it was *us* doing this, not just *me*.

"Our suspicion is that these events [what we have called sparks] are powerful because they are small and indirect. If we had told them this same information directly, if they had noticed it, it would have had less effect. It's not strategic; we don't think of it as being useful because we're not even thinking it at all. It's automatic."

What we are seeing at work here might be called *motivation by association*: a small, barely noticed connection searing deep into the subconscious and sparking a motivational response. In the case of the Yale students, the connection was a shared birthday, triggering a powerful jolt along the lines of: "I am similar to this guy; he has achieved really good things in math; I want to achieve those things, too!"

Here is Cohen: "The need to belong, to associate, is among the most important human motives. We are almost certainly hardwired with a fundamental motivation to maintain these associations."

Now, take a look at the following table, from Coyle's book *The Talent Code*:

Year	South Koreans on LPGA Tour	Russians in WTA Top 100
1998	1	3
1999	2	5
2000	5	6
2001	5	8
2002	8	10
2003	12	11
2004	16	12
2005	24	15
2006	25	16
2007	33	15

The rapid escalation in numbers over time almost forces one toward the conclusion that there must have been a spark somewhere around the year 1998. It is an inference that jumps off the page just by looking at the progression of data, even for somebody unacquainted with the idea of motivation by association. Happily, as Coyle has demonstrated, it is not difficult to identify the sparks.

On May 18, 1998, Se Ri Pak, a twenty-year-old Korean golfer, won the McDonald's LPGA Championships, lighting up a nation. Here is how her victory was reported by the *Boston Globe*: "Se Ri Pak fulfilled all the bright promise . . . by triumphing in yesterday's $1.3 million LPGA Champion-ship. . . . Followed by a huge gallery packed with supporters from her country and an army of Korean television and print journalists, she shot a final-round 68 for a record 11-under-par 273 to win $195,000 in the biggest sporting moment for her country [in years]."

For Russia that sporting moment came a few weeks later when Anna Kournikova, a seventeen-year-old tennis player with flowing blond hair, reached the semifinals at Wimble-don. It was one of the most watched television events of the year in her homeland, and partly because of her looks, her name topped Internet searches all around the world.

Now, consider the nature of the association: girls in South Korea will have watched the success of Pak in their masses; they will have been stunned by her triumph (as was most of the rest of the sporting world); and it will have registered in a detonation of national euphoria. The association in this case is one of patriotism, of shared nationality (rather than a shared birthday): a potent connection in any modern-day culture.

"I was very inspired by Se Ri Pak," said Inbee Park, winner of the 2008 U.S. Open. "At that time, not just me, but a lot of young girls like me picked up golf and wanted to be like her. It was very early in the morning. I was half asleep. There were replays, a thousand times after that. I was able to watch it quite a few times. I liked what she did for the people in Korea. . . . That's what really inspired me."

Connie Wilson, the LPGA spokeswoman, has made the same point: "Pak is the person who ignited the interest in women's golf in Korea back in 1998, and got South Korean girls thinking they could achieve this kind of success." In the

Korean media, the current crop of top homegrown female players are dubbed "Se Ri's Kids."

Now consider something else: the dates. Look at the pattern. Can you see something? Here is Coyle:

> Note that in each case the bloom grew relatively slowly at first, requiring five or six years to reach a dozen players. This is not because the inspiration was weaker at the start and then got progressively stronger, but for a more fundamental reason: deep practice takes time (ten thousand hours, as the refrain goes). Talent is spreading through this group in the same pattern that dandelions spread through suburban yards. One puff, given time, brings many flowers.

If we widen the perspective, we will see that this pattern (a powerful motivational spark followed, a decade or so later, by the flowering of success) reveals itself time and time again. In 1962 Hans Alser won the European Championship in table tennis for Sweden. It was, at the time, an unforeseen triumph that mesmerized a nation. Nine years later Stellan Bengtsson, who had marveled at Alser's success as a youngster, won the World Championships, ushering in two decades of Swedish success at the very highest levels of the game.

This pattern can even be seen in the phenomenal success of my hometown of Reading in table tennis in the 1980s. In 1970 local boy Simon Heaps won the European Youth Championships, by far the biggest and most prestigious competition in international junior table tennis. It was a remarkable victory, not least because Reading had no history or heritage in the game. But the motivational consequences of Heaps's success were dramatic and cumulative. Ten years later, one small street in Reading had more top players than the rest of the United Kingdom combined.

In each of these examples we are seeing two phenomena in operation. On the one hand, we are seeing the power of motivation: how a spark can ignite powerful consequences. This spark need not always be one of association—there is an almost endless array of motivational triggers that can suddenly cause us to care deeply, as we saw in the opening section of this chapter with the likes of Shaquille O'Neal and Carly Simon.

But on the other hand, we are seeing, once again, that the attainment of excellence is a long-term process. Ignition does not provide a shortcut; rather, it is the spark that starts one out on the long and arduous path to excellence.

All of which raises a further question. Many have been sparked by a particular event—associational or otherwise—and set off on a path toward a new destination with a fresh (often subconscious) sense of drive and purpose. But this, on its own, is insufficient to attain excellence. We have all met individuals who started out with gusto, only to fizzle away when encountering challenges and difficulties.

Why were some of the Korean girls inspired by Pak still striving for improvement five years later, while others were not? Why were some of the Yale students energized by a shared birth date still straining to solve the puzzle after most of the others had given up (remember, 65 percent represented the *average* increase in persistence)? Why is it that some people are open to the long-term consequences of ignition, while others seem to drift back into a state of motivational passivity?

To understand this, we have to explore the deeper question of how motivation is *sustained*. What psychological mechanisms are in operation, and how do such things as belief, confidence, and emotion influence them? Having widened the focus to look at the contours of motivational ignition, we have to narrow it again to delve into the individual mind. We do so using the groundbreaking research of Carol Dweck, a professor at Stanford University and one of the most influential psychologists of modern times.

The Talent Myth Revisited

The talent myth, as we have seen, is built on the idea that innate ability rather than practice is what ultimately determines whether we have it within us to achieve excellence. We have also seen that this is a rather corrosive idea, robbing individuals of the incentive to transform themselves through effort: Why spend time and energy seeking to improve if success is available only to people with the right genes?

In 1978 Dweck asked the question, Just how corrosive is it? Does a belief in the primacy of talent operate on the edges of our behavior, or does it define the way we interpret and respond to challenges? Does it sit in the background, only functioning at an intellectual level, or does it seep into everything we think, feel, and do? And do our beliefs about talent determine whether we persist on the road to excellence rather than fizzle out?

Dweck's experiment was simplicity itself. Along with a fellow researcher, she took 330 fifth- and sixth-graders and gave them a questionnaire to probe their beliefs about talent and, in particular, intelligence. Those students who held the belief that intelligence is set in genetic stone—i.e., those who subscribed to the talent myth—had what Dweck would later call a *fixed mind-set*. Those who believed that intelligence can be transformed through effort had a *growth mind-set*.

The students were then given a series of problems, the first eight of which were pretty easy, the next four formidably difficult. As the children toiled, two dramatically different patterns emerged.

Here is Dweck describing the kids in the fixed mind-set group (those who subscribed to the talent myth) when they came up against the tough puzzles:

> Maybe the most striking thing about this group was how quickly they began to denigrate their abilities and blame their intelligence for the failures, saying things like "I guess I'm not very smart," "I never did have a good memory," and "I'm no good at things like this."
>
> What was so striking about this was that only moments before, these students had had an unbroken string of successes. Their intelligence and their memory were working just fine. What's more, during these successes their performance was every bit as good as that of the mastery-oriented [growth mind-set] group. Still, only a short while after the difficult problems began, they lost faith in their intellect. . . .
>
> [T]wo thirds of them showed a clear deterioration in their strategies, and more than half of [them] lapsed into completely ineffective strategies. . . . In short, the majority of students in this group abandoned or became incapable of deploying the effective strategies in their repertoire.

And the kids with the growth mind-set? Here is Dweck again:

We saw that the students in the helpless [fixed mind-set] group blamed their intelligence when they hit failure. What did the students in the mastery-oriented [growth mind-set] group blame? The answer, which surprised us, was that they did not blame anything. They didn't focus on reasons for the failures. In fact, they didn't even seem to consider themselves to be failing. . . .

How did they perform? In line with their optimism, most of the students in this group (more than 80%) maintained or improved the quality of their strategies during the difficult problems. A full quarter of the group actually improved. They taught themselves new and more sophisticated strategies for addressing the new and more difficult problems. A few of them even solved the problems that were supposedly beyond them. . . .

Thus, even though they were no better than the helpless children on the original success problems, they ended up showing a much higher level of performance.

This is not just dramatic; it is extraordinary. Just to reiterate: this gaping schism in performance had nothing to do with intelligence and nothing to do with motivation. Indeed, Dweck actually made sure that all the students were equally motivated, by offering gifts they had personally selected.

Instead, the gap in performance was opened up by something completely different: their respective *beliefs* or *mind-sets*. Those who held the belief that abilities are transformable through effort not only persevered but actually improved in the teeth of difficulties; those laboring under the talent myth, on the other hand, regressed into a state of psychological enfeeblement.

Why such a striking difference? Consider for a moment

what was going on in the minds of the two groups of students. Both groups understood that the test was measuring their intelligence. So far, so good. But those in the fixed mind-set had a further belief: that the test was also measuring how intelligent they would be in the future.

How do we know this? Because, by definition, they believe that intelligence is fixed by innate talent. So the test is not merely a snapshot of an evolving capacity, but a measure that represents basic intelligence now and forever. Is it any wonder that they interpret failure as calamitous; that it saps their creativity and undermines future performance; that they will do anything to avoid challenges, even when challenges might be useful?

Perhaps the most stunning example of the destructive tendencies of the fixed mind-set was demonstrated by a study of freshmen at the University of Hong Kong in 1999. All classes at the university are conducted in English, but not all students arrive at the university with equal language skills. So Dweck and her fellow researchers identified a group of students with poor English and then gave them a questionnaire to sort them into fixed and growth mind-set groupings.

The students were then asked whether they would be interested in taking a remedial language class. This was a no-brainer, the kind of offer no sensible person could refuse, a chance to get a boost in one of the most important skills required by the university. But those with a fixed mind-set refused point-blank. They were no more interested in the class than students who spoke perfect English and who had, therefore, nothing to learn. The fixed mind-set students were imperiling their chances at university simply to insulate themselves from the possibility of failure.

Those with the growth mind-set, on the other hand, registered a high interest in taking the class, just as you'd expect.

As Dweck puts it: "In the growth mind-set, you don't feel the need to convince yourself and others that you have a royal flush when you're secretly worried it's a pair of tens. The hand you're dealt is just the starting point. . . . Although people may differ in every which way—in their initial talents and aptitudes, interests, or temperaments—everyone can change and grow through application and experience."

Take a look at that last paragraph again, because it may look familiar. The reason is that it is almost a perfect summary of everything we have learned about expertise so far in this book. The words could almost have been taken from the mouth of Anders Ericsson. What this is telling us is that individuals with the growth mind-set have a belief about the nature of talent that is actually corroborated by the evidence.

Now hold that thought and consider this one instead: remember Shizuka Arakawa, who fell down more than twenty thousand times on her odyssey from wannabe schoolgirl to Olympic figure-skating champion? When examining her story, the one question we failed to ask was: Why? Why would anyone endure all that? Why would she keep striving in the teeth of constant failure? Why not give up and try something else?

Dweck's research hands us the answer: *it is because she did not interpret falling down as failure.* Armed with a growth mind-set, she interpreted falling down not merely as a means of improving, but as evidence that she *was* improving. Failure was not something that sapped her energy and vitality, but something that provided her with an opportunity to learn, develop, and adapt.

This may seem odd, but it is central to the belief system of most top performers. Remember that famous Nike commercial where Michael Jordan says: "I've missed more than nine thousand shots. I've lost almost three hundred games. Twenty-six times I've been trusted to take the game-winning shot and missed"?

Many were bemused by the message, but to Jordan—a living, breathing testament to the growth mind-set—it expressed a deep and urgent truth: in order to become the greatest basketball player of all time, you have to embrace failure. "Mental toughness and heart are a lot stronger than some of the physical advantages you might have," he said. "I've always said that, and I've always believed that." Thomas Edison, the great American inventor, made precisely the same point: "If I find 10,000 ways something won't work, I haven't failed. I am not discouraged, because every wrong attempt discarded is another step forward."*

Think of life as having two paths: one leading to mediocrity, the other to excellence. What do we know about the path to mediocrity? Well, we know it is flat and straight. We know that it is possible to cruise along on autopilot with a nice, smooth, steady, almost effortless progression. We know, above all, that you can reach the destination without stumbling and falling over.

If you travel along this kind of path, it scarcely matters which mind-set you have. Both the fixed and growth mind-set groups will happily proceed toward their destination without any problems. Neither group will forge ahead, neither group will lag behind. They will both arrive at mediocrity with time to spare.

* Samuel Beckett, the playwright, also expresses this truth in his novella *Worstward Ho*: "Ever tried. Ever failed. No matter. Try again. Fail again. Fail better."

But the path to excellence could not be more different. It is steep, grueling, and arduous. It is inordinately lengthy, requiring a minimum of ten thousand hours of lung-busting effort to get to the summit. And, most important of all, it forces voyagers to stumble and fall on every single stretch of the journey.

How do we know that? Because this is the defining feature of purposeful practice, without which excellence is unattainable. Excellence is about striving for what is just out of reach and not quite making it; it is about grappling with tasks beyond current limitations and falling short again and again. The paradox of excellence is that it is built upon the foundations of necessary failure.

The implication hardly needs spelling out. A growth mind-set is perfectly suited to the achievement of excellence; a fixed mind-set, to the achievement of mediocrity. Even if the sparks that ignite us are sometimes enigmatic, lost in the deep and unfathomable mysteries of the mind, one thing is certain: if your chosen destination is within the domain of excellence, you'd better have a growth mind-set. Why? Because a spark ignited in a fixed mind is likely to be extinguished at the first sign of failure.

But is it possible to take control of your mind-set and those of your children or pupils? Is it possible to ditch the talent myth once you have fallen under its spell?

The Power of Words

In 1998, Carol Dweck and a colleague took four hundred fifth-graders and gave them a series of simple puzzles. Afterward, each of the students was given his or her score, plus something else: six words of praise. Half the students were praised for intelligence: "You must be smart at this!" The other half were praised for effort: "You must have worked really hard!"

Dweck was seeking to test whether these simple words, with their subtly different emphases, could make a difference to the students' mind-sets; whether they could mold the student's attitude to success and failure; whether they could have a measurable impact on persistence and performance.

The results were remarkable.

After the first test, the students were given a choice of whether to take a hard or an easy test. A full two-thirds of the students praised for intelligence chose the easy task: they did not want to risk losing their "smart" label by potentially failing at the harder test. But 90 percent of the effort-praised group chose the tough test: they were not interested in success, but in exploring a potentially fruitful challenge. They wanted to prove just how hardworking they were.

Next, the students were given a test so tough that none of them succeeded. But once again, there was a dramatic difference between the ways they responded to failure. Those praised for intelligence interpreted their failures as proof that they were no good at puzzles after all. The group praised for effort persevered on the test far longer, enjoyed it far more, and did not suffer any loss in confidence.

Finally, the experiment came full circle, giving the students a chance to do a test of equal difficulty to the very first test. What happened? The group praised for intelligence showed a 20 percent decline in performance compared with the first test, even though it was no harder. But those in the effort-praised group increased their scores by 30 percent: failure had actually spurred them on.

And all of these differences turned on the difference in six simple words spoken after the very first test.

Dweck and her fellow researcher were so stunned by these results that they repeated the experiment three times with students in different parts of the country and with very different ethnic backgrounds. On all three occasions the results were identical. "These were some of the clearest findings I've ever seen," Dweck said. "Praising children's intelligence harms their motivation, and it harms their performance."

The reason is not difficult to find: intelligence-based praise orients its receivers toward the fixed mind-set; it suggests to them that intelligence is of primary importance rather than the effort through which intelligence can be transformed; and it teaches them to pursue easy challenges at the expense of real learning. "Mindsets frame the running account that's taking place in people's head," Dweck has written. "They guide the whole interpretation process."

Take a look at the following expressions of talent-oriented praise:

"You learned that so quickly! You're so smart!"
"Look at that drawing. Martha, is he the next
  Picasso or what?"
"You're so brilliant, you got an A without even
  studying!"

They all sound wonderfully supportive and come across as precisely the kind of confidence-boosting statements that should be given to students or, indeed, anyone else. But now listen to the subliminal messages lurking in the background:

If I don't learn something quickly, I'm not smart.
I shouldn't try drawing anything hard or they'll see I'm
*   no Picasso.*
I'd better quit studying or they won't think I'm brilliant.

These examples, taken from Dweck's book *Mindset*, hint at a radical new approach to the way we interact with students, aspiring sports stars, or indeed, anyone else. That we should praise effort, not talent; that we should emphasize how abilities can be transformed through application; that we should teach others and ourselves to see challenges as learning opportunities rather than threats; that we should interpret failure not as an indictment but as an opportunity.

How, then, to praise a student who has just performed a task easily and quickly? How to avoid praising talent rather than effort when she has just accomplished something without breaking a sweat? Here's Dweck's advice: "When this happens, I say, 'Whoops, I guess that was too easy. I apologize for wasting your time. Let's do something you can really learn from!'"

The implications of Dweck's research are profound. Many educators have argued that lowering standards will boost the self-esteem of students and ultimately improve attainment. This was, indeed, the philosophy of the educational establishment in the United States and across Europe for much of the 1970s and 1980s, and it continues to exert a lingering influence.

But we can now see that, however well-intentioned, it is corrosive as an educational creed. "It comes from the same philosophy as the overpraising of students' intelligence," Dweck has written. "Well, it doesn't work. Lowering standards just leads to poorly educated students who feel entitled to easy work and lavish praise."

Citadels of Excellence

An eight-year-old girl in bubble-gum pink is thwacking balls on court no. 1 of the Nick Bollettieri Tennis Academy in western Florida. The balls are being fed from an iron-mesh vessel by one of the academy's many coaches, and the girl is playing double-handed backhands with such power that the follow-through revolves her through a half pirouette.

The coach switches the play and is now feeding balls to the girl's forehand while issuing instructions about the importance of rhythm and technique. Every now and again the steady flow of balls over the net is interrupted so that the coach can emphasize a particular point: "Don't hold the racket too tight" or "Try to think about the direction you are hitting the ball." The girl's brow furrows with concentration, sweat moistening her cheeks in the sweltering humidity.

A similar scene is being played on courts all the way into the distant horizon, like a chamber of mirrors chasing an image toward eternity, so that after a while one is no longer shocked at the sight of a child not much taller than a racket hitting the ball with such ferocity.

Bollettieri has become a byword for excellence since his academy was established in 1978 on Florida's west coast. But as I stride around the courts—indoor and outdoor—it becomes clear that it is not the quality of the *coaching* that sets this place apart from other tennis centers around the world. Rather, it is the quality of the *attitude*.

Here the youngsters train with devotion; they undertake physical training as if it is a privilege, not a chore; they eat food like it is fuel. This is simply not what it is like at other tennis centers. Sure, there is an appetite for practice and hard work at other venues, but it is not so visible, so raw, so voracious. It does not blow you away.

Why the difference? I watch Bollettieri, now almost eighty years of age, conducting a coaching session on one of the indoor courts, to search for clues. It is a revelation. He has never heard of Carol Dweck, he has never heard about her "praise" experiments, but everything he says and does is perfectly calibrated to evoke the growth mind-set in his pupil: a twelve-year-old French player called Yves.

He praises effort, never talent; he eulogizes about the transformational power of practice at every opportunity; he preaches the vital importance of hard work during every interruption in play. And he does not regard failure in his students as either good or bad, but as an opportunity to improve. "That's fine," he says as his student hits a forehand long. "You are on the right track. It's not the mistakes; it's how you respond to them."

This is Bollettieri's published creed, which must be signed by all residents: "Every endeavour pursued with passion produces a successful outcome regardless of the result. For it is not about winning or losing—rather, the effort put forth in producing the outcome. The best way to predict the future is to create it—therefore, we believe we have the best training methods to help each athlete achieve their dreams and goals and ultimately reach their ability level in the arena of sports and life."

It is difficult to imagine a more succinct description of the practice theory of expertise or a more eloquent means of promoting the growth mind-set. Is it any wonder that the Bollettieri Academy has produced such illustrious champions as Andre Agassi, Jim Courier, Martina Hingis, Maria Sharapova, Anna Kournikova, and Jelena Jankovic?

• • •

In Dweck's praise experiment we saw how praise for effort rather than talent helped to orient students toward a growth mind-set, with dramatic consequences. The problem is that further experiments by Dweck showed that those consequences were relatively short-lived: left to their own devices, children will eventually settle back into the default mind-set that predated the praise.

The only way for a growth mind-set to bed down is for effort-oriented praise to be constantly repeated—not easy in a world where the talent myth rules supreme. The Bollettieri Academy, however, shows how dramatic the results can be when the emphasis on the growth mind-set is constant, passionate, and relentless; when the message seeps deep into the subconscious of the students, altering the default settings.

"You know why this place is successful?" Bollettieri says in his growly drawl when we sit down to discuss his philosophy. "Because none of the kids leave here without their mind-set transformed. They may arrive thinking they can cruise their way to success, but they quickly learn that nobody has got anywhere in life without working hard, by showing tremendous discipline, and by taking responsibility for their actions. That is what ultimately separates the best from the rest."

Spend a few days at the Bollettieri Academy, and you will get a sense of the transformational drama being played out in the minds of his students as their subconscious minds slowly absorb, and eventually accept, the radical theory of the growth mind-set. Spend a few weeks there, and you will begin to sense, with strange exhilaration, your own mind-set gravitating toward the growth path.

The Bollettieri Academy is not alone in this respect. There are other citadels of excellence: places around the world where the growth mind-set has become embedded in the culture. Places where the causal relationship between hard work and excellence has been demonstrated and redemonstrated again and again. For generation after generation.

The fabled National Centre in Beijing is home to the China table tennis team. It is a gray concrete building within a security-controlled complex a few hundred yards from the Temple of Heaven. From the outside it looks no different from any other building in the Chinese capital. But inside is a beehive of activity, a living, breathing testament to the power of practice. On each floor is a different team: junior girls, junior boys, senior women, and senior men. And within each room are dozens of players playing on dozens of tables, moving, sweating, ingraining excellence: enough piston power to light up a city.

It is impossible to spend time in this building without realizing that the Chinese national team trains with more intensity, more devotion, and a more vivid belief in how hard work translates into medals than any other table tennis training team in the world. It is a place where every single player has gravitated toward the growth mind-set. It is the philosophy that permeates the entire building.

"It is difficult to exaggerate the power of these 'sporting homes,'" Peter Keen, a leading sports scientist and the architect of Great Britain's success at the 2008 Olympic Games, told me. "In the British Olympic movement we have a stated goal of trying to create places where the culture of personal transformation is so deeply embedded it rubs off on aspiring youngsters. I have no doubt that a significant part of the success of the British Cycling team [which won an astonishing eight gold medals at the Olympics in Beijing] is the culture of its training base."

That base is a building on the outskirts of Manchester, a city in England's industrial northwest. It is a rather drab location, surrounding by acres of concrete with little aesthetic beauty. As one arrives in a taxi, it is possible to feel a little underwhelmed. A little dispirited. A little vexed, even. And then you walk inside. You get talking to the coaches and athletes. And you begin to feel the magic. You feel the bite of the culture. You hear the echoing belief in the transformational power of hard work in almost every syllable of every sentence.

"I am convinced that world-class performance emerges from mind-set," says Keen. "Many of our greatest cyclists did not start out with obvious natural advantages, but they have transformed themselves through application. Perhaps the key task of any institution is to encourage the adoption of a growth mind-set. When that kind of philosophy becomes embedded in the culture, the consequences can be dramatic."

But if sporting citadels of excellence, constructed on the growth mind-set, are able to create world-class performers, what would a place that exalted the fixed mind-set look like? What would happen to an institution—a culture—deliberately and consciously founded on the talent myth? How would it perform, and how would its inhabitants behave?

Before answering that question, consider one final outcome of Dweck's praise experiment. In one of her studies, Dweck told the students that she would be conducting the same study at another school and that the children there might like to hear from students who had already taken the test. She gave the students a sheet on which they could record their thoughts along with a space where they could record how many problems they had got right.

When she looked at the children praised for effort, Dweck found that almost all of them had told the truth about their performance. Only one child in the group had doctored his score. But in the group praised for intelligence, an extraordinary 40 percent had lied about their scores. "Doing well was so important to them that they felt compelled to distort their performance in order to impress unknown peers," Dweck said.

When Talent Rules

On October 23, 2006, Jeffrey Skilling sat in the federal courtroom in Houston awaiting sentencing for his part in the Enron collapse, one of the most apocalyptic corporate failures in modern history. The former chief executive was smartly dressed in a dark suit and tie, his face grim as he contemplated a future behind bars. Alongside him, his small army of lawyers fidgeted in their seats.

All down the street and around the block, television anchors were ready with their microphones and earpieces. Newspaper reporters were poised with notebooks and mobile phones. A sprinkling of former Enron employees, many of whose retirement savings had been wiped out in the collapse, were also pacing around, hoping to be among the first to hear the sentence.

After listening to statements from Skilling—who continued to plead his innocence—and a number of those whose lives had been ruined by Enron's failure, the judge asked Skilling to rise. "The evidence established that the defendant repeatedly lied to investors, including Enron's own employees, about various aspects of Enron's business," he said. He then handed down the sentence: two hundred and ninety-two months in prison. Rebecca Carter, Skilling's second wife and a former Enron corporate secretary, broke down as the sentence was read out.

Skilling's trial attracted huge public interest, but it was difficult even for financial commentators to keep track of the evidence. Much of the time was taken up with the mind-spinningly complex financial devices that senior Enron executives had used to conceal the looming catastrophe from shareholders and the financial markets. Two, in particular, took up many hours as the court tried to penetrate the hidden activities of a corporate colossus that had ruled the world before collapsing like a house of cards.

The first was called mark-to-market accounting: this enabled Enron to book huge profits, not as a result of cash actually received, but on the basis of estimates of future income that might or might not accrue. The other was Enron's reliance on special purpose entities, or SPEs. These were specially created partnerships that existed at arm's length from the company, but which allowed Enron to borrow big without the debt showing up on company accounts. By the time of its collapse, Enron had created three thousand SPEs.

The court spent many days trying to unravel these mechanisms, but what was not considered in anything like as much detail was the possibility that these financial manipulations—which hoodwinked investors and shareholders for so long—were not the problem, but merely a symptom of a far deeper malaise; that they were, in effect, the consequence of a culture that had slowly but inexorably led a firm of 22,000 employees along a ruinous path to destruction.

• • •

In 2001 three senior executives of McKinsey, the world's largest and most prestigious management consultancy, published a book called *The War for Talent*. This book encapsulated a key tenet of McKinsey's philosophy: that talent is what ultimately determines success and failure in the corporate world; that pure reasoning ability matters far more than domain-specific knowledge.

"Bet on the natural athletes, the ones with the strongest intrinsic skills," one executive told the authors. "Don't be afraid to promote stars without specifically relevant experience, seemingly over their heads." Success in the corporate world, the authors contended, requires "the talent mind-set"—the "deep-seated belief that having better talent at all levels is how you outperform your competitors."

Although the McKinsey approach provoked debate within corporate America, one company embraced the philosophy, took it further, and pursued it more vigorously than any other. According to Malcolm Gladwell, in a seminal essay for the *New Yorker* magazine, "[Enron] was a company where McKinsey conducted twenty separate projects, where McKinsey's billings topped ten million dollars a year, where a McKinsey director regularly attended board meetings, and where the C.E.O. himself was a former McKinsey partner. . . . Enron was the ultimate 'talent' company."

Skilling's devotion to talent is perhaps best summed up by a famous incident: When he applied to Harvard Business School, he was asked by the interviewing professor, "Are you smart?" Skilling proudly replied: "F—— smart."

Not only did Enron recruit talent vigorously from only the very best business schools, it also exalted its leading lights as if they were superstars. Every year the top 15 percent of performers were handed huge bonuses, and the bottom 15 percent were often fired, in a process dubbed "rank and yank." Those considered to be in possession of talent were encouraged to move wherever they saw fit within the company, as if they had the ability to conjure profits for the company with the sheer quality of their superior reasoning.

"Fluid movement is absolutely necessary in our company. And the type of people we hire enforces that," Skilling told the authors of the McKinsey report. "Not only does this system help the excitement level for each manager, it shapes Enron's business in the direction that its managers find most exciting." It is hardly surprising that annual employee turnover from promotions reached close to 20 percent; that star employees ricocheted around the company like pinballs; that poaching from other business units was actually encouraged.

Enron's strategy was flawed for two independent reasons. The first is that it was based on the false premise so vigorously promoted by McKinsey: that talent matters more than knowledge. This is nonsense: as we saw in chapter 1, successful decision making in any situation characterized by complexity—whether in sport, business, or wherever—is propelled not by innate ability but by the kind of knowledge that can be built up only through deep experience.

But Enron's strategy was also flawed for a different, more insidious reason. Its core philosophy not only undermined productivity; it also served to create a very specific type of culture. A culture that exalted talent above the possibilities of personal development. A culture that mocked the idea that learning can transform ability. A culture that promoted, nurtured, and ultimately entrenched the fixed mind-set.

Here is Dweck:

Enron recruited big talent, mostly people with fancy degrees, which is not in itself bad. It paid them big money, which is not that terrible. But by putting complete faith in talent, Enron did a fatal thing: it created a culture that worshipped talent, thereby forcing its employees to look and act extraordinarily talented.

Basically, it forced them into the fixed mindset. And we know a lot about that. We know that people with the fixed mindset do not admit and correct their deficiencies.

Remember the experiment with the Hong Kong students? They turned down an opportunity to take part in an English-language booster course, something that would hugely benefit their education, because they lived in a psychological world where they did not dare to fail in public. Remember, too, how almost 40 percent of the students praised for intelligence actually lied about their score on the test? The fixed mind-set had made the public admission of their real result intolerable.

Now think back to mark-to-market accounting and the special purpose entities. Think of how Enron spent weeks leading up to the quarterly reports figuring out ways to conceal any bad news from the market. Think of how each employee became paranoid about admitting to any mistakes, fearful that he or she would be written off as untalented and yanked out of the company. Think of how the fixed mind-set came to permeate and define the daily existence of the executives and employees.

Here is Gladwell: "They weren't naturally deceptive people. . . . They simply did what people do when they are immersed in an environment that celebrates them solely for their innate 'talent.' They begin to define themselves by that description, and when times get tough and that self-image is threatened, they have difficulty with the consequences. They will not take the remedial course. They will not stand up to investors and the public and admit that they were wrong. They'd sooner lie."

The Garden Shed

In July 2002, I was invited to southwest London by Gideon Ashison, a table tennis coach with a remarkable track record of getting youngsters off the streets and away from crime through sports. "I have found a boy I want you to see," Ashison told me. "His name is Darius Knight."

Ashison took me to a shed in the back garden of one of his friends: small, cramped, poorly lit, but just about big enough to house a table tennis table. There, inside, Knight and another young boy from Ashison's group were training intensely.

Why the shed? The reason was simple: neither Ashison nor Knight could afford anywhere better. Knight hailed from a crime-ridden high-rise neighborhood; his father had been involved in drugs before walking out on the family. The shed represented a way out. Besides, it had one big advantage: it was available to use twenty-four hours a day.

Every afternoon, Knight would leave school, travel five miles across town on the bus, and then walk twenty minutes to get to the shed. There he would work with Ashison for hours at a time: honing his shots, learning footwork patterns, practicing his serves. By the time I went to watch him, his range of abilities was awesome, all the more so given the vivid contrast with the impoverished surroundings.

Over the next few weeks, I eulogized Knight: in my newspaper column, to friends, to the England table tennis establishment, to anybody who would listen. The reaction was highly enthusiastic. Within months, Knight was selected to attend the High Performance Centre in Nottingham: suddenly he found himself surrounded by state-of-the-art facilities, top coaches, specialized support staff, and schooling tailored around his training and competition schedule.

It was, as he said at the time, a dream come true.

But Knight also found himself surrounded by something less benign: a new kind of praise. With Ashison, Knight had only heard effort-based praise: this was Ashison's forte. His technical knowledge was basic, but he knew how to imbue his players with the growth mind-set: encouraging application, emphasizing personal responsibility, urging them to regard failure as an opportunity, not an indictment. His group of young players trained with an intensity unrivaled in English table tennis.

But in Nottingham, Knight—the hottest new property in English table tennis—kept hearing about how talented he was; how remarkable it was that he had achieved so much in so short a time; how he had been born to play table tennis. I was the loudest and most incautious in my talent-based praise (this was before I had read Dweck): "It is as if table tennis is encoded in his DNA," I wrote in *The Times*. "With talent like that, his progress seems assured."

It was not long before Knight started to go backward. His

training lacked intensity (Why train hard if I am so talented that things should come effortlessly?); he began to duck big matches (Why should I risk losing the talent label by losing to inferior opponents?); he even began to become deceptive about his results (Why be upfront when it might compromise all that gushing praise?).

Knight's story is interesting for all sorts of reasons, but it is, first and foremost, a parable about mind-set. When Knight trained in a humble shed, he improved at lightning speed: Equipped with the right state of mind, his appetite for hard work was ravenous, his enthusiasm palpable, his quest for personal transformation relentless.

But when he moved to one of the most prestigious sporting facilities in Europe, his development stalled. He had access to every conceivable advantage, but this counted for nothing because he had started to inhabit a very different psychological world: a world characterized by a preoccupation with talent, with wanting to look good, with fear of failure and an aversion to hard work.

Today, Knight is back on track. Why? Because Steen Hansen, the Danish-born performance director of English table tennis, realized that Knight's problem was not technical or tactical, but psychological. His problem was mind-set.

Hansen instructed the coaches to abide by the prescriptions of Dweck: to praise effort, not talent; to encourage Knight to embrace failure as a means of realizing his potential; to eulogize personal transformation. Knight's form has since soared, and he is near the top of the rankings for his age group, both in England and Europe. Will he win Olympic gold in 2016? Maybe, maybe not.

What is certain is that Knight is now equipped with the most important thing of all: the growth mind-set. It permeates his attitude not merely toward table tennis, but toward life: his relationships; his commitments; his responsibilities to friends, teammates, and sponsors. He does not duck challenges, and he does not regard failure as a reason to stop striving. "Mind-set is everything," Knight told me recently.

He is growing not merely as a table tennis player, but as a human being.

PART II

Paradoxes
of the
Mind

CHAPTER 5

The Placebo Effect

A Tin of Sardines

On September 25, 2000, Jonathan Edwards made his way to the Olympic stadium in Sydney to compete in the final of the triple jump. As the world record holder, the Englishman was the hot favorite for gold, but he was experienced enough to know that expectations can be a perilous thing. He took a deep breath as he walked through the athletes' entrance in the bowels of the stadium.

In his sports bag Edwards carried the equipment familiar to any top athlete: spikes, extra shirts, towels, special drinks. Nestling toward the bottom of the bag, however, was a rather unusual item: a tin of sardines. Why the sardines? A little more information about Edwards will help to explain.

Edwards was not merely one of the most admired athletes in the United Kingdom, he was also a born-again Christian.

Throughout his early athletic career he had refused to compete on Sundays, missing out on many top competitions, including the 1991 World Championships. Only after a long conversation with Christian friends—when he was convinced that competing on the Sabbath was God's will—did he relent.

But even as he traveled the world forging a reputation as the most brilliant triple jumper in history, he continued to preach and proselytize the gospel. Sport was, for Edwards, not about winning or losing, and certainly not about personal gain and glory; rather, it was about creating a platform for spreading the word of God. By the time of the Olympic Games in Sydney, his platform was just about as big as it gets.

So why the sardines? In Matthew 14, Jesus performed the miracle of the feeding of the five thousand.

> Taking the five loaves and the two fish and looking up to heaven, [Jesus] gave thanks and broke the loaves. Then he gave them to the disciples, and the disciples gave them to the people. They all ate and were satisfied, and the disciples picked up twelve basketfuls of broken pieces that were left over. The number of those who ate was about five thousand men, besides women and children.

This was one of Edwards's favorite passages from the Bible and provided him with deep reassurance about the power of the Lord. The sardines, then, were to symbolize the fish miraculously provided by Christ to the masses; they were, in effect, the physical representation of Edwards's faith in God.

As he walked out onto the field of play, Edwards whispered a silent prayer: "I place my destiny in Your hands. Do with me as You will." A few hours later he captured the gold medal with a majestic leap of 17.71 meters, securing his status as one of Britain's greatest athletes.

Many have questioned the rationality of religious belief, including Richard Dawkins in his best-selling book *The God Delusion*, but this chapter is not concerned with the rationality, much less the truth, of religious belief. It is, rather, concerned with the *potency* of beliefs of different kinds.

And can it be denied that religious beliefs have powerful effects?

The idea that the Creator is on your side, guiding your footsteps, taking a personal interest in your troubles, deriving pleasure from your victories, providing solace in your defeats, orchestrating the world such that, in the words of Saint Paul's Epistle to the Romans, "all things work together for good to those who love God"—all this must have a dramatic impact on the efficacy of an athlete, or indeed anyone else. As Muhammad Ali put it: "How can I lose when I have Allah on my side?"

Ali was talking in the buildup to his showdown with George Foreman in 1974, a bout that few, even in his own camp, believed he could win. Norman Mailer, Ali's most eloquent chronicler, feared that the boxer might lose his confidence and vitality in the buildup to the contest, such was the apparent gulf in ability between the aging former champ and his formidable young opponent. But Mailer failed to factor in the divine: How could Ali fall victim to self-doubt when his strength flowed, not from within, but from the Almighty?

Ali's God was, of course, different from Edwards's. The Black Muslims believed in the teachings of W. D. Fard, a door-to-door salesman turned Messiah, who preached that God—a divine being created from a single spinning atom 76 trillion years ago—will save blacks from the apocalypse in a wheel-shaped spaceship. Edwards, on the other hand, believed in Jehovah, the God of the Bible.

The key point is that these two belief systems say contradictory things, so only one (at most) can be true. Or, to put it another way, either Ali or Edwards (or both) has benefited powerfully from false beliefs.

Edwards made precisely this point when I went to see him at his home in the north of England. In the years since the Olympic Games in Sydney, his life has been something of a roller coaster. On his retirement from sport he landed the plum job of presenting *Songs of Praise*, the most high-profile religious program on British television. He also spent many weekends traveling to churches to preach and share his faith, with Christians flocking from around the country to hear his words.

But even as he clocked up the miles in dedication to his faith, Edwards was confronting a personal crisis. "I never doubted my belief in God for a single moment until I retired from sport," he told me. "But when I retired, something happened that took me by complete surprise. I quickly realized that athletics was more important to my identity than I believed possible. I was the best in the world at what I did, and suddenly that was not true anymore. With one facet of my identity stripped away, I began to question the others, and from there, there was no stopping. The foundations of my world were slowly crumbling.

"Once you start asking yourself questions like, 'How do I really know there is a God?' you are already on the path to unbelief. During a documentary I made for television on Saint Paul, some experts raised the possibility that his spectacular conversion on the road to Damascus might have been caused by an epileptic fit. It made me realize that I had taken things for granted without subjecting them to any kind of analysis. When you think about it rationally, it does seem incredibly improbable that there is a God. I eventually had to confess to myself that I no longer believed."

Edwards's apostasy rocked the Christian community in the United Kingdom and created understandable problems in his family life—he is married to a committed Christian—which happily seem to have been resolved. He also resigned from his position presenting *Songs of Praise* and his many other Christian commitments. But Edwards's religious about-face also provided him with a unique perspective with which to reflect on the impact of his beliefs on his sporting performances.

Were those beliefs, which he now thinks were without any objective foundation, helpful in the heat of battle?

"Without doubt," he said. "Looking back now, I can see that my faith was pivotal to my success. Believing in something beyond the self can have a hugely beneficial psychological impact, even if the belief is fallacious. It provided a profound sense of reassurance because I took the view that the result was in God's hands and that God was on my side. It enabled me to block out doubt in the moments before I was due to jump. Yes, it was vital."

If a born-again atheist can testify to the power of religious belief, who are the rest of us to doubt him?

Mind over Matter

In the opening chapters we saw how excellence is the consequence of thousands of hours of purposeful practice. But excellence is not, on its own, sufficient for success. It is also necessary to translate one's abilities into peak performance in the cauldron of competition and with one's livelihood, or at least one's ego, on the line. This, it turns out, is a strangely difficult art to master, and one that often separates the best from the rest.

We know it when we see it: that extraordinary ability of top sportsmen to rise above the anxieties and angst, the doubts and the tensions, that so often paralyze lesser performers. They retain their sureness of touch, their subtlety of mind, all those deep and complex motor skills built up over thousands of hours and which can so easily melt in the heat of the battle.

We see it in Tiger Woods sinking a twelve-foot putt to win the U.S. Masters without flinching; we see it in David Beckham bending the ball around a wall from thirty yards to save a match for the England soccer team. We see it in Barack Obama's seamless recall of facts and marshaling of complex arguments under the heat of the television lights and amid the glare of countless millions of voters during the presidential debates.

How do they do it? Where does the mental assurance come from? Can it be learned?

This chapter is about the psychology of *performance*. We will dig down into the minds of top performers and explore the relationship between mind and body under pressure. And we will arrive at the paradoxical conclusion that the thing that often separates the best from the rest is a *capacity to believe things that are not true but which are incredibly effective*.

That was the point of the story of Edwards and Ali. At

least one of them (or both) benefited from false beliefs. But those were anecdotes. Is there further evidence about how false beliefs can help to produce positive outcomes?

We start with the world of medicine and the placebo effect, one of the most perplexing phenomena in science. By the end of the chapter we'll see that the placebo effect provides a prism through which to understand how top athletes—and other top performers—are so consistently able to hit peak performance when it really matters.

In early 1944, Allied forces launched an offensive foray at Anzio in northern Italy during World War II. It turned out to be a disastrous maneuver, with American forces trapped in the caves of Pozzoli for over a week. Henry Beecher, a young doctor from Harvard, was the man responsible for treating the influx of injured American soldiers at a makeshift field hospital at the beachhead.

Such was the scale of casualties that Beecher soon ran out of anesthetic. Confronted with a soldier with gaping wounds and needing to operate quickly, he therefore instructed his nurse to administer a saltwater injection instead of morphine. The patient, assuming that a proper dose of anesthesia had been administered, lay back in preparation for his operation. What happened next would come to shake the medical world.

Beecher found that the soldier was not merely comforted by the injection of salt water; *he was able to tolerate the agonies of surgery as well as if he had been injected with "real" anesthetic.* Over the next few weeks Beecher was to replicate the result with dozens of wounded soldiers, each of whom could bear, with seemingly miraculous stoicism, the trauma of surgery with nothing more than salt water running through their veins. When he returned, Beecher wrote a paper called "The Powerful Placebo."

But Beecher was not the first doctor to have been astonished by the placebo effect. Theodor Kocher, a Swiss surgeon, successfully performed 1,600 thyroidectomies without anesthesia in Berne in the 1890s after taking careful steps to ensure that his patients believed that they had been fully anesthetized. According to journalist and doctor Ben Goldacre, "Surgeons from before the invention of anesthesia often described how some patients could tolerate knife cutting through muscle, and saw cutting through bone, perfectly awake, and without even clenching their teeth."

"You may be tougher than you think," Goldacre writes.

But if these examples provide compelling testimony to the power of mind over matter, only in the last few years has the full bizarreness of the placebo effect been revealed, leading doctors to radically rethink the connection between brain and body.

In 1972 an experiment was conducted in which students sitting through a lecture were provided with either a pink or a blue sugar pill. The students were told that the pill would either be a stimulant or a sedative, but were not told which (the pills, of course, were neither). It turned out that the pink placebo was better at maintaining concentration in students than the blue one. Or, to put it another way, the color of a pill matters.

Further experiments have shown that oxazepam, a drug like Valium, is more effective at treating anxiety when green and more effective for depression when yellow; that the sedative chlordiazepoxide is more effective in capsule form than pill form; and that invasive saltwater injections are more effective than sugar pills for blood pressure, headaches, and other pains, even though neither provides any known physical benefit. Another experiment compared two different placebo treatments for arm pain: one a sugar pill, the other a ritual modeled on acupuncture. The more elaborate procedure was significantly more effective.

All of which begins to hint at how the placebo effect works. The power of the placebo has nothing to do, by definition, with the pharmacological properties of the drug; rather, its effect derives from the *entirely false belief that the drug is effective*. But this belief is not created out of nowhere; it is manufactured within a cultural context. Anything that imbues the treatment with greater authenticity, that creates an illusion of credibility, will play on the mind of the patient, strengthening his misguided belief in the drug and, by implication, its efficacy.

One factor in the credibility of the placebo treatment is, of course, that the drug is administered by a qualified doctor. But there are countless others. Color, for example, is strongly connected in certain cultures with certain types of effect: red is buzzy, blue or white are cool and soothing. Drug companies play on these meanings. Goldacre reports that stimulant medication tends to come in red or orange, antidepressants in blue, and so on.

Packaging, too, confers cultural meaning that can bolster the placebo effect. Research has found that aspirins contained in snazzy, all-singing-all-dancing packaging are more effective than aspirins contained in dull, boring boxes. Aspirins are not, of course, placebos: the point is that packaging can itself deliver a placebo effect. So, too, can price. Dan Ariely, the behavioral economist, has shown that cheap painkillers are less effective than painkillers identical in every respect except for a more expensive price tag.

Again, it all comes down to belief. For obvious reasons, we find it easier to believe in a treatment when it burns a hole in our wallet: "At that price, it must be good!" As Ariely points out, this means that it may not be as crazy as it seems to pay more for a brand-name drug even when it is pharmacologically identical to the cheaper variety on the adjacent shelf. The very act of shelling out extra cash can instill the conviction without which the drug would be ineffective.

The key point in all this is that the power of the mind is exercised through the medium of belief, and it doesn't matter whether the belief is true or false or how the delusion is created—so long as it is created successfully. It doesn't matter if it is created by a reassuring doctor, slick packaging, price, advertising, color, invasiveness, ritual, or any of countless other possibilities. It does not matter if it is supported by fabricated evidence or no evidence at all. All that matters is that the patient *believes*.

Religion as Placebo?

In the 1960s a groundbreaking series of epidemiological studies found that heart disease is far less common among the actively religious than in the general population. At first this was thought to be because of secular factors such as religious types abstaining from unhealthy habits like cigarettes, and the reduced stress of being part of a supportive community.

But further studies, which controlled for these influences, continued to find that the actively religious have significantly better health outcomes. The scientific community was forced to accept the rather astonishing fact that religious belief, *in and of itself*, confers real and tangible health benefits.*

Christians were understandably quick to trumpet this phenomenon, proclaiming that God is actively involved in dishing out health benefits to his chosen few. The only problem with this view is that the impact of religious belief has been found to transcend denominational boundaries. It is not just Christians, but also those who hold beliefs that contradict the teachings of the Bible—such as Buddhists and Hindus—who benefit medically from their religious convictions.

As Herbert Benson puts it in his book *Timeless Healing*: "I describe God with a capital G in this book but nevertheless hope readers will understand that I am referring to all the deities of the Judeo-Christian, Buddhist, Muslim, and Hindu traditions, to gods and goddesses, as well as to spirits worshipped and beloved by humans all over the world and throughout history. In my scientific observations, I have observed that no matter what name you give the Infinite Absolute you worship, no matter what theology you ascribe to, the results of believing in God are the same."

In the context of the last section, it is not difficult to see what is going on: this is the placebo effect in action once again. But this time it is not the false belief in the efficacy of

---

* Final confirmation for the remarkable health effects of religious belief came in 1996 when Jeremy Kark of Hebrew University and fellow researchers undertook a pioneering study of mortality rates in a cluster of secular and religious kibbutzim in Israel. They found that mortality rates in the secular kibbutzim were nearly twice that of their religious counterparts. "There was no difference in social support or frequency of social contact between religious and secular kibbutzim," Kark wrote.

sugar pills that is generating the outcomes; rather, it is the belief in the healing power of God. And, as with sugar pills, it is those who believe most fervently who benefit the most.

Indeed, it could be argued that religion is the ultimate placebo. Instead of the authority of a doctor, belief is based on the authority of God, who is both infallible and omnipotent. Where belief in the medical placebo is based on slick advertising and snazzy packaging, belief in the healing power of God is derived from Holy Scripture. And it does not matter if your particular God is real or not (in the same way that it does not matter if a sugar pill has genuine pharmacological properties or not), so long as your belief is sincere.

What's more, many religions actively evoke the placebo effect within their theology. In Mark 9 of the Bible, for example, a father brings his ill son before Jesus for healing, saying: "If You can do anything, take pity on us and help us." Jesus replies: "If you can believe, all things are possible to him who believes." Jesus makes a similar point in the book of Matthew: "According to your faith, be it unto you."

What the Scriptures seem to be saying is that *God does not act in proportion to the worthiness of the intercessor, but in proportion to the intercessor's belief that God will so act.* Substitute "sugar pill" for "God" in the previous sentence, and you have just defined the placebo effect. "Nothing," writes Anne Harrington, professor of the history of science at Harvard University, "has contributed more to facilitating this innate capacity [of the body to heal itself] than belief in God's capacity to heal us."

Karl Marx called religion the "opium of the masses." He was almost right: religion is the sugar pill of the masses.

The Placebo Effect in Sports

In 1952 Norman Vincent Peale, a Protestant preacher, wrote what was to become arguably the single most important work of popular psychology of the twentieth century. Its title: *The Power of Positive Thinking*. It spent 186 straight weeks on the *New York Times* best-seller list and sold more than five million copies worldwide.

In the book, Peale tells the reader of the power of religious belief to heal, urging the reader to develop religious conviction through the techniques of imagery, affirmations, and reading the Bible. But Peale, despite his Protestant background, also makes it clear that the reader's religious background is irrelevant to the success of positive thinking. "It's not necessary to be born again," Peale said. "You have your way to God; I have mine. . . . Christ is just one of the ways."

Peale was, in effect, articulating the placebo effect: he was saying that it is *belief itself*, not its content, that matters. As Harrington puts it: "Peale actually probably spent more time than any other twentieth-century figure in the mind-cure movement downplaying the need to commit to any specific Christian or other specific faith tradition to enjoy the healing fruits of faith." It is hardly surprising that he was, for this reason, condemned by many within the Christian community.

But the genius of Peale's book lay in its recognition that the religious placebo (or, to use his words, the power of religious belief) extends far beyond the realm of health. He realized that it can also reduce anxiety, improve one's sense of belonging, boost self-confidence, and alleviate angst—all things that can, as Peale points out again and again, improve life and radically transform performance. Chapters in Peale's book include "Believe in Yourself," "Expect the Best and Get It," "I Don't Believe in Defeat," and "How to Draw on That Higher Power."

But it was in sport that the book arguably had its greatest impact. In the 1980s I lost count of the number of athletes who would turn up at competitions with a copy of the book in their gym bags; the athletes who suddenly turned to God for inspiration; the countless performers who would duck out before matches to spend fifteen minutes going through breathing exercises while quietly chanting affirmations from Scripture. More than half of the England table tennis team was actively using Peale's techniques by the mid-1980s.

Religion, which had once been out in the cold in the world of sports—not least because top athletes didn't think they had enough time for two separate realms of devotion—was suddenly center stage. Sportsmen entering the field of play would make the sign of the cross or lift their faces to their Creator above; victorious athletes would make a point of giving thanks to God, Allah, or some other deity. Watch closely, and you will see that many still do.

It was not long before researchers became deeply curious about all this, formally studying whether and how religious belief impacts performance. Like those who first checked out the influence of religious belief on health, they were highly skeptical of the idea that belief in an invisible God could have a tangible impact in an arena as brutally competitive as sport. But, as in medicine, the stats were unequivocal: religious belief bolsters performance. And it does not matter which god you are praying to, so long as the belief is sincere.

In 2000, for example, Jeong-Keun Park of Hoseo University studied the coping strategies of Korean athletes. He found that they identified prayer as a key factor in coping with stress and anxiety, attaining peak performance, and providing meaning to sports participation.

Park's work has been corroborated again and again. In a 2004 study by D. R. Czech and colleagues on nine former Division I Christian athletes, it was found that religious activity has a "powerful influence on athletes" and that they "use prayer as a coping mechanism to alleviate stress." Precisely the same findings were revealed in a study of Olympic athletes by Ralph Vernacchia of Western Washington University.

A quote from a participant in Park's study gets to the nub of the findings:

> I always prepared my game with prayer from the major games to the minor games. The content of my prayer to God is to help me do my best. . . . I committed all things to God, without worry. . . . These prayers make me calmer and more secure and I forget the fear of losing. It resulted in good play.

This speaks directly to the opening section of this chapter. We saw there that Muhammad Ali and Jonathan Edwards, according to their own testimony, benefited from their religious beliefs. They believed in different Gods and contradictory theologies, but the placebo effect is indifferent to such things. All that matters is that both men, in their different ways, were totally committed to their respective truths.

So, the obvious question for the new discipline of sports psychology (which, off the back of Peale's commercial success, was beginning to mushroom as a discipline in the 1980s, as was the wider field of "self-help") became: Is it possible to mimic the power of religious conviction in pursuit of top performance? Is it possible to secularize Peale's teachings? In short, is it possible to find a sugar pill for aspiring sports stars?

Listen to a top athlete talking in the moments before he is about to play a big match, and you will hear statements bordering on nonsense. After more than thirty years of sports psychology we have gotten used to this psychobabble, so we are, to a large extent, deaf to its specific kind of incoherence.

So let's dwell on some of the things that athletes are inclined to say. I wrote this chapter in spring 2009, and in that week there was a crucial soccer match between Newcastle and Middlesbrough. Alan Shearer, then the Newcastle manager, said: "I have not even considered the possibility of defeat. In my mind we are going to win and nothing will deter me from that fact."

This belief is, of course, wholly irrational. There was a strong chance, in advance of the game, that Newcastle would lose or draw to Middlesbrough. But Shearer is not interested in basing his beliefs on statistical truth; he is interested in cultivating beliefs that create success (which is a different kind of truth). Newcastle, incidentally, won the match 3–1.

In the same week, Andy Murray, the British tennis player, told us that he believes he will defeat whoever he is playing, wherever he is playing them. This is nothing less than crazy. If Murray is up against, say, Rafael Nadal on clay, he should (on mathematical grounds) believe he is going to lose. But Murray knows that doubt is a perilous thing when walking onto a tennis court.

Peale makes this point in *The Power of Positive Thinking*:

"I am now convinced that if you expect the best, you are given some strange kind of power to create the conditions that produce the desired results." Anne Harrington of Harvard University makes the same point: "There is an innate capacity for our bodies to bring into being, to the best of their ability, the optimistic scenarios in which we fervently believe."

This is what we might dub the "performance placebo," but the trick of sports psychology has been to divorce it from religion; to ground optimism not in the interventionism of the Almighty but in an exaggerated belief in the efficacy of the self; to remove uncertainty by building conviction in one's capacity to achieve. That is why athletes refuse to entertain the possibility of defeat—they are aware that doubt is as dangerous a thing when entering the field of play as it is when swallowing a sugar pill.

"Doubt is the fundamental cause of error in sports," Timothy Gallwey, author of the best-selling sports psychology book *The Inner Game of Golf*, writes. "The power of doubt lies in its self-fulfilling nature. When we entertain a lack of faith that we can sink a short putt, for example, we usually tighten, increasing the likelihood of missing the putt. When we fail, our self-doubt is confirmed. . . . Next time the doubt is stronger and its inhibiting influence on our true capabilities more pronounced."

Gallwey's solution is to eliminate doubt with a variety of mental techniques, the most important of which is a form of mental association. "The technique is simply to remember or associate with a seemingly difficult task (in this case the golf shot) some action that is simple, preferably one that has never failed. For example, when addressing a ten-foot putt, you might remember the action of simply picking up a ball out of the hole.

"By vividly associating with this easy act there is no room left in the mind to associate the upcoming putt with failure. . . . Each time I succeeded in totally immersing myself in this concept, there was not a trace of doubt in my mind about sinking the putt. . . . The true professional in every field performs from a base of solid faith in his potential to act successfully. He doesn't listen to self-doubt."

I am standing in a small, dimly lit corridor adjacent to the practice area at the Commonwealth Games in Manchester in 2002. It is quiet and tranquil, the sounds of the players training next door muffled by huge curtains draped from the ceiling. The corridor is a dead end: the door at the far end has been locked to keep out spectators. But that is perfect for my purposes. This is the place I come to work on my very own placebo.

At every venue I have ever played, I have found a place like this: a small, quiet space, away from prying eyes, in which to conduct my mental preparation in those last, crucial moments before competition. At the Olympic Games in Barcelona it was a small dressing room rarely used by other competitors; at the European Championships in Birmingham it was a roped-off area above the arena, away from the hubbub; at the Super Circuit in Tokyo it was a tiny space just behind the café on the top floor.

Sometimes I would discover the perfect spot, only to find it had been commandeered already. I once stumbled upon Zoran Primorac, the Croatian table tennis legend, in a tiny dressing room at the Swedish Open, dancing from foot to foot, his eyes closed, mouthing words to himself. On another occasion I snuck into a rarely used VIP area and bumped into

Dutch champion Trinko Keen, sitting on the floor, his head in his hands, his mind so deep in concentration he didn't even hear my approach. A quick whispered apology, and I left in search of a quiet place of my own.

I worked with three leading sports psychologists over ten years, and by the end of that period, I had my mental preparation down to a fine art. Precisely fifteen minutes before a match was scheduled to begin, and having already warmed up, got the feel of my paddle in the practice hall, and talked tactics with my coach, I would vanish out of the hall and make my way over to my carefully chosen retreat.

Once there, in the quiet and solitude, I would close my eyes and begin a carefully rehearsed sequence of deep breathing exercises. Inhale, relax; inhaaale relaaax; inhaaaaaale . . . re-laaaaaaaax. When one is first starting out, it can take a good few minutes to quieten one's mind, but after long practice it took me only ninety seconds or so to get my heart rate down and my mind into a state of deep relaxation.

With my mind nice and still, I would begin the process of what psychologists call positive imagery; in my case a series of vivid recollections of the greatest and most inspiring table tennis matches I had ever played. First I would be looking in from the outside, like a spectator, seeing the marvelous strokes, applauding the audacious attacks, marveling at the array and diversity of skills.

Then the perspective would switch, and I would be inhabiting my own body, feeling the sensuousness of the ball on the paddle, the uninhibited flow of my movement, and the exhilaration of playing to the best of my ability and beyond. Then I'd switch the focus and imagine myself playing my upcoming opponent, executing the tactics discussed with my coach and sensing a deep and growing feeling of optimism.

I can feel my confidence solidifying. I can feel the doubts dissolving. I am feeling better and better.

Then another mental switch to what psychologists call "positive affirmations." I am no longer seeing myself in action, but stating the following, strangely powerful words: "You *can* win." Over and over. With growing conviction. Note that I am not saying: "*I* can win." I am talking to my inner self, as if trying to talk him out of his default skepticism. The last few affirmations are ever so slightly different: "You WILL win! You WILL win!"

And with that, I open my eyes, my head actually nodding in agreement, my face etched with conviction and my lips smiling. Slowly I walk back into the competition arena, nod at my coach, exchange a high five, and walk onto court to shake hands with my opponent. I am in precisely the place, mentally, I want to be. I am at one with myself and my world.

There is only one problem: I can see from my opponent's face that he has also worked himself up into a state of deep and powerful conviction. He is oozing expectation and confidence. He is shorn of any visible sign of doubt. In short, he is also reveling in his own placebo effect.

Irrational Optimism

The great irony of performance psychology is that it teaches each sportsman to believe, as far as he is able, that he will win. No man doubts. No man indulges his inner skepticism. That is the logic of sports psychology. But only one man *can* win. That is the logic of sport.

Note the difference between a scientist and an athlete. Doubt is a scientist's stock in trade. Progress is made by focusing on the evidence that refutes a theory and by improving the theory accordingly. Skepticism is the rocket fuel of scientific advance. But doubt, to an athlete, is poison. Progress is made by ignoring the evidence; it is about creating a mind-set that is immune to doubt and uncertainty.

Just to reiterate: From a rational perspective, this is nothing less than crazy. Why should an athlete convince himself he will win when he knows that there is every possibility he will lose? Because, to win, one must proportion one's belief, not to the evidence, but to whatever the mind can usefully get away with. To win, one must surgically remove doubt—rational and irrational—from the mind. That is how the placebo effect operates.

As Arsène Wenger, one of the most successful soccer club managers of recent times, puts it: "To perform to your maximum you have to teach yourself to believe with an intensity that goes way beyond logical justification. No top performer has lacked this capacity for irrational optimism; no sportsman has played to his potential without the ability to remove doubt from his mind."

Tiger Woods is standing over a putt on the final hole of the 2008 U.S. Open at Torrey Pines, California. The air is still, and the mass of spectators surrounding the green is silent. Woods, as ever in the closing round of a major championship, is wearing a red polo shirt along with black slacks and a baseball cap. The putt is far from easy: twelve feet, a touch right to left.

This is one of the most important shots of Woods's season; a putt to take the second major of the year into an eighteen-hole playoff. Rocco Mediate, the competition leader, has already finished his round and is looking on from the clubhouse. Woods addresses the ball, then glances slowly and deliberately toward the hole in preparation for the stroke. The silence deepens. Woods glances at the hole once again and steadies himself for the putt. . . .

The 2008 U.S. Open was one of the most remarkable sporting events of recent years. It was Woods's first tournament since he underwent knee surgery, but as early as the opening round it was clear that the world number one was in great pain, wincing, grimacing, and sometimes even yelping during his swing as the desperately weakened cartilage in his left knee attempted to withstand torque of up to four times his body weight.

After one stroke on the third round he looked as if he might be physically sick, such was the pain of playing a long iron to the green. But Woods persevered, aware that a fourteenth major title was in offing. By the end of the third round Woods held a one-shot lead, but few thought, as his physical condition deteriorated, he would hold it together for the final round.

But Woods kept at it, recovering from dropped shots on the first two holes with birdies at nine and eleven. By the final hole thousands of spectators at the course, along with millions of television viewers around the world, were transfixed by the possibility of a man winning one of golf's majors on one leg. Nailing the twelve-foot putt on the seventy-second green would keep alive the possibility of arguably the most audacious victory in the history of golf.

As we have seen, self-belief sets up a powerful communication between mind and body. But perhaps the most striking thing about Tiger Woods is that his self-belief is so irresistible, his conviction so palpable, that he seems to be able to communicate with those around him. I spoke to eight leading golf writers following the 2008 U.S. Open, and all of them said they were "highly confident" he would make that crucial putt in advance of it being played.

That is quite extraordinary, given that, even for a player of Woods's ability, the probability of sinking a twelve-foot putt is well under 50 percent. But Woods's conviction about his own abilities is so total and his ability to communicate confidence with his body language so eloquent that even experienced golf writers are persuaded to back his judgment. I suspect that the vast majority of those looking on from the stands felt the same way.

So, too, did Mediate, the clubhouse leader. Interviewed in the moments after Woods nailed that putt (Woods would also go on to defeat Mediate in an 18-hole playoff), he said, "I knew he was going to make it."

This ability to instill belief in others is a vital facet of leadership—whether in politics or the military—but it can also create a huge advantage in sport through its impact on competitors. It is a remarkable fact that Woods (at time of writing) has lost only once on the fifteen occasions when he has led going into the final round of a major championship. Could it be that his nearest challengers, infected by the world number one's sense of assurance, find it difficult to sustain theirs? It often looks that way.

At the end of 2009 a number of problems in Woods's private life were revealed, with reports of philandering making headlines around the world. Neverthless, he remains a potent example of two of the main themes of this book: a man who has harnessed the incalculable power of purposeful practice over many thousands of hours and matched it with the equally awesome power of the placebo effect. His practice has imbued him with supreme abilities around a golf course; his self-belief has given him the ability to translate his abilities into peak performance under pressure.

As Jean Van de Velde, the top French golfer, puts it: "Woods is the most remarkable sportsman I have seen in terms of self-belief. He is able to fully commit to the shot. On ten-foot putts he believes he will nail them. On forty-foot putts, he knows, deep down, he is unlikely to hole them, but he is able to focus his entire mind on the possibility of success rather than the probability of failure. And at the moment he hits the putt, his conviction is total. It is a remarkable skill."

The best way to get an insight into the Woods psyche is to listen to him during interviews. Veteran Tiger watchers have gotten used to how his talk sounds strangely stilted, at least until one realizes that what he says is not directed at truth but at sustaining a particular mind-set. It is a mind-set that he worked on with his father over many years and has honed with psychologist Jay Brunza.

"I certainly learned it [mental toughness]," Woods has said. "Dad had all different types of techniques to get into my head. I actually asked him to do it because I wanted to be tough because I wasn't as physically gifted. I was playing against guys who hit the ball longer than I did, who were better players than I was, and the only way to get better was to get tougher. I figured if I didn't have the physical gifts, I could challenge them on a mental level, be tougher and out-think them."

Woods is a walking testament to the power of self-belief. As Morris Pickens, a sports psychologist whose clients include 2007 U.S. Masters champion Zach Johnson, says, "I don't think he doubts anything he does." It is an assertion that will be put to the test as never before, as Woods looks to rebuild his career and attempts to surpass Jack Nicklaus's record of eighteen major titles.

There is, however, a rather obvious problem with installing irrationally optimistic beliefs: they will all too often be contradicted by hard reality. Believing that one is going to defeat Rafael Nadal, for example, may ignite powerful psychological processes that make the outcome more likely, but it doesn't guarantee success—particularly given that Nadal is working on his own placebo.

Similarly, believing in God may confer myriad benefits on a person's health and so on, but it does not prevent terrible things happening. Many believers and their families still die of cancer and other illnesses. Many do not get healed of their ailments. Rather like the medical placebo (which works only with certain types of ailments), the "performance" and "religious" placebos operate within limits.

So, is it psychologically realistic for a person to sustain false (but useful) beliefs when they are so often contradicted by the evidence? Is it possible for Tiger Woods to retain the conviction that he is going to make his next forty-footer when he has missed the previous two? Can beliefs be slipped into and out of according to the occasion, like clothes?

As Nicholas Humphrey, professor of psychology at the London School of Economics, puts it:

> To discover a new placebo, all you need do is to *invent* it, and to invent it all you need do is *change your beliefs*. So it seems the way might well be open for everyone

173

to take *voluntary* control. . . . Yet, the truth is that—fortunately, perhaps—it's not that easy. When it comes to it, how *do* you change your own beliefs to suit yourself? No one can simply bootstrap themselves into believing what they choose.

Humphrey's point is both clear and pointed. But it is also wide of the mark. One of the most remarkable findings of modern psychology is the extraordinary capacity of human beings to mold the evidence to fit their beliefs rather than the other way around; it is our capacity to believe *in spite of the evidence* and sometimes in spite of our other deeply held beliefs. And it is this capacity, more than any other, which—psychologically speaking—distinguishes top athletes from the rest.

Doublethink

In 2002 Tim Henman, one of the world's top tennis players, lost to Jonas Bjorkman, an unseeded Swede, in straight sets at the Australian Open. It was a devastating blow, something that might have shattered Henman's confidence. He had played sluggishly, his shots lacking fluency and timing. But by the time of his postmatch press conference, none of this seemed to matter.

"I am going to take the positives out of the defeat and focus on the ways my game has improved," Henman said.

You may have heard this expression quite a lot—"taking the positives"—from top sportsmen and sportswomen. It is a psychological technique so universal that it has become a part of the lexicon. What does it mean? Well, it means what it says: it is about ignoring aspects of a performance that contradict one's prior optimism while focusing on the good tactics, the winning shots, etc., that support it.

To put it another way, top athletes have learned to filter out unwanted evidence in order to sustain an exaggerated belief in their own abilities.

This is, when you think about it, rather extraordinary. Henman played dreadfully in that match; it was one of the most discouraging defeats of his career. It could have knocked his confidence out of the ballpark. But Henman has trained his mind to ignore the evidence. He has learned to focus on tiny specks of optimism. He has learned to take the positives. Not long afterward Henman won his first and only ATP Masters title and reached a career-high ranking of fourth in the world.

I have sat through dozens of team meetings as a sportsman and have been consistently astonished at the capacity of teammates to dismiss all the negative happenings from their minds. I have interviewed dozens of top athletes and been astounded at how effortlessly and seamlessly they manipulate the evidence to conform to their beliefs rather than the other way around; at how they filter out experiences that might hamper their quest for top performance.*

* This is done with considerable subtlety, of course. If an athlete were to take only the positives, and neglect the negatives altogether, he would never adapt his training to correct the weaknesses exposed in competition. What happens—and this is explicitly taught by sports psychologists—is that athletes wield different beliefs as part of a cycle.

In stage one, the athlete "takes the positives" to protect self-belief; later, when training, he incorporates the insights gained from the negative aspect of the previous match to strengthen weaknesses; then, when the next match is looming, the focus returns to building self-belief once again, so that doubt is eliminated at the point of performance.

As Arsène Wenger, the widely admired manager of Arsenal soccer club, puts it: "Unless you have the ability to manipulate your beliefs over the performance cycle, it is difficult to perform well at anything, sport or otherwise."

"Taking the positives" is not the only psychological paradox at work with top performers. Reconsider the mental technique advocated by Timothy Gallwey in *The Inner Game of Golf*. You'll remember that he advises the golfer to associate a difficult putt with some action that has never failed, such as simply picking up a ball out of the hole. "By vividly associating with this easy act there is no room left in the mind to associate the upcoming putt with failure," he writes.

But any sensible golfer—including Gallwey and, for that matter, Tiger Woods—must putt with caution; he must putt in such a way that, in the event of a miss, the ball rolls only a couple of feet past the hole, so that the next shot is a tap-in. Playing the putt as if it is certain to hit the center of the hole is a recipe for disaster, as Gallwey would be the first to acknowledge.

So what Gallwey is really saying is that a successful golfer must attempt to create subjective certainty in his own mind that he will make the putt while simultaneously playing it at such a pace that acknowledges the possibility he might miss; he must execute a shot that is certain to drop in a way that concedes the possibility of failure. In other words, a golfer must juggle contradictory beliefs in order to maximize the placebo effect.

Anyone who has read George Orwell's *1984* will find this idea curiously familiar. In that remarkably perceptive novel, Orwell introduces the term *doublethink*, which he describes as follows:

Doublethink means the power of holding two contradictory beliefs in one's mind simultaneously, and accepting both of them. . . . [T]o forget any fact that has

become inconvenient, and then, when it becomes necessary again, to draw it back from oblivion for just so long
as it is needed . . . all this is indispensably necessary.

At the time of publication of *1984*, many critics argued
that doublethink was psychologically implausible, but it is, in
fact, commonplace. Doublethink is essential to the success of
leading athletes and other top performers.

Take top golfers again: they have to make to make scrupulously rational choices about shot selection (laying up, for
example, rather than going for the green), but once they have
committed to any given shot, they have to be—indeed, they
train themselves to be—irrationally optimistic about execution.

Nick Faldo, the six-time major winner, made precisely this
point when I interviewed him at the Open Championship in
2008. "You have to be very calculating in selecting the right
shot," he said. "You have to make a decision based upon a
realistic assessment of your own weaknesses and the scope
for failure. But once you have committed to your decision,
you have to flick the mental switch and execute the shot as if
there was never any doubt that you would nail it."

This is doublethink in action.

A Philosophical Conclusion

Not until 1996 was the performance placebo, as we have
called it, tested for directly. Psychologists took one hundred
participants and divided them randomly into two groups.
They then manipulated the beliefs of the two groups. Those
in group 1 were encouraged to believe they would complete

a set task even more quickly than they thought they would. Group 2 members, on the other hand, were manipulated in the opposite direction, so that their expectations were dampened down.

And guess what? The "positive thinking" group completed the tasks significantly more quickly than the "negative thinking" group, even though there was no difference in ability between the two groups. This proved what athletes, sports psychologists, and the self-help industry had long known: irrational beliefs can boost performance, provided they are held with sufficient conviction.

Why is this? What mechanisms are in operation? In the case of the medical placebo, there is evidence to suggest that sugar pills—in conjunction with strong beliefs—mimic the effects of real drugs. According to Ben Goldacre, when patients received a placebo for Parkinson's they showed extra dopamine release in the brain, just as they would if they had taken a "real" drug. But how does the brain state we call "belief" cause this outcome? Nobody has any idea.

In the case of the "performance placebo," we are even more in the dark. Does a belief that one will make a difficult putt create a more accurate motor program in the brain and central nervous system? And if so, why and how? My hunch is that the full answer will emerge only as we approach an understanding of consciousness itself.

The lesson in all of this, however, is that beliefs are aimed not solely at truth, but at *what works*. This lesson applies not just for athletes, of course: none of us can get by without beliefs that veer away from reality. We accentuate the positives; suppress the negatives; block out the traumas; create mini narratives about our lives and loves that, on honest reflection, have little basis in reality. We do this not merely to win, but to survive. Uninhibited reason can be a perilous thing, as anyone who has studied the lives of the philosophers will testify.

The difference is that world-class performers—often in conjunction with sports psychologists and "mind coaches"—take these mental manipulations to greater extremes. They have taught themselves to ratchet up their optimism at the point of performance; to mold the evidence to fit their beliefs rather than the other way around; to activate doublethink. And it is proficiency in these skills that often separates the best from the rest.

Muhammad Ali, Jonathan Edwards, Tiger Woods, Arsène Wenger, Nick Faldo: all, in their different ways, have found an irrational way to triumph in the strange game we call life.

CHAPTER 6

The Curse of Choking and How to Avoid It

Humiliation in Sydney

It seemed like an eternity standing behind the curtain, waiting to be announced to the crowd for my opening match at the 2000 Olympic Games in Sydney. I glanced at my opponent—a beatable but talented German called Peter Franz—and sensed his ambition. This was the most important match of our respective seasons, quite possibly the most important match of our careers.

I took a deep breath. I was twenty-nine, and this was likely to be my last Olympic Games, but it was also the first time I had been in with a realistic chance of progressing to the medal stages. My form was as good as it had ever been, and my confidence was soaring. My coach had spent the last two months trying to convince me that I could win a medal—a feat that would have been life-changing—and I had started to believe him.

My preparation had been highly effective, starting with a series of training camps at locations in Belgium and Sweden. Back in the UK I had regular sessions with psychologists, nutritionists, and physiologists. I was the only British table tennis player who had qualified for the Games, and no expense had been spared by the British Olympic Association to make sure my preparation was perfect.

I spent the final days before the games on Australia's Gold Coast, sparring with two international players who had been flown out specially. We practiced for four hours each day at a local club that had been decked out at extravagant expense with precisely the same specialist flooring that was being used in the competition arena at the Olympic Games. At times it seemed as if half the world had been mobilized to assist my preparation.

Finally the microphone struck up, and the crowd roared as I stepped through the curtains into the megawatt light of the competition arena. The Olympic Games! I noticed that a large group of British spectators was in the stands, waving the Union Jack, and I knew that back home my family and friends would be tuning in on television. This was the match I had saved for a career, a contest that could be life-transforming.

And then it happened.

Franz stroked the ball into play—a light and gentle forehand topspin. It was not a difficult stroke to return, not a stroke I would normally have had any trouble pouncing upon, and yet I was strangely late on it, my feet stuck in their original position, my racket jabbing at the ball in a way that was totally unfamiliar. My return missed the table by more than two feet.

I shook out my hand, sensing that something was wrong and hoping it would rectify itself. But things got worse. Each time my opponent played a stroke, I found my body doing things that bore no relation to anything I had learned over the last twenty years of playing table tennis: my feet were sluggish, my movements alien, my touch barely existent.

I was trying as hard as I could; I yearned for victory more intensely than in any match I had ever played; and yet it was if I had regressed to the time when I was a beginner.

I walked to the back of the court at the end of the opening game: I had lost 21–8, an absurdly one-sided score line for a contest between two evenly matched players. My coach, normally calm and assured, was bewildered. This would typically be a time for highly refined tactical advice—the amount of spin to use, when to go for drag rather than disguise—but why talk tactics when I could barely keep the ball in play? He tried to reassure me, to bolster my confidence, but the problem went far deeper, and he knew it.

The second game was even more catastrophic: 21–4. It was as if an impostor had taken over my body and was playing in my stead. I was fumbling around, stilted and sluggish, as the audience murmured in disbelief. This was more than a defeat, it was humiliation: a collapse both graphic and inexplicable. My movements were sometimes lethargic, sometimes jerky, my technique lacking any semblance of fluency and coherence.

By the time the match ended, my opponent had no emotion except sympathy. He put his arm around my shoulders as we shook hands. "What went wrong?" he asked. I shrugged. My one thought was to get out of there. To get away from the arena of my humiliation. Only when I got back to my room in the Olympic village and sat down with my head in my towel did I realize what had happened.

As my coach put it with brutal and characteristic honesty: "It is simple, Matthew," he said. "You choked."

The Great White Shark Drowns

In basketball it is called "the bricks"; in golf it is sometimes termed "the yips." In more academic domains it is called "cracking"; in England in the 1970s and '80s, it was termed "bottling." Today, all these labels—each of which carry deeply pejorative connotations—fall under the now-familiar term: "choking."

In chapter 5 we saw that self-doubt can lead to a dip in performance that, although small, can be the crucial difference between success and failure. Sometimes a lull in form just happens by chance. But choking has nothing to do with either of these phenomena: it is a species of failure so absolute that it looks as if there is an entirely different player on view.

Sometimes choking is condensed into a single (and often fateful) instant of time, such as when Bill Buckner of the Boston Red Sox inexplicably let the ball run through his legs in game six of the 1986 World Series, handing victory to the New York Mets. Sometimes it lasts an entire match, such as my humiliation at the Olympic Games in Sydney.

But there is one aspect of choking that is universal: it occurs only under conditions of severe pressure, often when an athlete is confronting a career-defining moment. It hardly needs stating that this is precisely the time when you would least want to choke; when you are striving hardest for top performance; when playing well matters most.

Choking is surreal to observe because it often involves a world-class performer, someone who has spent a lifetime honing his skills and touch, suddenly looking like a novice. His highly refined technique is replaced by a curious mixture of twitching and lethargy; his demeanor is overhauled with confusion; his complex motor skills, built up over thousands of hours of practice, seem to vanish into the ether.

But choking is not limited to top athletes. Musicians, politicians, actors, artists, surgeons, painters, and all manner of other performers have, at times, been afflicted by the curse of choking, suddenly and inexplicably unable to execute the skills they have spent a lifetime perfecting. You may have choked at some point, too—unable to utter a word on a hot first date, unable to string a sentence together when giving a big presentation.

But why does it happen?

Before examining one of sport's greatest mysteries, consider the ways in which we describe the choking phenomenon. When Greg Norman fell apart before the eyes of the world during the final round of the 1996 U.S. Masters, some journalists wrote that he didn't want it enough, others that he wanted it too much; some said that Norman had played too aggressively, others that he had not played aggressively enough.

But do any of these often contradictory "explanations" hit home? Do any of them do even partial justice to what happened over the course of the closing few hours at the Augusta National?

Consider that Norman, nicknamed the Great White Shark, was the number-one player in the world and arguably the most gifted player of his generation: a man who had played a succession of dazzling shots around the fabled Georgia course to take the lead on the seventeenth hole of the opening round and to hold on to it throughout the next two and a half days.

By the start of the final round Norman led by a gaping six shots from Britain's Nick Faldo, and many insiders felt that the outcome was a formality as the final pair teed up at the opening hole on Sunday morning.

Then, on the fairway of the ninth hole, it happened.

Norman's fabled technique deserted him as he hit his approach to the elevated green, his hips and shoulders moving out of sync, taking crucial pace out of the ball. He then watched, pupils dilating, as the ball rolled back thirty yards down the hill. Golf's most infamous choke had begun.

At the tenth hole, Norman hooked the ball off the tee, causing yet another dropped shot. On the eleventh, he hit his approach to within fifteen feet of the pin and looked like he might recover a shot. Instead, he knocked his putt three feet past the hole and then missed coming back as the audience gasped. He shook his head slowly, his confusion escalating, as he walked slowly toward the next tee.

At the twelfth tee, Norman's lips were pale and his eyes glassy as Faldo hit his tee shot to the middle of the green. The Australian seemed like the loneliest man in the world. He shook his hands and rocked his shoulders, trying to get some life—some semblance of normality—back into his body. But it was no use. He was shot. He was choking, bottling, yipping, bricking, cracking, call it what you will—and there was no way out.

He took the club away for his backswing, but his hips were

again curiously out of kilter with the rest of his body, lulling back toward the impact point too early. His clubhead was fatally short of acceleration, and the Australian looked up forlornly as the ball stalled in the air. It landed on the bank at the front of the green, paused for an instant, and then began to roll slowly back toward Ray's Creek. Norman's challenge had drowned.

He had held the lead for sixty hours, across forty-eight holes, but he had gone from three up to two back over the course of four fateful holes.

By the time Norman put his ball into the water for a second time, at the par-three sixteenth, the spectators seemed unsure whether to greet the Australian with sympathetic applause or funereal silence. They averted their eyes as he trudged down the fairway, fearful of catching his gaze in his moment of infamy.

Even Faldo, a feisty competitor, was deeply conscious of the humiliation being endured by his adversary, and when the Englishman knocked his final putt into the hole to win the title on the eighteenth green, his celebrations were muted. Putting a long, sturdy arm around Norman, he murmured: "I don't know what to say. I feel horrible about what happened. I'm so sorry."

Seen in this context, explanations focusing on Norman's aggressiveness (or caution) seem trite. Norman was scarcely able to *play*, let alone play aggressively. Explanations focusing on his tactics also fail to address the enormity of what occurred. The Australian was virtually unable to swing the club properly, let alone execute tactics of any kind. The club ought to be an extension of the body, but to Norman, for those crucial holes, it was an alien object.

"I am a winner," Norman said defiantly at his press conference, but for the rest of his career he was labeled a loser.
This may seem paradoxical given that the Australian won
countless titles on tour, but this was a label with a very specific meaning. It was that Norman collapsed on the grandest
stage of all; that he had spurned a career-defining victory
even as it beckoned to him; that he had choked in spectacular fashion.

His only consolation—and it is not much of one—is that he
is not alone. Jimmy White choked in the final of the 1994 World
Snooker Championships; Scott Norwood choked in Superbowl
1991; Todd Martin choked in the men's singles semifinals of
Wimbledon in 1996; dozens of unfortunate athletes choke in
career-defining contests across the planet every day. I choked
at the Olympic Games in Sydney. Perhaps you choked in your
last big job interview.

But why?

A Tale of Two Brain Systems

I am standing toward the back of the hall at the Cippenham
Club, the most prestigious table tennis facility in the south
of England. Ken Phillips, the club coach, is working with a
large group of twelve-year-olds who are relatively new to the
sport, and he is barking instructions at them.

They are learning how to play the forehand topspin, one of
the most important strokes in the game. "Keep using the wrist,"
Phillips shouts from his position at the front of the large hall.
"Don't forget that it is the wrist that creates the spin on the
ball."

Lauren, a brown-haired, ponytailed girl on the table nearest me, furrows her brow with concentration. She repeats the coach's instruction under her breath—"Use your wrist, Lauren!"—and then, on the next rally, makes an effort to get her wrist rotating. She misses the ball completely. Phillips comes across, takes her hand, and guides her through the correct movement, and she gives it another go.

This time she connects with the ball, but now she has neglected to rotate her shoulders and bend her knees. Her forearm has also gone out of kilter, as has the connection between the hips and the torso. Phillips, however, does not mention any of this: he is preoccupied simply with getting the wrist moving in the right way.

As I watch, I begin to get a sense of the sheer complexity of the forehand topspin: the symphony of moving parts, the requirement for synchronicity between each of them. Phillips has broken it down into a few simple instructions, but over time his young players will have to integrate literally hundreds of biomechanical rules into the construction of their motor programs.

"It normally takes around six months for a player to get the basic of the forehand topspin technique, and it is then that we can start trying to integrate it into footwork patterns involving other strokes and new spins," Phillips says. "There is no shortcut."

I ask Lauren to try something new—to count the number of times I tap my foot on the floor during the next rally—but she immediately breaks down, her stroke petering out even as she starts it. She looks confused. "I can't do it," she says. "I can hit the ball or count the number of taps of your foot, but not both at the same time."

A couple of hours later, Phillips is coaching a new, smaller group of youngsters: fourteen-year-olds who have been playing for at least six years each and who are vying for a place on the England team. Phillips asks them to play along the forehand diagonal—as he had done with the earlier group—and this time all the youngsters play their topspins with elegance, making the infinitesimal adjustments to technique and position as each new ball is fired toward them.

I repeat the experiment I had attempted with Lauren, asking a boy called James to play his topspin while counting the number of times I tap my foot on the ground. It is not even a challenge. He nails fifteen topspins, during which I have stamped my foot seventeen times. He smiles as he gives me the correct answer. On the next rally, I talk with James about what he has been doing at school today, but once again the distraction makes no difference to his ability to play the rally.

The reason is simple: James has "automated" his stroke-making. Many hours of practice have enabled him to encode the stroke in implicit rather than explicit memory. It wasn't always like this: when he started out, he was just like Lauren, consciously monitoring the way he was hitting the ball as he painstakingly built up the neural framework supporting the shot. Only after many hours was he able to execute the shot without even having to think about it.

When I ask James to explain the way the different parts of his body relate to each other during his stroke, he shakes his head and shrugs his shoulders. "I'm not sure how I do it," he says, smiling. This, as we saw in chapter 1, is what psychologists call expert-induced amnesia. Contrast this with Lauren, who explicitly repeated her coach's instructions under her breath between rallies.

James and Lauren are, in effect, using two entirely differ-ent systems of the brain to play the forehand topspin. Russell Poldrack, a neuroscientist at UCLA, has conducted a number of brain-imaging experiments to trace the transition from explicit to implicit monitoring that occurs over many hours' practice. He has discovered that the prefrontal cortex is acti-vated when a novice is learning a skill, but that control of the stroke switches over time to areas such as the basal ganglia, which is partly responsible for touch and feel.

This migration from the explicit to the implicit system of the brain has two crucial advantages. First, it enables the expert player to integrate the various parts of a complex skill into one fluent whole (this "motor chunking" is akin to the perceptual chunking described in chapter 1), something that would be impossible at a conscious level because there are too many interconnecting variables for the conscious mind to handle. And second, it frees up attention to focus on higher-level aspects of the skill such as tactics and strategy.

This transition between brain systems can be most easily understood by thinking about what happens when you learn to drive a car. When you start out, you have to focus intently in order to move the gearshift while keeping the steering wheel in the right place, pushing on the clutch, and keeping an eye on the road. In fact, at the beginning these tasks are so difficult to execute simultaneously that the instructor starts you off in a parking lot and helps you slowly to integrate the various elements.

Only after many hours can these various skills be per-formed effortlessly, without any conscious control, so that you are now able to arrive at your destination without even being aware of how you got there, your mind having been on other things, such as what to make for dinner. Your skills have moved from the explicit to the implicit, from the conscious to the unconscious, and your ability has graduated from novice level to proficiency.*

But now imagine if an expert were to suddenly find himself using the "wrong" brain system. It wouldn't matter if he were the greatest player of all time or merely a decent club player because he would now be at the mercy of the explicit rather than the implicit system. The highly sophisticated skills encoded in the implicit part of his brain would count for nothing. He would find himself striving for victory using neural pathways he last used as a novice.

This situation has been re-created by Robert Gray, a psychologist at Arizona State University. He took a group of outstanding intercollegiate baseball players and asked them to swing at a moving ball while listening for a randomly presented tone to judge whether the tone was high or low in frequency. As expected, the tone-listening task had no detrimental effect on the efficiency of their swings (just as counting the number of foot taps had no impact on James's forehand topspin). Why? Because the baseball hitters have automated their shot-making.

But when the hitters were asked to indicate whether their bat was moving up or down at the instant the tone sounded, their performance levels plummeted. Why? Because this time the secondary task forced them to direct their attention toward the *swing itself*. They were consciously monitoring a

* In order to improve a skill once it has been automated, it is vital to continue to undertake tasks that exceed current limitations, as we saw in chapter 3. This requires the performer to exert conscious control over certain parts of the skill during practice, thus building additional expertise. If you simply cruise along on autopilot, improvement stalls.

stroke that was supposed to be automatic. Explicit monitoring was vying with implicit execution.

Their problem was not a *lack of focus*, but *too much focus*. Conscious monitoring had disrupted the smooth workings of the implicit system. The sequencing and timing of the different motor responses were fragmented, just as they would be with a novice. They were, effectively, beginners again.

Psychological Reversion

In 1989 Scott Hoch stood on the tenth green of the Augusta National with an eighteen-inch putt to win the U.S. Masters. It was the second hole of a sudden-death playoff with Nick Faldo (the same player who seven years later would capitalize on Greg Norman's spectacular choke on the very same course). Faldo had bogied the hole, and Hoch, a rank outsider from North Carolina, stood before a simple putt that could transform his life.

Had he faced such a short putt on the opening hole, or the seventh or the fifteenth, the American would have knocked it in without a great deal of forethought, but with the Masters title within his grasp, Hoch spent what seemed like an age checking and rechecking the line. Only after two minutes of analysis did the American settle over his putt. Then he rechecked the line. And rechecked his grip. And refocused his mind. Rechecked everything, in fact. The putt didn't even touch the lip—and Faldo won the title at the very next hole.

Unsurprisingly, the American was known thereafter as "Hoch the Choke."

Unlike the baseball hitters in the previous section, Hoch

hadn't been asked by a researcher to explicitly monitor his hitting action. But his desire to win the Masters was such that his attention to the line, the wind, and every other conceivable variable spilled over into a very different—and fatal—kind of attention. He consciously monitored the *stroke itself*. He yearned for the ball to drop so much that he inadvertently took explicit control of a putt that would surely have dropped had he but left it in the hands of the implicit system.

He jabbed at the ball, just as Norman would jab at so many of his putts and long irons seven years later, just as I had jabbed and jerked during that humiliation in Sydney, my shots becoming un-chunked as I vainly tried to consciously control the disparate movements of a task that can only be executed unconsciously. Each of us lacked touch, finesse, and control because these are elements of a skill that reside in the implicit part of the brain. The years of practice counted for nothing. We were novices again.

Think of some of the other iconic chokes in sporting history and you'll notice they follow the same pattern. When Jana Novotna led Steffi Graff 4–1 and 40–30 in the women's singles final at Wimbledon in 1993, the result seemed like a formality. Novotna had been playing tennis from the heavens: serving, volleying, and passing her German opponent almost at will.

But standing on the threshold of her first Wimbledon title, Novotna stalled. She double-faulted, her service action losing any semblance of normality. The toss was too low, there was insufficient arch in her back, her swing lacked conviction.

Over the next few games, she went from bad to worse. Her movements slowed drastically, her strokes became stilted, her movements disconnected. The explicit system had taken over. Novotna was trying to consciously organize hundreds of moving body parts into one seamless whole. That is why she was sluggish on some shots (her conscious mind failing to keep pace with changing circumstances), jerky on others (as she made belated readjustments).*

Novotna's failure was not a lack of *courage*, which is the way chokes are often described. She would love to have attempted some audacious shots: that, indeed, was her nature in normal circumstances. It was mine, too; and Norman's. But when the brain switch occurs, neither courage nor cowardice makes the least bit of difference. Choking is a problem of psychological reversion: the flipping from a brain system used by experts to one used by novices.

Why does it occur? Consider what happens when executing a simple task, like keeping a cup of coffee upright under pressure—say, because you are walking across a very expensive carpet. In these circumstances, explicit attention is *just what you need*. By focusing on keeping the cup vertical, you are far less likely to spill the contents because of inadvertence or a lack of concentration. On simple tasks, the tendency to slow down and take conscious control *confers huge advantages*.

But precisely the opposite applies when executing a *complex* task. When an expert hits a moving table tennis ball or strikes a fade on a golf shot, any tendency to direct attention toward the mechanics of the shot is likely to be catastrophic

---

* As Sian Beilock, a psychologist at the University of Chicago, has put it: "Once [a motor skill] is de-chunked, each unit must be activated and run separately. Not only does this process slow performance, but it also creates an opportunity for error at each transition between units that was not present in the integrated control structure."

because there are too many interconnecting variables for the conscious mind to handle (this is another example of combinatorial explosion).

Choking, then, is a kind of neural glitch that occurs when the brain switches to a system of explicit monitoring in circumstances when it ought to stick to the implicit system. It is not something the performer does intentionally; it just happens. And once the explicit system has kicked in (as anyone who has been afflicted by choking will tell you), it is damned difficult to switch out of.

Now think of the way in which chokers are sometimes admonished. When the England soccer team lost to Germany at the 1996 European Championships, Gareth Southgate was given a hard time by parts of the British media for having missed a crucial penalty. His shot lacked assurance, his technique all leg and no hips and torso. The various parts of the skill had become unchunked: a classic choke.

"Why did Southgate kick the ball so feebly?" one commentator asked. "You could understand a beginner screwing things up under pressure, but not a man who has spent his life playing football."

But we can now see that the truth is precisely the reverse. It is only an expert performer—someone who has practiced long enough to automate a skill—*who has the capacity to choke*. For a novice—still wielding the explicit system—any additional attention is likely to *benefit execution, not hinder it*.

This outcome has been demonstrated by Charles Kimble, a psychologist at the University of Dayton. He took some highly skilled players of the Tetris video game and also some novice players and then created a high-pressure environment by getting them to play in front of a big audience. The expert players got worse, exhibiting clear choking effects; the beginners actually improved.

Doublethink Revisited

The tension is rising in the heat box as the clock ticks down to the opening race of the 500-meter speed skating at the Olympic Games in Salt Lake City in 2002. The heat box is the small area where the competitors assemble in the moments before their race, the glare of the stadium hidden behind curtains that run from the ceiling to the floor.

Some of the athletes are pacing around, steely-eyed; others are sitting down and shaking out their hands and feet; still others are in earnest conversation with their coaches, rehearsing their tactics and strategy one last time. The roar of the crowd through the curtains is an ever-present reminder that their moment of truth is approaching.

But one competitor is not engaged in any of the familiar last-minute activities. Sarah Lindsay, a twenty-one-year-old British skater, is sitting, breathing slowly, her eyes staring forward—and all the while she is saying something audibly to herself. "It's only speed skating!" she says. "It's only speed skating! It's only bloody speed skating!"

This is a very curious thing to say, given that speed skating is Lindsay's life and that she is about to compete in the most important race of her career—her first Olympic experience. She has spent the last four years building up to this moment. She has endured hardship, innumerable hours of training, and countless personal sacrifices. But once again she says it—

"It's only speed skating!"—as the race officials beckon the competitors into the arena.

We have seen that choking is a neural glitch that occurs when individuals are under pressure; when they find themselves explicitly monitoring skills that would be better executed automatically. We have also seen that this is a deeply confusing and often surreal experience for the performer—unable to execute the smooth and refined actions he or she has spent a lifetime mastering.

So, how to overcome choking? How to prevent the explicit system taking over? Considering that choking only ever occurs in highly pressurized circumstances, what better way than to convince oneself that a career-defining contest doesn't really matter? After all, if the performer does not *feel* any pressure, there *is* no pressure—and the conscious mind will not attempt to wrestle control from the implicit system.

That is why Sarah Lindsay kept repeating, "It's only speed skating!" She was trying to convince herself that the final of the Olympic Games was a triviality; that it did not matter any more than a training session. By alleviating the pressure, she was giving herself the opportunity to compete without inhibition—and without choking. "Just do it," as the Nike commercial puts it.

"The problem at the Olympics is not that you want it too little, but that you want it too much," Lindsay told me. "You are so desperate to win that you can become unhinged. I remember walking into the stadium and seeing twenty-two thousand spectators and banks of television cameras. But instead of getting uptight, I repeated once again: 'It's only bloody speed skating!' "

It worked. Lindsay, a talented skater who had suffered from episodes of choking, placed way above her ranking in Salt Lake City and finished in the top eight four years later at the Olympics in Turin, a brilliant performance that stunned her family, friends, and teammates. Choking normally leads to a catastrophic decline in performance, but Lindsay had actually *upped her game*. She had conquered the curse of choking by manipulating her beliefs in the last few moments before competition. To use the terminology of chapter 5, she had wielded a form of doublethink.

As Mark Bawden, the sports psychologist who worked with Lindsay, puts it: "In order to make all the sacrifices necessary to reach world-class levels of performance, an athlete has to believe that performing well means everything. They have to cleave to the belief that winning an Olympic gold is of life-changing significance.

"But that is precisely the belief that is most likely to trigger a choking response. So, the key psychological skill for someone with a tendency to choke is to ditch that belief in the minutes before competition and to replace it with the belief that the race does not really matter. It is a form of psychological manipulation, and it takes a lot of work to master."

I worked with Bawden for many years after the Olympic Games in Sydney to ward off choking. My method was to think about all the things that are so much more important than sport: health, family, relationships, and so on. During my prematch routine, I would spend a few minutes in a deeply relaxed state, filling my mind with these thoughts, finishing with an affirmation just like that used by Lindsay: "It's only table tennis!" By the time I reached the court, my beliefs had altered: the match was no longer the be-all and end-all.*

Sometimes, the ruse worked brilliantly. At other times, I still experienced some interference from the explicit part of my brain, with partial choking effects. But I never again choked in the graphic and overwhelming way I had in Sydney; I never again suffered the humiliation of being virtually unable to hit the ball during a career-defining contest.

To use the wonderfully evocative phrase of Steve Davis, six-time World Snooker Champion, I had learned the art of "playing as if it means nothing when it means everything."

* Many athletes are able to perform without having to artificially ease the pressure. That does not imply they do not care about what is happening; rather, it is that they are fortunate enough not to be a victim of the neural glitch that triggers choking; they are able to direct their conscious attention to tactics and strategy even under severe pressure, leaving the complex motor skills to the implicit system.

CHAPTER 7

Baseball Rituals, Pigeons, and Why Great Sportsmen Feel Miserable After Winning

Superstition

Tennis players are a strange bunch. Have you noticed how they always ask for three balls instead of two; how they keep using the towel between points, not to remove sweat but to erase the demons from their minds; how they bounce the ball the same number of times before serving, as if any deviation from their routine might bring the world down on their heads? It sometimes seems as if Wimbledon is less a tennis competition than a giant OCD convention.

But the superstitions, tics, and rituals so beloved by the world's top players are not confined to the court. They take even more bizarre twists when the players get home after their matches. Goran Ivanišević got it into his head that if he won a match, he had to repeat everything he did the previous day, such as eating the same food at the same restaurant, talking to the same people, and watching the same TV programs. One year this meant that he had to watch Teletubbies every morning during his Wimbledon campaign. "Sometimes it got very boring," he said.

Perhaps the most revealing insight into the surreal inner lives of top tennis players was provided by Serena Williams. Having exited the 2008 French Open in a shock third-round defeat, she was asked what went wrong. Was it her misfiring forehand? Her lack of fitness going into the competition? Her nonappearance at many top events during the season? Here's what she had to say: "I didn't tie my laces right and I didn't bounce the ball five times and I didn't bring my shower sandals to the court with me. I didn't have my extra dress. I just knew it was fate; it wasn't going to happen."

Superstition is not, of course, limited to tennis players, but extends across the world of sport. Tiger Woods always wears a red shirt in the final round of competitions; Mark Shwarzer, the Australian soccer goalkeeper, has worn the same shin pads since he was sixteen; cricketer Mark Ramprakash would chew the same piece of gum throughout an innings, sticking it to the top of his bat at the end of a day's play; legendary rugby player David Campese always sat in the seat next to the bus driver on the way to matches out of town.

But for sheer variety of superstitions, there is nothing to match baseball, a sport in which it sometimes seems as if a bizarre ritual is a condition of entry into the major leagues. Pitcher Greg Swindell would bite the tip off one of his fingernails before each start and hold it in his mouth for the entire game. Jim Ohms put a penny in the pouch of his jockstrap after each win—the pennies would clang against the plastic cup as he ran the bases toward the end of a winning season. Richie Ashburn slept with his bat.

Wade Boggs ate chicken before every game during his career and would take batting practice at precisely 5:17. Former Oriole pitcher Dennis Martinez drank a small cup of water after each inning and then placed the cups upside down under the bench, in a line. His teammates could always tell what inning it was by counting the cups. Mike Hargrove, the former Cleveland Indians first baseman, had so many time-consuming elements in his batting ritual that he was known as "the human rain delay."

All of which raises some intriguing questions: Why are so many top athletes deeply superstitious? Do these superstitions work? If not, why are they clung to so fiercely? And what does all this tell us about ritual and rationality in the wider world?

The answer is to be found in the world of pigeons. This may sound a little strange, but it was the firm opinion of B. F. Skinner, the man widely regarded as the father of modern psychology. "If we want to understand the basis of superstition in humans, the best place to start is by looking at the behavior of pigeons," he said.

Skinner's view was based on a groundbreaking experiment in 1947 in which he placed some hungry pigeons in a cage attached to an automatic mechanism that delivered food "at regular intervals with no reference whatsoever to the bird's behavior." He discovered that the pigeons associated the delivery of the food with whatever chance actions they happened to be performing at the moment it was first delivered. So what did the pigeons do? They kept performing the same actions, even though these had no effect whatsoever on the release of food.

Here is Skinner: "One bird was conditioned to turn counterclockwise about the cage, making two or three turns between reinforcements. Another repeatedly thrust its head into one of the upper corners of the cage. A third developed a 'tossing' response, as if placing its head beneath an invisible bar and lifting it repeatedly."

Of course, this is nothing compared with the strange behavior going on in major league baseball, but the connection is clear. The pigeons were acting as if they could influence the mechanism delivering the food in just the same way that Dennis Martinez thought he could influence the outcome of his next match by placing his cups under the bench upside down in a line. To put it a tad formally, they both witnessed a random connection between a particular kind of behavior and a desired outcome, and (wrongly) inferred that the relationship was causal.

Here is George Gmelch, an anthropologist at Union College and former baseball player:

> Most rituals grow out of exceptionally good performances. . . . Outfielder John White explained how one of his rituals started: "I was jogging out to centerfield after the national anthem when I picked up a scrap of paper. I got some good hits that night and I guess I decided that the paper had something to do with it. The next night I picked up a gum wrapper and had another good night at the plate. . . . I've been picking up paper every night since."

> Outfielder Ron Wright of the Calgary Cannons shaves his arms once a week and plans to continue doing so

until he has a bad year. It all began two years before when after an injury he shaved his arm so it could be taped, and proceeded to hit three homers over the next few games. Wade Boggs' routine of eating chicken before every game began when he was noticed a correlation between multiple hit games and poultry plates (his wife has over 40 chicken recipes).

The fact that pigeons and human beings share superstitious tendencies suggests that this kind of behavior emerged quite early in evolutionary history. What is certain is that it is widespread, particularly within *Homo sapiens*. In a recent poll, more than half of Americans admitted to being superstitious, and it is not just silly and gullible types either. At Harvard, students frequently rub the foot of the statue of John Harvard for good luck.

Even cricketers, sometimes described as the most sensible of sportsmen, are not immune to superstition. Jack Russell, the former England wicketkeeper, was among the most notorious, refusing to change his hat or wicketkeeping pads throughout his career, even though they became threadbare and smelly.

On one occasion in 1998, during an England tour of the West Indies, Russell was asked to wear the blue England cap instead of his favorite white hat. He refused, and according to Mike Atherton, one of his teammates, this is how the conversation unfolded.

ATHERTON: Jack, will you wear an England cap?
RUSSELL: No.
ATHERTON: Is there any way we can find a compromise
    solution?
RUSSELL: No.

ALEX STEWART (the captain): Well, if Jack's going to
wear his hat, I'm going to wear my white, not blue,
helmet.

NASSER HUSSAIN (another teammate): If the Gaffer's going
to wear his white helmet, I'd like to wear my favorite
baseball cap to field in.

Of course, some rituals may have a genuine impact on
performance. The very fact that they have become part of
a well-established routine may help an athlete to relax and
feel comfortable, aiding clear thinking and reducing anxiety. Rituals may also exert a placebo effect: as we saw in
chapter 5, believing strongly that something works can, in
circumstances where the outcome is under personal control,
make it more likely that it actually *will* work.

But the fact that superstitions exist in circumstances where
they can have no conceivable impact on performance suggests
there is something deeper at work. As Skinner said, "Rituals
for changing one's fortune at cards are good examples. . . .
So is a bowler who has released a ball down the alley but
continues to behave as if she were controlling it by twisting
and turning her arm and shoulder. These behaviors have,
of course, no real effect upon one's luck or upon a ball half
way down an alley, just as in the present case the food would
appear as often if the pigeon did nothing."

So the question remains: Why is it that so many athletes—
and the rest of us—maintain myriad rituals when they have
no real connection with the desired outcome? Or, to put it another way, why is superstitious behavior so widespread when
it seems to confer no tangible benefits? It's here that things
get really interesting and a little complex. And, as with many

interesting things, the answer is to be found in deep evolutionary history.

Let's start by imagining a caveman going to pick some berries from some bushes near his rocky abode. He hears some rustling in the bushes, wrongly infers that there is a lion lurking in there, and runs away. He even gets a little superstitious about those bushes and makes an effort to avoid going near them in the future. Is this superstition a problem to our caveman? Well, not if there are plenty of other berry-bearing bushes from which to get his five-a-day.

But suppose that there really is a lion living in those bushes. The caveman's behavior now is not just precautionary but life-saving. To put it another way, a tendency to perceive causal connections that don't actually exist can confer huge evolutionary benefits, providing a cocoon of safety in a turbulent and dangerous world. The only proviso (according to some devilishly complicated game theory) is that your superstitions must not impose too much of a burden on those occasions when they are without foundation.

And this is almost precisely what superstitions look like in the modern world. Some people believe in horoscopes, but few allow them to dictate their behavior; some like to wear the same lucky shoes to every job interview, but it is not as if wearing a different pair would improve their chances of success; some like to bounce the ball precisely seven times before serving at tennis, but although they are wrong to suppose that this ball-bouncing is implicated in their success, it does not harm their prospects (even if it irritates those of us watching).

It is only when a superstition compromises our deeper aspirations that we have moved along the spectrum of irrationality far enough to risk a diagnosis of obsessive-compulsive disorder. Take Kolo Touré, the former Arsenal soccer defender, who insists on being the last player to leave the dressing room after the halftime break. No real problem, you might think, except that when William Gallas, his teammate, was injured and needed treatment at halftime during a match in February, Touré stayed in the dressing room until Gallas had been treated, forcing Arsenal to start the second half with only nine players.

When a superstition that is supposed to help you actually harms you, it is probably time to kick out the ritual. Using a rabbit's foot, obviously.

Anticlimax

At the Olympic Games in Athens in 2004, renowned British track cyclist Victoria Pendleton failed to win a medal, coming sixth in the time trial and ninth in the sprint. She was bitterly disappointed. Although she bounced back to win a succession of World Championships, she knew deep inside that everything hinged on the Olympics in Beijing in 2008. The Great Britain cycling team has always been up front about its raison d'être: winning Olympic gold is everything, all else is detail.

Pendleton worked harder than ever in 2008, rising early to do the lung-busting cardio work, pumping weights, making sacrifices in her personal and family life, you name it. Her entire being was directed at a few minutes of pedaling around an indoor track in China. That was her destiny and her ambition, her be-all and end-all. That is what it is like—that is what it has to be like—if you are serious about becoming the best. Then, in Beijing, in the theater of dreams, calamity struck.

She won.

Consider her words, as honest as they are perplexed, just a few months after achieving her lifetime ambition. "You have all this buildup for one day, and when it's over, it's: 'Oh, is that it?'" she said. "People think it's hard when you lose. But it's almost easier to come second because you have something to aim for when you finish. When you win, you suddenly feel lost."

Steve Peters, the British cycling team's mind coach, has revealed that many other Olympic champions—as well as some among the support teams—have also struggled with severe anticlimax. "This is true not just in cycling but across the sports I've worked with," he said. "A number of people I've been in touch with following the Olympics, people who'd succeeded, said the same. They felt quite depressed, almost like a sense of loss."

I know what he means. During my table tennis career, there were few things more terrifying than getting my hands on a coveted prize. A defeat offered such a pleasing variety of emotional options: vengefulness, stoicism, anger, resignation, sadness, exasperation. But the metaphysical hollowness that often accompanies a long-desired triumph is something that nobody can prepare you for. The champagne I swilled after winning my first Commonwealth gold medal was not so much to soak my euphoria as to numb a spiraling sense of angst.

For months I had nurtured an ambition so precious it had become like a dear friend. But now it had vanished in a detonation of euphoria. No wonder Peters spoke of a sense of loss, almost like a bereavement.

Have you been there—not the Ping-Pong, the emptiness? Bought a shiny convertible, only to glimpse its superficiality? Won a promotion, only to discover that the job was not all you had dreamed of? As Robert Louis Stevenson, a man who knew a thing or two about the ironies of the human psyche, wrote: "To travel hopefully is a better thing than to arrive."

I have seen it again and again in sport, an arena that, more than any other, crystallizes what it means to reach one's destination. James Toseland wept in the privacy of his hotel room after winning his first Superbike world title. Martina Navratilova was afflicted with bouts of melancholy at many high points during her career. Marty Reisman, the table tennis hustler from New York's Lower East Side, bemoaned the futility of sporting achievement after his career-defining triumph at the English Open in 1949.

One of the most famous episodes of anticlimax, sporting or otherwise, descended upon Harold Abrahams after he won a gold medal in the 1924 Olympics 100 meters. In one of the closing scenes of the film *Chariots of Fire*, he is portrayed in his dressing room looking sullen and confused, refusing to talk to anyone. One of his friends, who had lost in a previous race, asks what is wrong. "One of these days you are going to win yourself—and you are going to find that it is pretty difficult to swallow," comes the response.

But what would it be like if we could eliminate this perplexing facet of the human condition; if we could somehow get the emotional highs without the lows; if we could arrive at our chosen destination—Olympic gold or otherwise—without falling victim to an echoing sense of anticlimax?

Psychologists, many of whom seem to regard all disagreeable mental states as viruses that should be deleted from consciousness, would doubtless embrace this vision. But would it really make us happier, healthier, more successful people?

In the late 1960s, Paul Ekman, an American psychologist, took a trip to Papua New Guinea to conduct a series of interviews with the Fore, an isolated tribe living in an ancient, preliterate culture. He was seeking to test the cultural theory of emotion: the idea that emotions are learned behaviors that are picked up from family and friends, like languages.

According to this theory—which was almost universally accepted at the time—in order to experience joy or bitterness, you first need to see others being joyful or bitter. Without that social transmission, you would never experience those emotions.

Ekman's experiment was remarkably simple: he told the Fore tribesmen various stories and then asked them to choose, from photographs of Americans expressing various emotions, the photo that most closely matched the story. One story, for example, involved coming across a wild animal in a hut, a situation that would create fear in westerners.

Given that the Fore had never had any contact with westerners, Ekman did not expect them to have any idea about the kinds of emotions experienced by westerners or the facial expressions associated with them. But to his astonishment he found that when they were shown the photographs, the Fore tribesmen picked out precisely the expressions that westerners linked to the stories.

Ekman then reversed the experiment, asking the Fore people to make facial expressions appropriate to the various stories, which he videotaped. After he arrived back in San Francisco, he asked Americans to link the Fore faces to the stories. Once again, the judgments coincided perfectly.

Ekman's experiment sounded the death knell of the cultural theory of emotion. His findings showed that many emotions are universal: hardwired into the brain at birth rather than learned through contact with any particular culture. Why? Because they are evolved traits rather than cultural creations, designed by natural selection to facilitate survival and gene propagation.

As Dylan Evans writes in his book *Emotion: A Very Short Introduction*, "Our common emotional heritage binds humanity together in a way that transcends cultural difference."

Seen in this evolutionary context, emotions start to look very different. So-called negative emotions, while they may seem unnecessary and unpleasant, are vital mechanisms that guard our long-term health and survival (rather like physical pain, which warns of damage to our bodies). Indeed, according to Evans, it would be impossible for anyone to make it far through life without emotions: "Lacking fear, the creature might sit around and ponder whether or not the approaching lion really represented a threat or not. Without anger, it would be picked on mercilessly. Lack of disgust would allow it to consume faeces and rotting food."

Other so-called negative emotions can also be seen from this perspective: anxiety facilitates escape from dangerous situations and helps us to avoid them in the future; mild depression enables us to disengage from unattainable goals; humiliation is triggered when we are faced with the threat of losing social status; sexual jealousy is aroused by the imminent (or perceived) loss of a partner's fidelity.

From this vantage point, anticlimax begins to make perfect sense: millions of years of natural selection have sifted sequences of DNA just so that we can feel miserable in the aftermath of long-coveted triumph. Why? So that we are able to disengage from our triumph, enabling us to focus on the next challenge. If goal fulfillment induced indefinite periods of contentment, we would be robbed of all future motivation.

For a triumphant athlete, then, anticlimax is the emotional lull that lays the psychological foundations for the next tilt at gold. For an award-winning writer, it is the melancholy that provides the creative impetus for the next literary adventure. For a lottery winner, it is the sense of hollowness that makes her want to go out to work again.

This cuts to the heart of one of the deepest questions of humanity, long debated by writers and philosophers: What is it about certain people—top athletes in particular—that makes them so relentless? What causes them to set their eyes on the next summit so soon after scaling the last one? Why are they so driven? So unsated by success?

At one time the answer seemed to be inexplicable, lost in the unfathomable mysteries of the human psyche. But we can now see that the answer may hinge on something far simpler: an evolved capacity to experience anticlimax faster, sharper, and deeper than the rest of us. After all, anticlimax is something we have all experienced, but it is striking just how quickly top performers come down to earth after winning a major title; remarkable how rapidly they emotionally disengage from a goal they may have spent years striving for.

As Sir Alex Ferguson, the manager of Manchester United soccer club, put it just a few moments after holding aloft a record ninth Premier League soccer trophy in 2007: "I'm already looking forward to next season. Let's get on with it. I'm looking forward to going on to win a European trophy as well as pushing for the league."

The very next season Manchester United not only won the Premier League, but also the hugely prestigious European Champions League. It was a double triumph that cemented Ferguson's reputation as the greatest British soccer manager in history.

PART III

Deep Reflections

CHAPTER 8

Optical Illusions and X-Ray Vision

Illusion and Reality

Take a look at the Charlie Chaplin mask on the next page. In Photo A it looks precisely as you would expect it to look, as it does in Photo B, where it has been rotated 90 degrees. But now look at Photo C: this is the mask rotated 180 degrees so that we are looking in at the hollow end—but somehow the mask continues to look convex. Photo D is particularly surreal, with the hollow part of the mask seen as convex and the truly convex part also seen as convex.

In this chapter we are going to explore the mysteries of human perception and why it is that top athletes seem to perceive faster, smarter, and deeper than the rest of us. But in order to get there, we first need to figure out what is going on

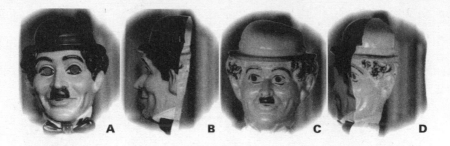

with the mask illusion. Why does the hollow end of the mask look like a perfectly normal face? And why does the illusion remain intact, even when we have been told about it?

Think about the mechanics of vision for a moment or two. We all have an intuitive understanding of how this works: light bounces off objects, enters our eyes, and is focused on the retina by the lens. This retinal image is then sent to the brain, where it is "experienced." In this account of perception, the eye operates as a kind of camera, with the brain getting access to the picture via the delivery system of the optic nerve.

But a little reflection shows that this account must be flawed. After all, if the retinal image is like a photograph, which is sent to the brain, who is sitting in the brain to "see" the incoming picture? This is the Terminator fallacy: you may remember in the movies starring Arnold Schwarzenegger that the machine-assassin sees the world as a computer readout on a screen. But this makes no sense, given that there is nobody inside the Terminator's brain to see the screen. Besides, if vision is about the brain getting access to a two-dimensional retinal image, why is it that we see and experience the world in three dimensions?

These reflections hint at the rather surprising truth that the information provided by our eyes and ears is only very loosely connected to the way we experience the world. Retinal images, for example, are vague, fragmentary, and highly ambiguous, and it takes a huge amount of work by the brain to transform them into the vivid, three-dimensional "movie" that constitutes waking experience.

To get an idea of just how much work the brain does in perception, consider a remarkable acoustic experiment by Makio Kashino of the NTT Communication Science Laboratories in Japan. He recorded a voice saying "Do you understand what I'm trying to say?" then removed short chunks and replaced them with silence, thus making the sentence virtually unintelligible. But when he filled the gaps with loud white noise, the sentence—astonishingly—snapped back into focus.

"The sounds we hear are not copies of physical sounds," Kashino said. "The brain fills in the gaps, based on the information in the remaining speech signal." It is our *knowledge* of language—drawn from many years of experience—that enables us to renovate the sensory information into a comprehensible form.

In the case of the Chaplin mask, it is our knowledge that *misleads* us into seeing the hollow side of the mask as convex. Our experience has taught us that faces are pretty much always convex, so when the brain gets to work on the retinal image, it embroiders it so that we see the inside of the mask as convex even though the sensory information (shadows, shading, etc.) is telling a different story. As psychologist Richard Gregory, who has conducted some of the most pioneering research on illusions, puts it: "Bottom-up sensory information is overridden by top-down knowledge."

The role played by top-down knowledge can be seen in the

"plumbing" of perception: in the case of vision, there are more downward fibers from the cortex to the brain's relay stations than there are bottom-up from the eyes. So when we look at, say, a face, there is more data traveling downward from the knowledge areas of our brains than traveling upward from our eyes. Perception is what happens when the two interact.

This is, of course, deeply counterintuitive. After all, how does the brain "know" what information to send downstream in response to upstream sensory data in order to create a meaningful perception? This is a question that neuroscientists continue to grapple with. What is known is that the process is extraordinarily complex, with the visual system containing an extensive web of feedback connections projecting from higher cortical areas to lower areas.

What would the perception of faces be like without top-down knowledge? We can get an idea from the remarkable cases where blind people gain sight late in life. Sidney Bradford, a British man, developed sight at the age of fifty-two after receiving corneal grafts at the Wolverhampton and Midland Counties Eye Infirmary. Here is how researchers reported his experience when he looked at the face of his surgeon after the bandages were removed:

> He heard a voice coming from in front of him and to one side: he turned to the source of the sound, and saw a "blur." He realized that this must be a face. Upon careful questioning, he seemed to think that he would not have known that this was a face if he had not previously heard the voice and known that voices came from faces.

That's right: When Bradford looked at a face, he saw a blur. He had access to the same visual information as everyone else (the light entering his retina was identical, as was the retinal image), but he *saw it differently* because he lacked the knowledge—drawn from experience—to mold the sensory data into a meaningful form. Even after a few months, Bradford was unable to recognize people through vision alone, even when meeting them for the third or fourth time. Instead, he had to rely on acoustic information such as tone of voice.

This may sound bizarre, but it is actually familiar. Precisely the same phenomenon happens to the rest of us when we hear people talking. When we listen to a conversation in our own language, we hear a series of distinct words separated by tiny gaps of silence. But no such silences actually exist.* It is our knowledge of the grammatical structure of our language that enables us to retouch the acoustic information so that we *hear it* in a neatly structured form.

Now contrast this with listening to people talking in a foreign language: this time we hear a confused and undigested influx of noise without any noticeable gaps or structure. That is what it is like for a blind person who has recently attained her vision trying to see a face. She is looking at her friend, but she sees only confusion and haziness because she lacks the top-down knowledge with which to create a meaningful perception.

The key point in all this is that knowledge is not used merely to make sense of perceptions; *knowledge is embedded in perception*. As the great British philosopher Sir Peter Strawson put it, "Perception is thoroughly permeated by our concepts."

---

* This has been demonstrated by analyzing the energy profile of the voice signal. Researchers have found that the regions of lowest energy (the moments closest to silence) do not line up with the word boundaries.

X-Ray Vision

A key difference between experts and novices is that experts are better at extracting information from what is going on around them, as we saw in chapter 1. Roger Federer, for example, can anticipate the movement of a tennis ball more efficiently than the rest of us, not because he has better eyesight but because he knows where to look and how to interpret the movement patterns of his opponent.

Similarly, expert firefighters are able to figure out how to combat a raging blaze because they have a deep knowledge of fires and have learned to grasp subtle visual cues revealing their dynamics.

But we can now see that truth is even more radical. When Roger Federer plays tennis, he does not make better inferences from a universally accessible pool of sensory information; rather, he *sees and hears the world in an entirely different way.* His deep knowledge of tennis transforms the very fabric of his perceptions.

This dramatic difference between experts and nonexperts can be most easily seen in the world of medicine. Clinicians with long experience are able to make better diagnoses from X-rays and mammograms than medical students. But this is not because they make more astute inferences from the pictures, but because they can actually see patterns and structure that are invisible to their less experienced colleagues.

You can get a sense of what is going on from the picture on the next page: your knowledge of faces enables you to see the image embedded in the collection of dots, but someone with no experience of looking at faces would see only the dots, not the face. The retinal image is the same in both cases, but the perception is entirely different.

The ability of experts to see things that are invisible to the rest of us may sound a little weird but is actually quite familiar. It is the reason why Eskimos, with their long experience of arctic conditions, can discern shades of white invisible to westerners; it is why Charles Revlon, head of the cosmetics chain, was able to see four shades of black; it is why highly trained musicians are better than nonmusicians at detecting very small differences in the pitch and loudness of notes.

It also explains the seemingly miraculous skills of chick spotters. Poultry owners once had to wait until chicks were five to six weeks old before differentiating male from female (gender became visible only when adult feathers started appearing). But they now hire expert spotters, who are able to instantly determine the sex of day-old chicks, even though, to amateurs, they look identical. This is of serious commercial value, enabling egg producers to avoid feeding unproductive males.

But none of these expert spotters have superior eyes or ears; rather, they have the knowledge drawn from long experience with which to sculpt sensory information into a dramatically new form.

These insights help to unlock some of the deepest mysteries of sport. It is why top table tennis players are able to spot variations of spin that novices cannot see even when they are looking at them. It is why Wayne Gretzky is able to perceive patterns of movement in the players around him that are invisible to the rest of the world. It is why Garry Kasparov is able to see the right move just by looking at the configuration of a chessboard.

It is as if top athletes are wearing X-ray goggles, providing perceptual access to a realm of spins, shapes, curves, and patterns denied to the rest of us. Is it any wonder we marvel at their abilities? We cannot see what they see. We are like recently healed blind people looking at faces and seeing confusion, or visitors to a foreign land listening in on a conversation and hearing only noise. We lack the top-down knowledge to construct meaning from our senses.

It normally takes many thousands of hours of purposeful practice for this kind of perceptual makeover to take place, and the process is so gradual that the expert rarely notices the changes along the way. But we can get a sense of the kind of transformation that takes place by looking at the picture on the next page. You will see either a young woman with her face turned away or an elderly woman with a hood.

But if you look long enough, the perception will snap from one to the other, even if you keep your eyes stationary so that the retinal image remains exactly the same. In this case, the perceptual transformation takes place instantaneously because we possess knowledge of both young girls and old women. But suppose you had only ever met old women. In those circumstances the perceptual flip would occur only once you had spent lots of hours in the company of young girls.

It is not difficult to understand why, over evolutionary time, we have developed the ability to sculpt perceptions using top-down knowledge: it provides immediacy. Instead of having to *infer* the existence of a face in a pattern of dots or the structure in a mammogram, you can *see* it. It is *there*. The inference is, as it were, embedded in the perception.

This not only saves time but also frees up psychological resources to focus on other elements of a task. A top table tennis player who can "see" where the ball is going just by looking at his opponent's movement patterns has greater available "bandwidth" to think about tactics and strategy than a player who is consciously striving to figure out what the postural cues mean.

This ability of experts to free up attentional resources has become one of the hottest new topics in psychology, and it is not confined to perception, but is also seen in the automation of movement. Because many of the strokes and movements used by experts are encoded within implicit memory (as we saw in chapter 6) and can be executed without conscious control, this frees up mental resources for other key tasks.

But if experts have the ability to free up attention, it raises the question: what happens to perception when attentional bandwidth is exhausted?

Inattentional Blindness

Suppose you were to watch a tape of two teams of basketball players—one in blue and the other in white—throwing to each other. And suppose you were asked to count the number of passes made by one of the teams: say, the team in white. This, I am sure you will agree, is a pretty straightforward task, and you would have little difficulty managing it.

But now suppose that while you are watching the two teams, a man in a gorilla costume walks into the middle of the action, actually brushing shoulders with the players, turns toward you, beats his chest, and then slowly walks out the other side. Do you think you would notice the gorilla? It seems like a ridiculous question. Of course you would. Wouldn't you?

In fact, when this experiment was conducted at Harvard, more than half the participants failed to spot the guy in the ape costume. They were so absorbed in counting the passes, they didn't see the gorilla in their midst. Afterward, when the participants watched the tape again, they were so surprised when the gorilla was pointed out to them that many accused the experimenters of having doctored the tape between viewings.

A similar phenomenon can be seen in another Harvard experiment. This time a student walking through campus is asked for directions by a passerby. As the student is answering, two workmen barge past, carrying a door. Then something peculiar happens: in the moment or two the passerby is behind the door, he switches places with one of the workmen. The student is left providing directions to a different person: older, taller, different clothes, different voice.

Does the student notice? Would you? In fact, more than half of those taking part in the experiment merrily continued issuing directions, totally oblivious to the fact they were talking to a different person.

What this shows is that attention is a resource with severe capacity limitations. As we make our way through the world (or take part in a sports contest), we are bombarded by so much sensory information that it is impossible to process it all consciously. Attention acts as a kind of filter system that permits only a certain amount of information to hit conscious awareness. But if attention is at overload (because, say, we are scrupulously counting the number of passes made by a basketball team), we are unable to perceive things that are actually there, right in front of our noses.

Most of us have roughly the same amount of bandwidth available for conscious processing, but experts, by automating perceptual and motor programs, are able to create spare capacity. When the gorilla basketball experiment was repeated with basketball experts, for example, they had no problem seeing the gorilla. Their deep knowledge of basketball meant that they had spare capacity to devote to tasks beyond merely counting the passes.

Blindness That Kills

It is December 29, 1972, and Eastern Air Lines Flight 401 has just taken off from the bitter cold of New York City and is heading out to Miami. One hundred and sixty-three passengers are on board, most of them hoping to enjoy a New Year's vacation in the sun. Ann-Margret is on stage at the Fontainebleau, Woody Allen at the Deauville, and the King Orange Parade is happening on New Year's Day.

The flight is smooth and without incident as, a little before midnight, the plane makes its final approach into Miami International Airport. The wheels are lowered in preparation for landing, the captain informs the guests of the local temperature, and the passengers fasten their seat belts.

But then the captain notices that something is wrong. On most aircraft, there are three sets of wheels: one set beneath each of the two wings, and another just below the nose. When the wheels are lowered into place and lock into position for landing, indicators in the cockpit light up. But the green light linked to the wheels beneath the nose has failed to illuminate.

This could mean one of two things: either the light itself is faulty or the wheels have failed to lock into place. Either way, the captain has no choice but to abort his landing to figure out what has gone wrong. He informs air traffic control at just after half past eleven:

CAPTAIN: Well ah, tower, this is Eastern, ah, 401. It looks like we're gonna have to circle, we don't have a light on our nose gear yet.

AIR TRAFFIC CONTROL: Eastern 401 heavy, roger, pull up, climb straight ahead to two thousand, go back to approach control, one twenty eight six.

What happens next will ultimately cause one of the biggest civil aviation disasters in history. *The crew members fixate on the faulty light.* They pull it from its fitting, they turn it around in their hands, they blow on it to remove dust, they get it jammed when trying to put it back in its fitting. They devote so much attention to the light, they fail to notice the gorilla in their midst.

The gorilla, in this case, is the fact that the autopilot has been inadvertently disengaged, and the airplane is losing altitude. As the crew continue to focus their attention on the light, the plane is now taking the crew and passengers on a downward path toward disaster in the Everglades.

CAPTAIN (*talking about the faulty light fixture*): Put it in the wrong way, huh?

COPILOT: In there looks square to me.

CAPTAIN: Can you get the hole lined up?

As the plane drops through 1,750 feet, an altitude warning alarm rings through the cockpit. The alarm is part of a sophisticated warning system, informing the pilots of their mortal danger. But although the alarm is clearly audible on the black box recording, neither the pilot nor the copilot hears it. Their attention is so wrapped up with the light, they have no spare bandwidth with which to consciously register the noise. They are now less than one hundred seconds from death.

COPILOT: The tests didn't show that the lights worked anyway.
CAPTAIN: That's right.
COPILOT: It's a faulty light.

Altitude is declining every second. The pilots can't feel it because their senses are deceived by the plane's motion. They can't see it through the windows because it's a moonless night, and there is no visible horizon. But right in front of the pilot's noses, the altitude meter is spinning downward. It is within their line of sight. It is possible that both pilot and copilot actually look at the meter and see it moving. But they can't *perceive* what it is saying. Why? Because it never hits conscious awareness.

Only when the plane is seven seconds from impact with the ground does the copilot finally realize that something is seriously wrong.

COPILOT: We did something to the altitude.
PILOT: What?
COPILOT: We're still at two thousand, right?
PILOT: Hey, what's happening here?

The pilot takes evasive action, pulling hard on the lever, but it's too late. A moment later the plane crashes, killing 101 people.

Perhaps the most remarkable thing about Eastern Air Lines Flight 401 is that the plane's detailed warning systems *worked.* The altitude meter told the pilots that the plane was descending, and the alarm system provided the same information in acoustic form. But neither made the slightest bit of difference. The pilots had insufficient bandwidth. They were inattentionally blind. For the pilots, focused on the faulty light, it was as if the warnings never happened. They vanished into the realms of the unconscious.

Crash investigators would later establish that the nose wheels had, in fact, locked into place: the plane could have landed. The only piece of faulty equipment was the lightbulb in the nose gear assembly fixture, which had burned out. One journalist said, "The crash occurred due to the failure of a $12 piece of kit." In a way, he was right, but the deeper truth is that a warning system, however sophisticated, is often only as good as the attentional resources at the disposal of the crew.

Eastern Air Lines Flight 401 has become a seminal event in aviation safety history, changing the way crashes are investigated and the way pilots are trained. A key innovation in crew training systems is a clear procedure of delegation between the pilot and the copilots in order to free up attentional resources.

The problem with the faulty lightbulb was not just that the captain fixated on it, but that the rest of the crew did, too: the pool of attention was exclusively focused on a single problem. Had just one of the crew focused on the light fitting, there would have been plenty of available attention for the others to have picked up on the visual and acoustic cues indicating the plane's descent.

This system of crew delegation is not unlike that wielded by a top athlete using the "crew" of her own mental resources. Top-down knowledge enables a world-class tennis player to see where the ball is going before her opponent has actually hit it. She has, in effect, delegated the inference to the higher areas of the brain. Long hours of practice mean that she can initiate and execute the motor programs to play her shots without thinking about it. She has, in effect, delegated the stroke to the brain's implicit system.

This means that she has plenty of available attention with which to think strategically and to deal with looming emergencies, such as a sudden switch in tactics from her opponent. It is often the difference between success and failure. In aviation, clever delegation to avoid inattentional blindness can sometimes be the difference between life and death.

CHAPTER 9

Drugs in Sport, Schwarzenegger Mice, and the Future of Mankind

Heidi Krieger

In the summer of 1979 Heidi Krieger received the letter she had been dreaming of: a card emblazoned with official stamps inviting her to join the fabled Dynamo Sports Club in East Berlin. For a thirteen-year-old who had recently fallen in love with shot-putting at her local athletics club, it was a dream come true.

Heidi showed the invitation to her mother and three brothers, who were as excited as she was. This was a once-in-a-lifetime chance to pursue her ambition of becoming an international sportswoman and, who knows, traveling the world to compete in big competitions, bringing glory to the motherland. That night she found it difficult to sleep: her young mind was racing with anticipation.

A few months later Heidi arrived at the club. She was put on a schedule of two periods of school classes and two training sessions per day. For the first year she was observed by coaches, whose objective was to identify the most talented athletes from the new intake. She was thrilled to see that they seemed satisfied with her progress.

Toward the end of her second year Heidi was told that she was being brought under the supervision of a specialist throwing coach and a sports doctor, concrete proof that the club regarded her as a major prospect.

It was then that they started giving her blue pills. They were bright and round and looked like sweets. Heidi was told they were vitamin tablets that would keep her healthy and protect her from the sometimes chill temperatures during training. She was handed one every morning and one every evening and was observed as she swallowed them with a glass of water.

Almost immediately Heidi's body began to change: her muscles expanded and her face, nose, and hands started to enlarge. Her mood, too, went haywire: one moment she was afflicted with depression, and then, in an instant, she was overwhelmed with feelings of aggression. Her girlfriends also found strange things happening to their bodies and minds: hair started to sprout across their bellies and faces, their voices became deeper, and their libidos swung violently.

The coaches and doctors soothed the concerns of the girls and their parents, explaining that the strange alterations were a consequence of the extra training sessions and would be temporary. Those who voiced doubts were told that they would be punished if they persisted with their questioning. This was East Germany at the height of communism: citizens, young and old, did what they were told.

Gradually the number of blue pills increased, so that after a few years Heidi was being fed five to six tablets a day plus regular injections of what her coaches told her was glucose. The teenager seemed, even to herself, a different person: aggressive, depressive, and with anatomical and facial characteristics that were almost unrecognizable compared to the photo of the slight girl who arrived at Dynamo, which she kept in a drawer near her bed.

But while Heidi's life fell apart, her shot-putting soared. At the European Championships in Stuttgart in 1986, she reached the pinnacle of her career, winning the gold medal with a putt of 21.1 meters. It ought to have been a moment of celebration, a vindication of her many years of hard work. But it wasn't. Heidi was in despair, estranged from herself and her body, unable to cope with her crippling mood swings and chronic knee pain.

In 1990 she retired to join the ranks of the unemployed—a broken woman, her childhood dreams shattered.

It is June 2008 and a beautiful summer's day in the East German town of Magdeburg. In an army surplus store on the high street a middle-aged man is standing behind the till, waiting for his next customer. Business is slow, and the man is enveloped by a faint air of loneliness. He is tall, with a large, round face, powerful forearms, and huge hands. His dark hair, brushed back from the forehead, is flecked with gray and is thinning just a little; his four-day stubble is shaped in a goatee.

His face brightens noticeably as I come through the door, and he bounds across to shake hands. He is friendly and tactile, with a booming voice and plenty of boyish charm. At the back of the shop is a small kitchen, and he gestures me through to join him for a coffee.

The room is stacked with supplies, but he is not trying to sell anything—instead he goes to the cupboard under the sink and heaves out a red crate. It is full of medals, images, and other sporting mementos. He pulls from the pile a large photo of Heidi Krieger being presented with the European Championship gold medal from 1986 and grins as he examines it.

I look from the face of the man in the shop to the face of the woman in the photo and the truth is strange but unmistakable: they are one and the same person.

It took many years for Andreas Krieger—the name Heidi chose following her sex-change operation in 1997—to discover what had been perpetrated at the Berlin Dynamo Club. Top-secret documents relating to the sporting system in East Germany were uncovered only after the fall of the Berlin Wall, and it took almost a decade to excavate the full, mind-bending story.

At the heart of the infamy were those bright blue pills. Krieger discovered that they were not vitamin tablets but anabolic steroids called Oral-Turinabol: powerful prescription drugs that built muscle and induced male characteristics. Krieger was not unusual in having been fed those pills: according to secret files uncovered at a military hospital on the outskirts of Berlin, more than ten thousand athletes were doped with Oral-Turinabol over a twenty-year period.

Experimentation by the authorities demonstrated that the effects of the steroids were more pronounced on women, who naturally lacked androgens (male hormones). The East

German political establishment realized that they had happened upon a powerful means of boosting the prestige of their "enlightened" system of government.

Secrecy was paramount. In a classified document, which proves that the doping program was approved at the highest level of the political establishment, the Central Committee of the Communist Party decreed that the administration of steroids should be organized centrally under the auspices of the Sports Medical Service and classified as an Official Secret. Concealment was maintained by requiring coaches and sports doctors to sign confidentiality agreements and by engaging more than three thousand spies reporting directly to the Stasi, East Germany's secret police.

Such were the financial incentives offered to coaches to produce champions that a black market emerged in Oral-Turinabol. Coaches attempted to get their hands on extra supplies of the drug, using them to dope girls and boys as young as twelve years of age.

But it did not take long for the risks to manifest themselves. Manfred Höppner, the head of the Sports Medical Service, who was already aware of the dramatic changes in terms of hair growth, mood swings, clitoris growth, and severe acne, wrote of the risk of liver damage in one of his regular reports to the Stasi: "Liver damages have appeared, including considerable increases in the size of the organ (heptaomegaly). In female athletes these damaging effects are additionally promoted by contraceptive pills [which female athletes were forced to take to guard against pregnancy]. In two of the athletes tested, liver damages were diagnosed in such an advanced stage that one could not take the responsibility to let them continue with high performance sport."

But to those in the political elite, the results of East

German athletes justified the means. By 1972 a nation with a population of 17 million had forced its way to third in the medal table at the Munich Olympic Games, behind the Soviet Union and the United States. Four years later East Germany surpassed the United States and trailed the Soviet Union by just nine gold medals. Erich Honecker, the political leader of East Germany, hailed his athletes as paragons of the nation.

By the time Krieger arrived at the Dynamo Club, the officials heading the doping program—intoxicated by the runaway success of its athletes—had lost all inhibition. An average teenage girl produces around half a milligram of testosterone per day. By the midpoint of her sporting career Krieger was being fed 30 milligrams of anabolic steroids each day, far in excess of Ben Johnson, the Canadian sprinter, at the height of his drugs program.

State-sponsored scientists had also developed STS 646, an anabolic steroid that caused male characteristics in women at a rate sixteen times that of Oral-Turinabol. It was distributed to coaches even though it had not been approved for human use, not even in Stage 1 clinical trials. Even Höppner expressed his doubts, telling the Stasi that he was not willing to be held responsible. But Manfred Ewald, president of the Sports Federation, insisted they were necessary and ordered 63,000 tablets from the state pharmaceutical plant. Krieger was almost certainly one of the recipients.

Krieger's unease over his sexual identity predated his doping program, but he now says that the androgenic abuse left him with little choice but to undergo a sex change operation. "I had no sympathy with my body; it had changed beyond all recognition. It was as though they had killed Heidi. Becoming Andreas was the next logical step." Krieger underwent surgery in 1997—and then he prayed for justice to take its course for those who had wrought havoc with his life.

It was not until May 3, 2000, that Höppner and Ewald, the men who had masterminded the doping program, were brought before a court in Berlin to face charges of causing actual bodily harm. Krieger was in the courtroom alongside many of East Germany's most successful athletes, all listening intently as the charges were read out.

Krieger was the only female athlete to undergo a sex-change operation following the years of androgenic abuse, but other female athletes suffered from complications ranging from cancer to ovarian cysts. Male athletes, too, suffered from the side effects of excess steroid use, including heart damage and high blood pressure. All yearned for a successful prosecution that might enable them to obtain some kind of closure from one of the darkest chapters in the history of sport.

The trial lasted almost three months and was covered extensively by the world's media. Höppner and Ewald were eventually both convicted of causing actual bodily harm. Ewald was sentenced to twenty-two months probation, and Höppner to eighteen months' probation.

"It was not as severe as the athletes had hoped," said Krieger. "But at least we had the satisfaction that they were convicted of what they had done."

To Ban or Not to Ban?

The horrors of the East German doping system provide a powerful case for why drugs in sport should always remain prohibited. Surely no sane person would want to see any return to a situation where adolescents are doped up to the eyeballs by state-sanctioned coaches. Surely nobody would want to actually legalize such activity within the domain of sport.

But are the atrocities that took place in East Germany the last word in the debate? This question is worth considering for at least one simple reason: the battle against drugs in sports is failing. Despite thousands of athletes being doped in East Germany, only one was ever caught by the antidoping authorities. Since then, despite the introduction of out-of-competition testing, the authorities continue to chase shadows.

As Victor Conte, the head of Balco, a controversial sports nutrition center in California which distributed steroids to many top athletes before coming under investigation in 2003, said: "It is as easy to evade the testers as it is to take candy from a baby."

The essential problem for WADA (the World Anti-Doping Authority, which leads the fight against drugs in sport) is that the cheats are always one step ahead—able to use chemically altered substances and other deceptions that elude conventional testing procedures—putting honest athletes at a severe disadvantage. As British sprinter Dwain Chambers puts it: "It's simple: science always moves faster than the testers."

One way to eliminate drug cheating, of course, would be to legalize drug taking (without rules to break, cheating would cease to exist by definition), but this would surely be an intolerable solution. Success would be determined not by ability and hard work but by a willingness to trade future life expectancy for present glory. The dangers of excessive doping were comprehensively demonstrated during the doping trials after the fall of the Berlin Wall, as we have seen.

The question, therefore, is whether there is a middle road between prohibition and full-scale legalization. According to Julian Savulescu, professor of practical ethics at Oxford University, there is. In a radical new approach, he argues that we should not legalize *all* performance-enhancing drugs; rather we should legalize *safe* enhancers. That way the dangers of former athletes developing medical complications are eliminated (or, at least, minimized), and at the same time, the way is paved to greater transparency in the way drugs are administered and detected.

How? Let's take a couple of examples. Perhaps the most widely used drugs in sport are in endurance events, where success is determined by how efficiently oxygen can be transported to the muscles via the red blood cells. The percentage of red cells in the blood is known as the hematocrit level (HCT), and it can be increased by injecting EPO (a hormone banned by WADA) or by training at altitude (a training technique that is not banned).

Increasing HCT to around 50 percent carries no significant health risks, whether it is achieved by altitude training or EPO. It is only when HCT is elevated above 55 percent that the risks begin to escalate: the increased concentration of red cells thickens the blood to the consistency of jam, increasing the risk of heart attack. In recent years a number of Tour de France cyclists have died as a result of unexpected heart attacks consistent with possible EPO abuse.

WADA has spent millions of dollars in a doomed attempt to find a foolproof test for EPO. One of the latest is a joint blood-urine test that can easily be cheated on by the use of plasma expanders (which increase the fluid in the blood) and diuretics. But even if WADA managed to develop a miracle test for EPO, athletes would simply respond with blood transfusion, an illegal but virtually untestable procedure in which an athlete withdraws some of his own blood and then reinfuses it just before a big competition, thus increasing the number of red blood cells.

WADA's banning of HCT enhancement, then, is not only futile but also morally perverse. The logic of WADA's position is that it is acceptable to boost HCT from 55 to 60 percent by training at altitude, even though this is potentially fatal, yet it is not acceptable to increase HCT from 40 to 45 percent using EPO, even though it is perfectly safe. By focusing on the *means* by which athletes boost HCT, WADA has lost sight of the impact upon the athlete's health.

Would it not be more effective to legalize all blood-altering techniques and simply test directly for HCT? Setting a safe limit (50, say, or 55) would give the authorities a foolproof procedure that would also protect health.

This system would also be fairer. The problem with unenforceable rules is that they reward cheats and penalize the honest. Under the present system, those who refuse to transfuse blood or use EPO are at a disadvantage during competition because they have no means of increasing HCT. By permitting all safe methods of increasing HCT to the legal limit, WADA would level the playing field between the honest and dishonest.

The same logic applies to steroids. It is said that steroids are unsafe, but this is simplistic. Drugs are not safe or unsafe; it is the quantities in which they are taken that are either safe or unsafe. Moderate steroid use improves strength and aids recovery without significant damaging side effects. Permitting safe usage would still require the authorities to test for excessive use, but this could be made more effective if testers focused on the symptoms of overuse (such as left ventricular hypertrophy—a marker for heart disease) rather than testing directly for the elusive substances.

A policy of "regulated permissiveness" would also create a safer environment for athletes by giving them an opportunity to choose drugs under conditions of informed consent. The problem with prohibition is that it forces the problem underground, with athletes taking unlicensed drugs in collusion with dubious suppliers. A reformed policy would also provide huge incentives for drugs companies to create safe drugs: at present, as in East Germany in the 1970s and '80s, the pressure is simply to create undetectable drugs.

It hardly needs stating that Savulescu's proposal would not in any way condone the atrocities perpetrated in East Germany; rather, it would condemn the East German system, not merely because drugs were pushed on children but also because the protocols were dangerously unsafe.*

But many will still feel uncomfortable about Savulescu's approach. They will feel that even if the practical difficulties could be overcome and the safety of the athletes guaranteed, it would still be morally wrong to permit doping in sport; that the performances of athletes pumped up on drugs—even safe drugs—would be artificial and less worthy of admiration than the performances of athletes who had relied exclusively on their God-given ability and hard work.

This viewpoint has been forcefully articulated by Dick

---

* Savulescu's proposal hinges on the ability of the doping authorities to test for the symptoms of drug overuse rather than the drugs themselves. In the case of blood doping, it is pretty easy to test directly for HCT. But with other drugs, the symptoms may be as tricky to identify as the substances themselves. That would open the door for athletes to cheat by using drugs and then disguising the symptoms. Savulescu and his colleagues are currently working through the practicalities of his proposal.

Pound, a former head of WADA. "I don't want my grand-children to become chemical stockpiles in order to become good at sports and to have fun at it," he has written. "It's a completely antithetical view to what sport should have been in the first place. It's essentially a humanistic endeavor to see how far you can get on your own talent."

Pound is not concerned here with safety, fairness, coercion, deception, health, or cheating. Rather, he is condemning the *very essence of doping*; he is arguing that there is something *inherently wrong* with manipulating human abilities by arti-ficial means. He is asserting that sport is about seeing how far you can get without access to these "pharmacological distortions."

Pound's views have been echoed by some of the world's most influential voices, including the President's Council on Bioethics, a body set up in 2000 by George W. Bush. Report-ing to the president in 2002, in their hugely influential report *Beyond Therapy*, the council wrote, "It seems that some performance-enhancing agents call into question the *dignity* of the performance of those who use them. The performance seems less real, less one's own, less worthy of our admira-tion. Not only do such enhancing agents distort or damage other dimensions of human life, they also seem to distort the athletic activity itself. . . . The runner on steroids is still, of course, a human being who runs. But the doer of the deed is, arguably, less obviously *himself* and less obviously *human* than his unaltered counterpart."

Do these arguments demonstrate that all performance-enhancing technologies are suspect? Do enhancements com-promise the "dignity" and "humanity" of those who use them? Before answering these questions, consider this one instead: What if performance-enhancing technologies were available, not merely to athletes, but to you and me? What if they offered the prospect not merely of greater strength and speed but of increased intelligence and longer life?

Would you still be opposed? Would you refuse to take them on moral grounds? Would you want them to be banned by the state in the same way that performance-enhancing drugs are banned by sporting authorities?

The issue of drugs in sport is important on its own terms, but it is also at the center of a more momentous debate. It is a debate about the extent to which it is legitimate to enhance human beings through artificial means; a debate about whether it is acceptable to alter our innate capabilities via technology: in short, it is a debate about the future of mankind itself.

Genetic Enhancement

In a laboratory in Philadelphia is a series of cages containing mice. These are no ordinary mice, however: they have twice as much muscle, are longer-lived, and can recover from injuries that would kill their weaker cousins. But these impressive physiques have not developed through extra exercise or steroid injections. Rather, they have been genetically engineered using techniques that, transferred to humans, could transform the evolutionary future of our species.

The technique is quite simple. Viruses are dangerous because they are able to infiltrate the body and introduce their genetic material into host cells. So scientists came up with the nifty idea of modifying viruses so that instead of transporting disease, they deliver beneficial genes directly into the genome. In the case of the so-called Schwarzenegger mice, the viruses were duped into delivering the gene that codes for insulin-like growth factor 1 (IGF-1)—a chemical that stimulates muscle growth.

The results were spectacular: the increased production of IGF-1 boosted muscle mass by 15 percent in young mice and 27 percent in older mice. Indeed, the continued presence of extra IGF-1 genes prevented the deterioration of strength familiar in older mice. Successfully transferred to humans, the procedure could transform the lives of the elderly and those afflicted with muscle-wasting diseases.

Other gene transfer technologies currently under development include a radical attempt to engineer resistance to AIDS and some cancers like melanoma by researchers at the California Institute for Technology. Meanwhile, scientists in Europe and elsewhere are attempting to develop a pioneering treatment for inherited human blindness and a potential cure for deafness.

So far, the motivation for gene transfer research has been therapeutic, but it is not difficult to see how the techniques could be used to enhance human capacities. Athletes, never slow to take advantage of scientific advances, have been transfixed by the possibilities. In a German court investigation into steroid violations in 2006, prosecutors uncovered an e-mail exchange between Thomas Springstein, the husband of Grit Breuer, the two-times European 400-meter champion, and the doctor of a Dutch speed-skating club.

Buried in the exchange was mention of Repoxygen, a trade name for a gene therapy procedure that releases EPO in response to low oxygen concentration in mice. Professor Werner Franke, a doping expert, said at the time: "We have been expecting gene doping in sport, but not so soon. This is the crossing of the Rubicon." The risks of gene doping are immense, because many of the treatments have yet to complete clinical trials. But it is anticipated that safe gene doping techniques could be available within years. Some experts believe that genetically modified athletes are already among us.

Genetic manipulation forms the cornerstone of the debate over enhancement. Athletes will doubtless seek to exploit genetics to improve performance, but it is almost certain that nonathletes will also demand access to these technologies as they become available. Biotechnology may eventually provide the means of enhancing intelligence and extending lifespan. Some experts on cell regeneration believe the first thousand-year-old human may already be alive.

Should these technologies be permitted? Should they be encouraged? Or would their use "dehumanize" us, calling into question the "dignity" of those who take them? And is there a moral difference between taking enhancements in sport and taking them beyond the field of play?*

These are deep ethical waters, but let's start by considering an enhancement that might be useful to athletes and non-athletes alike: say, an enhancement that boosts intelligence. This is currently hypothetical (no such enhancement exists at the moment) but will help us to explore the moral issues.

Perhaps the key thing to note is that we seek to enhance intelligence through the education system all the time. As the philosopher John Harris has noted, if a politician improved average educational attainment by 5 percent by restructuring

---

* WADA acted early to ban all forms of gene doping and is investing millions of dollars in research aimed at detection. This may well prove futile because gene doping enables the body to produce performance-enhancing chemicals from within. WADA's difficulties are increased by the possibility of germline gene transfer. This is where germ cells—sperm and eggs—are modified so that genetic alterations are passed on to children. This technology is particularly exciting to the medical profession because a single procedure engineering resistance to a disease would benefit all future generations.

the curriculum, he would be hailed as a hero. So why not attempt to achieve precisely the same outcome via genetic engineering? The answer—according to the President's Council on Bioethics—is that there is something objectionable about using "artificial" *means* to achieve an otherwise desirable *end*.

But we can test the credibility of this objection by taking a different example. We saw earlier that scientists at the California Institute for Technology are seeking to genetically engineer resistance to cancer. Should this research be banned on the grounds that the means are objectionable? Should we deny cancer sufferers the opportunity to benefit from this "artificial" cure?

If moral conservatives answer yes to this, their position seems crazy. Why allow people to suffer great pain simply because the remedy is, in some sense, "artificial"? Surely it is the *end* that is important, not the *means*. But if this is true of a genetically engineered cure for cancer, why is it not also true for other genetic procedures that lead to desirable ends, such as enhanced intelligence or extended life?

Conservatives usually respond to this argument by shifting ground. They argue that there is a moral difference between therapy and enhancement. The former—such as a cure for cancer—returns the patient to "normal functioning," whereas the latter—such as gene therapy to boost intelligence—takes the individual "beyond normality."

But this distinction is, when you think about it, rather shaky. It is precisely because susceptibility to cancer is so tragically normal that scientists are keen to find a cure. Illness and disease are, and have always been, normal aspects of the human condition. Besides, on the wider point, surely the reasons we have to enhance our abilities are synonymous with the reasons we have to cure disease: *they enable us to lead better and fuller lives.*

What about the objection that genetic enhancement—like chemical enhancement—is artificial? Again, this objection seems flimsy. Telescopes are also artificial—they artificially enhance our ability to see across large distances. But does that make them immoral?

As Harris has put it, "I wonder how many of those who have ever used binoculars thought they were crossing a moral divide when they did so? How many people thought (or now think) that there is a moral difference between wearing reading glasses and looking through opera glasses?"

It's noteworthy that many of the contemporaries of Galileo (inventor of the modern telescope) really *did* think there was something morally dubious about the telescope; that it was taking humanity beyond the powers expressly sanctioned by God. They were the moral conservatives of their day. It is not difficult to imagine that those currently opposing genetic enhancement may one day be seen in the same light.

Much of the resistance to genetic enhancement seems to hinge on a kind of squeamishness, the idea that it is both a little creepy and a little presumptuous to interfere with the fabric of human DNA. But this squeamishness is surely misplaced. After all, the human genome is the product of an arbitrary process of evolution. Is it not time to embrace any safe genetic intervention that can improve lives or reduce suffering?

Zero-Sum Games

Suppose there was an enhancement that engineered immunity to the common cold. This is an enhancement that would make my life go a lot better. As someone who regularly suffers from colds, I would love to take advantage of any technology that helped me avoid my annual bout of sniffling and shivering.

But given the choice, I would want others to benefit from this technology, too. This is an enhancement that I benefit from whether or not others benefit from it at the same time. I would want to take advantage of it, not because it gave me an edge over those who didn't have it, but *for its own sake*. It is *inherently* valuable.

But now suppose that I am a 100-meter athlete with access to an enhancement that helps me to run faster. In this case, I benefit from the enhancement *only if it is denied to others*. If everyone has access to the drug and improves their time by 10 percent, I will find myself in precisely the same position as I did before taking the drug. In sport (or any other zero-sum game), an enhancement that is available to all is practically equivalent to an enhancement that is available to none.

This tells us something of great importance about the morality of enhancement. It tells us that the reasons we have to embrace enhancements *beyond* sport are infinitely more powerful than the reasons we have to embrace enhancements *within* sport. As we saw earlier, the reason for permitting safe enhancers in sport is that the system would be fairer and less hazardous for athletes. But the arguments in favor of safe enhancement beyond sport are far more compelling: they can make *everybody's life go better simultaneously*.

The human race stands at the dawn of a new era of evolution, which, instead of being driven by the forces of natural selection, is directed by biotechnical intervention. Wouldn't you want to benefit from this remarkable technology?

Wouldn't you want your children to benefit from it, too? I know I would.

Krieger's Happy Ending

At the commencement of the trial of Manfred Ewald and Manfred Höppner in the summer of 2000, the athletes whose lives had been shattered by the East German doping system watched intently as the evidence was compiled by the prosecution. Up in the public gallery, Ute Krause, a talented former swimmer, gazed across the packed courtroom, and her eyes alighted on Andreas Krieger, the shot putter formerly known as Heidi. It was love at first sight.

I meet Krause when she comes to pick up Krieger after he has completed his day of work at the army surplus store in Magdeburg. She is tall with keen eyes and a warm smile, and she is remarkably open both about her own experiences on the East German doping program and her improbable romance with Krieger.

"I was very good at swimming at school, and I was invited to join SC Magdeburg in 1973," she says. "The coaches there were very happy with my progress, and in 1977 they started to give me the blue pills. I put on fifteen kilos in weight in a matter of weeks. I thought the reason was that I was eating too much, so I became bulimic. I felt like I was living in somebody else's body."

Krause, one of the fastest 200-meter backstroke swimmers in the world, began to suffer from severe depression. After a suicide attempt in 1983, when she woke up in a pool of vomit after an overdose, she realized it was time to get out and retire from swimming. Four years later, in her new job as a trainee nurse, she looked in on a patient and suddenly encountered, again, the blue pills she had taken as a young athlete.

"I couldn't believe it when I saw those pills," she says. "I had been led to believe they were vitamins, but when I looked at the information, I realized they were powerful prescription drugs for people recovering from chemotherapy. I was in a state of shock."

In the evening I take Krieger and Krause for dinner at an open-air restaurant in a cobbled courtyard near Magdeburg's famous cathedral. Krause talks of their early romance. "I saw Andreas in court, and it was like, wow!" she says. "At the end of each day the athletes would meet in small groups to talk about what we had seen in court. I immediately clicked with Andreas: we had similar experiences and the same vocabulary. We were able to empathize with and comfort each other. We talked and talked. I knew he was the man I wanted to spend the rest of my life with."

Krieger moved to Berlin to live with Krause and her daughter from a previous relationship soon after the end of the doping trials. They have since enjoyed a mutually rewarding relationship over the past eight years, and their love shows no sign of diminishing. "We married at Hundisburg Castle [near Magdeburg] in front of seventy guests," Krause says, glancing with a warm smile toward Krieger. I ask if she still struggles with depression. "Since meeting Andreas, it has got less and less. With his help I will overcome it."

Krieger wolfs a huge salad followed by duck and potatoes and regales us with affectionate tales about the woman in his life. He invariably refers to Krause as "my wife," as though he has long wished to use those words and has yet to exhaust the novelty factor. His regular injections of male hormones, necessary to maintain his stubble and other male characteristics, are administered by Krause, a qualified nurse.

Krause comments wryly that Krieger now receives male hormones voluntarily, having previously been duped into taking them. Krause's irony makes Krieger giggle. It is, perhaps, the ultimate twist in one of sport's most mind-bending stories.

CHAPTER 10

Are Blacks
Superior Runners?

Lightning Bolts

There is nothing quite like the hush that descends on a stadium when eight men are limbering up to do battle for the mythic title of Fastest Man on Earth. I was in Beijing's Bird's Nest Stadium in 2008 as Usain Bolt kneeled on his blocks, shoulders rocking, his competitors twitchy, as if they were all too aware of the capabilities of the tall Jamaican in Lane 4.

Bolt exploded from the blocks and found himself so far clear at eighty yards that he jived his way to the line, waving his arms, pumping his fists, and sending 80,000 spectators into delirium. It was not until a few moments later, when the time went up on the giant screen, that a gasp began to reverberate around the stadium. Bolt kneeled in the flashbulb light and pointed to the electronic timer: it read 9.69 seconds, a new world record.

Bolt's demolition of his competitors was a thing of beauty, his spontaneous celebration yards from the tape providing the iconic image of the twenty-ninth Olympiad. But it was also a continuation of a trend stretching back more than four decades. In 1968 in the sweltering heat of Mexico City, Jim Hines became the first man to duck under ten seconds using an electronic timer. Since then ten men from three nations have broken the world record. All, including Hines, have been black.

The dominance of black men in the sprints is not limited to record breaking. Every winner of the 100 meters at the World Championships since the inaugural event in 1983 has been black, as has every finalist from the last ten championships, with the solitary exception of Matic Osovnikar of Slovakia, who finished seventh in Osaka in 2007. No white athlete has reached an Olympic final for over a quarter of a century.

There's a natural conclusion to be drawn from all this: that blacks have a genetic advantage over whites when it comes to sprinting. This is an assertion that has been made by many writers and scientists, to the fury of liberals who fear that any acknowledgment of natural differences between the races might usher in a new era of racism.

But are such differences real, and what would it mean if they were? The answer cuts to the heart of our understanding of race and human diversity at the beginning of the twenty-first century.*

The prototypical argument for black superiority in sprinting can be found in *Taboo: Why Black Athletes Dominate Sports and Why We're Afraid to Talk About It* by Jon Entine, an American writer. Entine's central thesis is that it is not blacks as a whole that are good at sprinting, but rather a subset of people who can trace their origins to western African coastal states. Indeed, he has made the point that "no white, Asian or *East African* runner has ever broken" ten seconds in the 100 meters" (my italics).

East Africans, it turns out, have a different skill set: distance running. As has been well documented, male runners from Kenya have been strikingly successful in races of 800 meters and above, collecting fifty-three medals at the Olympic Games, seventeen of them gold, since 1968 (despite not participating in the boycotted games of 1976 and 1980). In addition, between 1986 and 2000 Kenyans triumphed twelve times out of fourteen in the men's World Cross Country Championship.

Let's assume—for the purposes of argument—that this pattern of results has genetic causes. Can we conclude that blacks are naturally better athletes? Well, no. All we are entitled to say is that East Africans are naturally better at distance running, West Africans are naturally better at sprinting, and whites are probably somewhere in the

---

* In the opening part of the book we saw that in any complex task, success is primarily determined by practice rather than genes. Running is not complex in this sense. It is a simple sport testing a single dimension: speed or, in the case of distance running, endurance. That does not mean practice is irrelevant, merely that individual differences in athletic ability are, at least in part, genetically determined. The question for this chapter is: Are the differences in ability between *population groups* also genetically determined?

middle in both disciplines. So why make the further claim that "blacks" are naturally better at sprinting and distance running?

The logical fallacy may not seem obvious because we are so used to thinking that "black" and "white" refer to biologically distinct types. So let's imagine a similar argument using the Central African Bambuti, a tribe commonly referred to as Pygmies. With an average height of four feet, we can safely assert that the Bambuti have a natural superiority when it comes to walking under low ceilings. Would it be legitimate to extrapolate from this that blacks in general have a natural advantage at walking under low ceilings?

Finding genetic differences between populations is common. Small populations have genetic traits that are often different from those of other populations: the short-limbed Inuit, for example, are different from the Australian Aborigines. Such differences exist across the planet. But why lump together all the diverse populations that happen to share similar skin pigmentation?

The problem for the racial scientist is his yearning to generalize.

Flawed Generalizations

Eldoret is a town lying in the Great Rift Valley, the vast geographical depression that runs from Syria in southwest Asia to Mozambique in East Africa. Lying south of the Cherangani Hills, it was once inhabited by the Masai and the Sirikwa, although by the start of the colonial era it had been occupied by the dark-skinned Nandi, a subset of the Kalenjin tribe.

We have seen that, according to Entine's own data, distance

running is not a "black" phenomenon, but an East African phenomenon focused on the nation of Kenya. Now we are going to ratchet up the magnification some more. Take a look at the map below, adapted by Jon Entine from *Kenyan Running*, the classic work by John Bale and Joe Sang. It shows with the aid of numbering the geographical distribution of Kenya's running success.

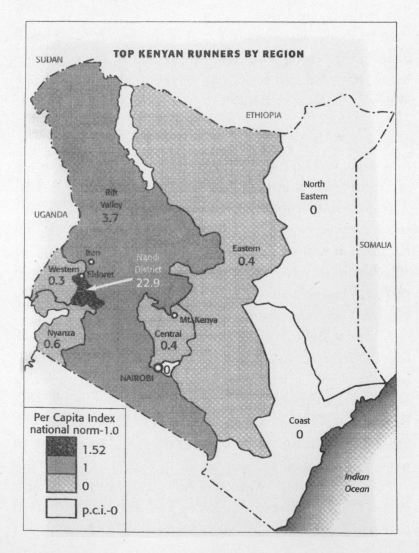

You will immediately notice that Kenya's top runners are not evenly spread across the nation but are highly concentrated on one tiny area in the Rift Valley, in and around Eldoret. As Fred Hardy, a retired American college track coach, put it: "If one were to circumscribe a radius of sixty miles around the town of Eldoret, you would get about 90 percent of the top Kenyan athletes. Something special has happened here in the Nandi Hills."

In his book *Taboo*, Entine makes this point. "One small district, the Nandi, with only 1.8 per cent of Kenya's population, has produced about half of the world-class Kalenjin athletes. . . . Most of Kenya's runners call Eldoret home," he writes.

Seen in this context, the theory that "blacks" are naturally superior distance runners seems not merely dubious but bizarre. Far from being a "black" phenomenon, or an East African phenomenon, or even a Kenyan phenomenon, distance running is actually a Nandi phenomenon focused on the town of Eldoret. Or, to put it another way, much of the "black" distance running success is focused on the tiniest of pinpricks on the map of Africa, with the vast majority of the continent *underrepresented*.

A similar story emerges when looking at the "black" success in sprinting. According to Entine himself, the vast majority of African nations have had no success in sprinting whatsoever. Instead, the top performances are limited to what he calls "blacks who trace their ancestry to West Africa" who hold "494 of the top 500 100-meter times and 98 per cent of top sprinting times."

But not even this "West African" success is quite what it seems. Many of these world-beating performances are limited to two population groups: African Americans and Jamaicans.

It is true that both these groupings have West African ancestry (as well as a smaller proportion of European ancestry), but it makes no sense to describe their success in sprinting as a West African "trait."

Why? Because virtually no West African nations share their success. Look at Mauritania, Guinea-Bissau, Sierra Leone, the Republic of Guinea, Liberia, Ivory Coast, Togo, Niger, Benin, Mali, the Gambia, Equatorial Guinea, Ghana, Gabon, Senegal, Congo, and Angola—all West African states but whose combined inhabitants have never won a single medal in the 100 meters at either the Olympic Games or World Championships.

Just like the "East African" success in distance running, the "West African" success in sprinting is highly specific.

How, then, can Entine and others talk of a "racial" superiority in athletics? How is it that he failed to notice the contradiction between the title of his book and the data he was using to justify it? How is it that these kinds of racial generalizations continue to be approvingly cited by many writers and journalists?

It would seem that the notion of race is so deeply embedded within the human psyche that there is a collective blind spot when it comes to its use and meaning. We automatically put people of dark skin in a box marked "black," and assume that any trait shared by some (even a tiny minority) is shared by all.*

Some scientists have resorted to smuggling in racial generalizations under an epidemiological guise. For example, blacks are said to be more predisposed to sickle cell anemia.

---

* In a radio debate on the BBC in September 2009, Entine accepted that the description of athletic prowess as a "racial" or "black" phenomenon is misleading.

The truth, again, is more complex. Sickle cell anemia disproportionately affects the descendants of populations who lived in malarial zones, which means a higher risk for those whose ancestors came from certain parts of sub-Saharan Africa. But it also implies a higher risk for those who hail from areas in the southern Mediterranean. Genetic diseases are not racial per se. Many other so-called black diseases are in fact diseases of poverty with well-established environmental causes.

As Jonathan Marks, an anthropologist at the University of North Carolina at Charlotte, puts it: "All human groups, however constituted, have particular medical risks. African Americans, Ashkenazi Jews, Afrikaners and Japanese, poor people, rich people, chimney sweeps, prostitutes, choreographers, and the Pima Indians all have their particular health risks. And race is not the cause of it; in fact, race will positively obscure it. Providing health care can obviously benefit by knowing something of the self-identification of the subject . . . but that does not presuppose that there are fundamental biologically based divisions between the groups."

The reason why racial scientists are able to get away with statistically flawed generalizations is because they tally with our natural inclination to regard "black" as a biological type distinct from "white" or "yellow" or "red." Indeed, this inclination is so powerful that it requires an effort of will to free oneself from its clutches.

But it's worth the effort. The findings of population genetics over the course of the last four decades prove beyond doubt that the notion of race held for most of the last two and a half centuries—that humanity can be divided into a set of subspecies with crisp genetic boundaries—is entirely without foundation.

Genetic Variation

In 1972 Richard Lewontin, then a young scientist working in Chicago, took a bus to a scientific conference in Carbondale, Illinois. Instead of idling away on the long journey, he used his time to examine the burgeoning data on human genetic differences. This was a time when scientists lacked the technology to look at the human genome itself, but instead examined the protein products of genes, such as blood and other types of human tissue.

The relevant protein was crushed and stuck in a slab of jelly, and an electric current was passed through it (a technique called gel electrophoresis). If two proteins (from, say, the blood taken from two different people) moved at a different rate in the electric field, it meant that they derived from a different form of the gene. This is what is known as genetic variation.

For more than two hundred years, humans had been categorized according to the classic races—Negroid, Caucasoid, Mongoloid, and so on: the ones we're familiar with today. It had long been known that the visible differences between the races—essentially skin color, hair texture, nose shape, and so forth—were determined by genes. That much was clear from the fact that black Africans born in Europe or the United States were the same color as their parents.

But the vast majority of biologists believed that these surface differences were matched by other, more fundamental disparities. As George Ferguson wrote in *The Psychology of the Negro* in 1916: "The colour of the skin and the crookedness of the hair are only outward signs of many far deeper differences."

Lewontin realized that the results obtained from gel electrophoresis would enable him to test these arguments for the
very first time. If the races really were significantly different
beneath the surface, they would display a high level of genetic
differentiation.

Hunched over logarithmic tables and books containing
the data from the experiments that had been conducted,
Lewontin made his calculations as the bus drove south. His
efforts were well rewarded: the results caused a sensation and
remain among the most widely cited findings in the field of
human genetics.

Lewontin found that for the vast majority of genes, pretty
much every person on the entire planet has the same form of
the gene. But he also found that for those genes where there
is variation, the vast majority of that variation—around
85 percent—exists between individuals *within* population
groups. Of the remainder around a half is accounted for by
the differences between small population groups, with the
remainder—a mere 7 percent—between the so-called races.

To put it another way, if some nuclear nightmare wiped
out the entire human race apart from one small population—
say, the Masai tribe in Africa—virtually all the genetic variation that exists in the world today would be present in that
one small group.

This is, of course, deeply counterintuitive, and many have
dismissed these findings for lacking in common sense. How
can racial differences be minor when we can each see with
our own eyes that blacks and whites diverge dramatically?
But in this case, seeing is not believing. Why? Because only a
tiny fraction of a person's genes has effects the eye can see.

As Henry Harpending, a professor of anthropology at the
University of Utah, has put it: "Personal computers are divis-

ible into major races—Compaq, Dell, Gateway, Micron—as well as many minor populations. Are there deep essential differences between clone X and clone Y? Hardly. Take the cases off and we can barely tell them apart. The components of PCs are commodities that are completely interchangeable. The important differences among PC races are the labels on the outside of the box. Human race differences are like that."

This blows the conventional view of race out of the water. For decades scientists and laypeople believed that racial groups possessed unique genetic traits not shared by other groupings, but this has proved to be entirely without foundation.

As Luigi Luca Cavalli-Sforza of Stanford University, perhaps the most influential population geneticist of modern times, puts it: "Classification into races has proved to be a futile exercise. . . . All populations or population clusters overlap when single genes are considered, and in almost all populations, all alleles [gene types] are present but in different frequencies. No single gene is therefore sufficient for classifying human populations into systematic categories."*

The findings of population genetics—and in particular the finding that pretty much *all the genetic variation* that exists on the planet is contained *within* racial groups—demonstrate how absurd it is to engage in racial generalizations; how crazy it is to witness a tiny group of blacks winning at, say, the 10,000 meters and to infer that all people who happen to

---

* This does not quite imply that "race" is an entirely meaningless term. If I tell you that a person is "black," you will be able to make a good guess about the likely color and curliness of his hair, and a few other things with a genetic basis. This is what A. W. Edwards, a Cambridge mathematician, was hinting at in a now-famous paper in which he showed that even if the genetic differences between the races are very small, the correlation of racial characteristics makes a person's race at least a little informative.

have similar skin pigmentation share an aptitude for 10,000-meter running.

It's only because we see the world through race-tinted glasses that we're inclined to describe all sorts of things—and not just running prowess—as having a racial basis.

Let's take stock. We have seen that success in distance running is not a "black" phenomenon at all, but a Nandi phenomenon concentrated around the town of Eldoret. We have also seen that success in sprinting is concentrated among African Americans and Jamaicans. The question we are left with is: Why? Why are these population groups so successful, in their different ways, at running?

One possible answer is that these abilities are genetic: the Nandi have a natural advantage when it comes to distance running, and African Americans and Jamaicans have a natural advantage when it comes to sprinting. This conclusion does not constitute a dubious racial generalization, since it does not contain the inference that *all blacks* share this genetic advantage.

But is there any evidence for it? Is there anything in the genome of these groupings that reveals biological advantages? Let's start by focusing on the Nandi and their success in endurance running.

John Manners, an expert on Kenyan running, has constructed an elaborate theory to support the idea of genetic superiority. His theory involves such things as cattle raiding, the ritual of circumcision, and certain assumptions about marriage practices. In short, he believes that the forces of natural and sexual selection have operated in a unique and forceful way over two thousand years to sculpt a tribe with incredible athletic stamina.

Manners admits that his hypothesis is not verifiable (which might be considered a bit of a weakness) but argues that it must hint at the truth, for how else to explain how a tiny population has come to dominate the world in a sport accessible to all?

Fortunately, one man has devoted his working life to searching for the answers.

The Indiana Jones of Sports

A medium-build white man is hiking through the vast expanses of the western Rift Valley. He is wearing blue jeans, a red T-shirt, and brown boots and is carrying a battered knapsack. The sun is high in the sky and beating down in waves as he looks from side to side. His eyes affix on a particular mud hut, one of many such dwellings on the farmland where he is trekking, and he consults a scrap of paper. Satisfied that he has found his destination, he knocks on the door.

A few moments later a tall, elegant black man comes to the entrance; behind him his wife is craning her neck to see who has arrived. They are expecting their white visitor and beckon him through the small opening. Inside the hut is a single room containing a broken table, four chairs, and some magazine cuttings pinned to the wall: the basic items that you might find in any Kenyan rural dwelling. The guest is offered a drink by his hosts, and they begin an animated conversation.

The presence of a white man in this part of Kenya is strange enough, but what happens next is stranger still. The visitor reaches into his knapsack, pulls a swab from a sterile tube, and proceeds to scrape it along the inside of his host's cheek. He then places the swab into a container, seals it, and carefully place it into his bag. He then undertakes the same procedure with the man's wife. Afterward, the three of them talk for a few minutes and then rise to shake hands. Then the white man is off, out of the door, in dogged pursuit of his next destination.

Yannis Pitsiladis is one of the most remarkable academics I have ever met. As a teenager, he was an enthusiastic volleyball player, making it to regional level in his homeland of Greece. But it was only after retiring from sports that Pitsiladis discovered his life's ambition: to figure out why certain ethnic groups excel in running.

It is a question that many academics have pondered from the comfort of their armchairs, but Pitsiladis wanted hard evidence. So he set about harvesting genetic data from the greatest athletes in the world. The mud hut described earlier is eight miles to the south of Eldoret, the epicenter of the Kenyan running phenomenon, and his hosts were Amos Biwott, gold medal winner in the 3,000-meter steeplechase in the 1968 Mexico Olympics, and his wife Cherono Maiyo, who participated in the Olympics in Munich in 1972.

Pitsiladis has spent the last few years of his life like a latter-day Indiana Jones, zigzagging across the Rift Valley in search of nuggets of athletic talent that lie embedded in the region, with swabs at the ready to harvest the precious DNA sequences hidden within the living cells of the athletes. The journey has not been easy, nor has it been cheap.

"You have no idea how difficult it has been to get this far," he says. "I had to remortgage my house twice to get the money for the research because the funding institutions were not interested. One of my recent field trips was paid for by an Indian restaurant in Glasgow [where Pitsiladis is a lecturer at the city's university]. I was eating when the owner came out to ask if the meal was okay, and we got chatting; I told him about the difficulties of raising funds for my research. He told me that he would pay for the trip himself."

But finding the cash was, in many ways, the easy part. Pitsiladis did not merely have to travel to some of the remotest corners of the planet in search of the world's greatest athletes; he also had to go through the painstaking process of securing the necessary ethical consents. First he would approach the local Olympic Committee to secure their permission and would then have to convince often suspicious athletes to sign consent forms for their genes to be analyzed.

The minefield he has had to negotiate is revealed by one of his field trips to Ethiopia. A few weeks after his return to the UK he heard that the secretary-general of the Ethiopian Olympic Committee had been forced to resign. Why? Because the press had run outraged stories of how the secretary-general had authorized a white scientist to steal the DNA of two-time Olympic champion Haile Gebrselassie, in order to create a new breed of white superathletes.

But while Pitsiladis's odyssey of intellectual discovery has been tough, it has also been revelatory. We have seen that superiority in distance running is not a "black" phenomenon, but a singularity concentrated upon the Nandi region of Kenya. The question that has been left hanging is whether the explanation for the success of this tiny population is genetic.

The biological theory of Nandi athletic superiority is pretty simple to understand. Distinctive body types are the consequence of population isolation, enabling the gene pool to drift apart from neighboring populations, aided and abetted by the forces of natural and sexual selection.

Back in his laboratory in Glasgow, Pitsiladis took the swabs gathered from his field research, extracted the DNA, and then began to examine whether the genes revealed the supposed isolation. He started by focusing on mitochondrial DNA, which is inherited exclusively from the mother, and Y chromosome DNA, which is inherited exclusively from the father, both of which are convenient for analyzing ancestry and genetic relatedness.

As he gazed at his data, Pitsiladis realized that, far from being an isolated population, the Nandi are remarkably diverse, indicating that the tribe has been subject to many migration events over the centuries: precisely the opposite of what he expected to find. The notion of a fiercely independent tribe subject to unique selection pressures is not borne out by the evidence.

The genetic theory of Nandi distance-running success has also come under threat from recent results in major championships. In the last couple of decades runners from Morocco and Algeria have started to challenge Kenyans in the middle distances, while Ethiopians have done the same in longer races.

This is not what you would expect if the primary driver of the Nandi success in distance running was genetic. Evolution operates over an incredibly lengthy time frame, so natural advantages do not shift from population to population and from region to region decade by decade, or even century by century.

Pitsiladis has also journeyed to Ethiopia to gather the DNA of their very best athletes, like Gebrselassie, the man universally regarded as the greatest distance runner of all time. And guess what? DNA analysis shows that this grouping is—just like the Nandi—very genetically diverse. Indeed, many top Ethiopian athletes share a more recent mitochondrial DNA ancestor with many Europeans than they do with each other. The Ethiopians are also genetically very distant from the top Nandi runners, despite having similar skin color (which shows how misleading pigmentation can be as a marker for genetic similarity). This gives the genetic theory yet another major problem. Put simply: If these two groups are genetically distant, how can their mutual success be driven by the same underlying biology?

"The more we have studied the phenomenon, the more we have realized that the patterns of success are not genetic despite being specific to certain populations," Pitsiladis says. "So far we have only checked specific genes, and it may take a few more years to look across all thirty thousand genes in the genome, but we can already say with reasonable confidence that social and economic factors are the primary factors driving the success of Kenyan distance running."

Scott Thomas, an expert in exercise and performance science at the University of Toronto, agrees. "It's looking like there is some genetic component to performance, but *it's not race linked*" (my italics), he has said. He points out that there is "tremendous variety" in the genotypes found in Ethiopian and Kenyan populations, which produce the top distance runners, and that this variety "overlaps with varieties we find in other places."

Take a long enough perspective, and you will see that there have been many major shifts in dominance in distance running success. In the early part of the twentieth century, Scandinavian runners won twenty-eight of thirty-six possible Olympic medals over 5,000 and 10,000 meters. Thirty years later, Australasians held the ascendancy, then Kenyans. Now Ethiopians and North Africans are in the hunt. On the women's side, China has broken several world records in recent years (although doping is believed to have played a part in this success).

None of this rules out a role for genetics in shaping patterns of success and failure between population groups, but it strongly suggests that other, more powerful forces are at work.

If Not Genes, Then . . . What?

Why are the Nandi so successful, then, if not primarily because of their genes? According to Pitsiladis, a key thing to note is that the top Kenyan athletes are predominantly from areas of high altitude, even relative to the rest of East Africa. Altitude training has long been used by endurance runners to improve performance because the thin air forces the body to produce more oxygen-carrying red blood cells, which, in turn, boosts endurance.

The importance of altitude is even more persuasive if you widen the perspective to look at the success of top Ethiopian runners. It turns out that, just as with Kenya, the "Ethiopian" distance running phenomenon is highly specific. In a recent study it was found that 38 percent of the elite marathon runners were from the region of Arsi, which accounts for less than 5 percent of the Ethiopian population. Arsi, like Eldoret, is at one of the highest altitudes in East Africa.

Living at altitude is not, of course, sufficient to create running success all on its own, as the dearth of elite Nepalese and Peruvian runners demonstrates. But when you also factor in the remarkable fact that many of Kenya's top runners ran extraordinarily long distances to school, sometimes in *excess of twenty kilometers per day*, it is possible to see the beginnings of a persuasive explanation for the Nandi running phenomenon.

Kenyan youngsters do not run to school for fun, of course, but out of necessity—public transportation is virtually nonexistent—but the cumulative consequences have been dramatic. At a speed of fifteen kilometers per hour, this adds up to eighty minutes of running per day, more than ninety hours per week, five hundred hours per year, and in excess of six thousand hours by the time of their sixteenth birthday.

Here is Pitsiladis: "We found that elite distance runners ran farther to school as children, and more had done so by running exclusively at high altitude. Many of the distances were incredible, with many exceeding twenty kilometers each day. Recently we measured the running economy of Kenyan children who use running as a means of transport to a school located in an area of extreme elevation [the Pemja Primary School in South Nandi] and found values typical of well-trained endurance athletes."

Pitsiladis's research has been corroborated by Professor Bengt Saltin and colleagues. In a landmark study, they found that East African children who had used running as a means of transport to school had a maximum oxygen uptake (VO_2 max) some 30 percent higher than those who had not. Just to be clear: it was not their genes that created this aerobic advantage but thousands of hours of running.

When you add to this that athletics has become a national obsession in the years since the Olympic success of Kip Keino in 1968 (trained by John Velzian, a top British coach); that almost every young person aspires to replicate his success; that Kenyans are often too poor to get involved in other types of sport; that scientists have found that the traditional Kenyan diet is nutritionally optimal for running success; that Kenya has an outstanding system for nurturing top runners: put all that together and you have an alliance of forces that is extremely powerful.*

What About the Sprints?

Entine's argument for the superiority of blacks in the sprints rests, as we have seen, on data showing that success is, in fact, concentrated among African Americans and Jamaicans. But do these population groups have a genetic advantage? Is there anything in their DNA that suggests a natural superiority when it comes to sprinting?

Research undertaken in 2003 found that variation in a particular gene called ACTN3 is associated with sprinting success (through its impact on fast-twitch muscle fibers, which assist explosive lifting and running), and that the "sprint" version of this gene is more common among Jamaicans than other populations. This led to a spate of headlines in the media suggesting that Jamaican sprinting success is genetic.

But, as so often, the reality is rather more complex. It was soon discovered that, although 98 percent of Jamaicans have the relevant gene, so too do 82 percent of Europeans. That

---

* The Kenyan diet consists of small amounts of roasted meat, fruit, cooked vegetables, milk, and *ugali*, a thick, polenta-style porridge made from water and cornmeal. It is a diet that is high in carbohydrate, low in fat, and matches recommendations for protein intake.

is to say that both populations have a huge majority of individuals with an ACTN3 status compatible with sprinting success. Further research found that Kenyans (who win distance events but have *virtually no success in sprinting*) have an even higher frequency of the "sprint" gene than Jamaicans. As Daniel MacArthur, the Australian geneticist who has conducted much of the research on ACTN3, puts it, "There's simply no clear relationship between the frequency of this variant in a population and its capacity to produce sprinting superstars."

In the absence of a genetic explanation, scientists have focused on the cultural forces underpinning Jamaican sprinting success. MacArthur, for example, has noted the "importance of Jamaica's impressive investment in the infrastructure and training system required to identify and nurture elite track athletes, the effects of a culture that idolizes local track heroes, and the powerful desire of young Jamaicans to use athletic success to lift themselves and their families out of poverty."

Research by Pitsiladis also failed to find a genetic explanation for sprinting success among Jamaicans and African Americans. "Genetic studies of elite sprinters from Jamaica and the USA have not found that these athletes possess a unique genetic makeup; rather, they highlight the high degree of genetic diversity among ethnic groups," he said. "It is unjustified, therefore, to regard ethnic differences in sporting success as genetically determined; to justify doing so one must identify the genes that are important. Until now, that has proven elusive."

In *Taboo*, Entine does not present any substantive genetic evidence to support his racial claims, but he does spend a great deal of time documenting the disproportionate success of African Americans in sports such as basketball and American football. Once again, he argues that this represents an innate superiority in blacks. But this is also flawed: as we saw in the first section of the book, success in these complex sports is primarily determined by practice, not genes.

So, how do we explain the success of African Americans in sports? Why do they perform so well, not just in sprinting but beyond? Perhaps the key thing to note is that the over-representation of African Americans in professional sport is almost precisely mirrored by an underrepresentation in positions of economic power. This suggests that the sporting success of African Americans is the consequence not of genetics but of unequal opportunity; that blacks are driven into professional sport due to barriers to entry in other spheres of economic life.

This explanation becomes compelling when you consider a groundbreaking experiment in 2003 by Marianne Bertrand and Sendhil Mullainathan, two leading economists. They drafted five thousand CVs and placed archetypal black names such as Tyrone or Latoya on half of them, and white names such as Brendan or Alison on the other half. They then divided the white CVs into high and low quality and did the same with the black CVs.

A few weeks later the offers came rolling in from employers, and guess what? The "black" candidates were *50 percent less likely* to be invited to interview. Bertrand and Mullainathan also found that although high-quality whites were preferred to low-quality whites, the relative quality of black CVs made no difference whatsoever. It was as if employers saw three categories: high-quality whites, low-quality whites, and blacks.

Is it any wonder that black children fail at school, given

that success is often ignored by employers? Is it any wonder they end up going into sports instead?*

The Meaning of "Black" Sporting Success

Is it such a terrible thing for blacks to be described as superior athletes? Sure, the claim may be scientifically dubious, but does it do any real damage? Indeed, could it not be considered a benign claim, undermining old notions of "white" supremacy?

It's noteworthy that the success of black athletes over the decades is often regarded as having been a powerful force for good. Sports journalists regularly eulogize the successes of the likes of Joe Louis, Muhammad Ali, and Jackie Robinson, arguing that they acted as a battering ram for racial equality by striking at the ideology of racists and bigots.

As Simon Barnes of *The Times* put it following the election of Barack Obama,

[Obama] has a debt to great American athletes across the 20th century. Sport not only reflects society, it is a significant force in changing it. The road that led to the election of Obama has black athletes as its milestones, but sport was also one of the bulldozers that shaped it. . . .

Sport is perhaps the closest thing we have as a public and objective measure of worth. There was no on-the-other-hand and look-at-it-this-way when [Joe] Louis

---

* The barriers to black economic advancement are clear from the statistics: according to the U.S. Census Bureau, blacks are twice as likely to be in poverty as nonblacks and make nearly $5,000 a year less, on average.

smashed [Max] Schmeling or when [Althea] Gibson walloped her way to victory in five grand-slam tournaments. Sometimes blacks are better than whites; and no one can duck that truth.

As an analysis of the power of sport to change the world, this is stirring stuff. But it also misses an essential point. By misconstruing the way black sporting success has been interpreted down the ages, it fails to recognize the dangers in the stubborn idea that blacks are naturally superior athletes. To see how, we need to take a fresh look at the history of race and sports.

The first scientist to argue that there are biological differences between the races was a Swedish botanist called Carolus Linnaeus. He claimed in a famous 1792 paper that the indigenous Indians of America are "red, ill-tempered with hair black, straight, thick; nostrils wide, obstinate . . . contented . . . ruled by habit"; Europeans are "hair blond, eyes blue, very smart . . . inventive . . . ruled by law"; and Africans are "impassive, relaxed . . . hair kinked . . . crafty, slow, foolish . . . ruled by caprice."

Linnaeus's work sparked an obsession with the idea of a racial hierarchy, but it was only with the publication of Charles Darwin's *On the Origin of Species* in 1859 that these various ideas were grafted onto the hot new theory of evolution. Scientists wielded Darwin's ideas to argue that blacks were less developed, from an evolutionary perspective, than whites.

What did this claim amount to? Two things: first, that blacks are less intelligent than whites. As Henry Edward Garrett, a psychology professor at Columbia University, put it as late as 1963: "[The Negro] has less of what I call 'abstract intelligence' than the white man. He functions at a lower level." The second part of the claim was that blacks are stronger and faster than whites. Here is Garrett again: "Those black Africans are fine muscular animals when they're not diseased."

The connection between the (supposed) intellectual primitiveness of blacks and their athletic superiority was, perhaps, most powerfully articulated by Dean Cromwell, leader of the American team at the Berlin Olympics in 1936: "The Negro does well in certain disciplines because he is closer to primitive man than white people. It is not long since his ability to run and jump meant the difference between life and death in the jungle. He has supple muscles and his light-minded disposition is useful in the mental and physical relaxation necessary for someone who runs and jumps."

The fact that such views had no scientific basis didn't seem to matter, particularly as the idea of black primitiveness coincided with the economic interests of the white majority. The notion of the black brute—strong, athletic, but mentally dull—provided moral cover for the use of blacks in the cotton fields of the rural South.

The key point is that the merging of black athletic superiority and intellectual inferiority within a single theory proved to be one of the most powerful ideas of the last two hundred years and was the prism through which the vast majority of black athletic achievements were interpreted. To put it another way: the successes of black athletes did not undermine the theory of white supremacy; they were taken to confirm it.

Take the success of Jesse Owens at the Berlin Olympic Games of 1936. His multiple gold-medal-winning feats have gone down in popular imagination as having dealt "a hammer blow to the theory of Aryan supremacy." But this is a historical fiction. The reality is that the German public were already well versed in the theory of black athletic superiority, with Nazi intellectuals arguing that the Americans had cheated by selecting a black man with "abnormally large animal heel bones."

Far from being a disaster, the Berlin Olympics were a propaganda coup for Hitler. As Guy Walters has demonstrated in his book *Berlin Games*, support for the Führer's policies hardened, state persecution of racial minorities escalated, and preparations for World War II continued unabated.

Similarly, Jack Johnson, who became the first black heavyweight champion in 1908, offended white sensibilities not by defeating white men in the ring but by cavorting with white women at a time when miscegenation was illegal across the South and by mocking his opponents with a swagger that led to rioting after his demolition of the white boxer Jim Jeffries in 1910. White reaction to Johnson sprung not from his victories, but from a fear that blacks might respond to them by demanding social and political reform.

Joe Louis, a boxer who defeated many more white opponents than Johnson, was positively embraced by many racists precisely because his success went hand in hand with the social deference—deliberately cultivated as a means of reassuring white America—which they demanded of an "intellectual inferior."

The same analysis applies to Jackie Robinson's debut for the Brooklyn Dodgers. His principal achievement was not to demonstrate that blacks could play baseball—this was already well known from the strength and depth of the Negro leagues. The subversive aspect of Robinson's debut season was not sporting but symbolic: here was a high-profile and deeply evocative act of desegregation, involving a man of extraordinary character and forbearance.

Muhammad Ali drives the point home. Can it be argued

that his chief contribution to racial equality was to exhibit black "worth" by winning the heavyweight championship of the world, given that he won the title from a black man, who, in turn won it from another black man?

No, Ali's political and cultural influence was wielded not *inside* the ring, but because of his capacity to *transcend* the ring. His fists provided the platform, but it was his tongue that helped to alter the course of twentieth-century American history by articulating a black radicalism that struck fear into the white majority. This would prove a vital force for change amid the complex dynamics of the civil rights era. In short, it was Ali's capacity to shatter the stereotype of black intellectual inadequacy that shook up the world, not his ability to shatter white men's jaws.

None of this is to deny the wider importance of black sporting success, but merely to contend that its contribution to racial equality is far more complex than is often claimed. Its central impact was not to undermine the ideology of racism but to bolster the self-esteem of an oppressed minority. Sport was a focal point of racial pride because it was just about the only area of public life where blacks—protected from discrimination by sport's objectivity—could get ahead. In this sense, it provided a launching pad from which blacks could strike at the true foundation of white bigotry: the myth of white intellectual superiority.

The only occasions when black sporting success subverted the old stereotypes were in those sports considered to have an intellectual dimension. In the UK in the 1960s and '70s, for example, blacks were considered to lack the mental sophistication to undertake the creative role of playmaker in soccer, a prejudice challenged by the performances of brilliant black soccer players such as John Barnes.

Similarly, in the United States there was a long-standing view that blacks lacked the intellect to cope with the demands of such positions as quarterback in American football. As former Arizona state athlete director Gene Smith put it, "There was a stereotype that black quarterbacks weren't well-rounded enough intellectually to run an offense." Again, it was the performances of black athletes—such as Doug Williams and Donovan McNabb—that helped to confront this dogma.

But these successes represented, in the wider battle for racial equality, only partial victories. Take the way Kip Keino's triumph in the Olympic 1,500 meters in 1968 (four years after the signing of the Civil Rights Act) was described in the popular press. One journal described him as "half man, half hartebeest" who could "beat a leopard to a zebra carcass." Jim Murray of the *Los Angeles Times* wrote, "Keino came off the slopes of Mt. Kenya about a decade ago with no more idea of how to run formally than a rhinoceros. You can reconstruct how they must have found him. They came into a clearing one day and here was this pride of lions with their tongues hanging out and a rich lather of sweat on their flanks—and the tracks show they had been on the spoor of this man who is calmly staying safely ahead of the lions relay team while munching on a sandwich."

From this vantage point, the notion of black athletic superiority can be seen, not as a harmless scientific error, but as an idea with a powerful and pernicious history.

Stereotype Threat

Between 2001 and 2005 Jeff Stone, a psychologist from the University of Arizona, and a colleague interviewed 1,500 students to uncover prevailing attitudes to race and sports. They found, among other things, that black athletes were rated by the participants as being higher in natural athletic ability than in sports intelligence. White athletes, on the other hand, were rated in precisely the opposite way: better in terms of sports intelligence than natural ability.

This provided compelling evidence that the old idea linking sporting talent and intellectual inferiority in blacks (and vice versa in whites) is not merely a historical curiosity, but finds an echo in the collective consciousness of today.

But the researchers wanted to check something further: Do these stereotypes really matter? Do they influence the way we interact with each other, both in sports and beyond? Or do they simply operate in the background with no tangible effects?

To find out, they took a group of white participants and asked them to listen to a radio broadcast of a basketball game to evaluate the performance of a particular player. In the first test, the participants were led to believe the player was black. After listening to the broadcast, the participants rated the player as high in athletic ability and as a superior player.

But in the second test the researchers reversed the experiment, telling participants that the player was white. What happened? You guessed it: they now considered the player to be *low* in natural athletic ability, and considered him an inferior player. Just to reiterate: these almost contradictory viewpoints came in response to the very same broadcast.

This demonstrates just how powerfully stereotypes influence the way we perceive the world. It shows how a high school teacher could see two equally able athletes in action, but nevertheless *perceive* the black athlete to be the more naturally gifted player simply because of underlying (and possibly subliminal) racial assumptions. And remember that such assumptions run so deep they infect all ethnic groups, including blacks.

We saw earlier in the chapter that employers tend to discriminate against applicants with black-sounding names. Now we can see why: it is because they are likely to perceive a black applicant as less intellectually qualified for the job, even with a CV identical to the successful candidate's. This discrimination may occur at a subconscious level, but the consequences are very real. Remember that black-sounding applicants were 50 percent less likely to be invited to interview than whites with precisely the same CVs.

Perhaps the most pernicious problem is that these stereotypes have the tendency to be self-perpetuating. If black people observe that educational success is being overlooked by employers, they may make a (perfectly rational) decision to focus their efforts elsewhere, causing a further decline in black educational standards. Over time, this will mean that the background assumptions of employers (that blacks are less intellectually qualified than whites) will be permanently reflected in hard reality.

When it comes to sports, the direction of racial bias is reversed. Now the prevailing assumptions favor blacks while deterring whites. Whites will tend to be overlooked (particularly in sports involving strength and speed) because of the assumption that they lack natural aptitude in these areas. Blacks, on the other hand, will be perceived as naturally gifted, and encouraged, leading to extra practice and better performances, thus seeming to confirm the original assumption.

Perhaps the most graphic demonstration of the power of

stereotyping occurred in an experiment undertaken by Stone and colleagues in 1997. They took white and black former high school athletes and gave them a golf putting task. They found that the two groups performed equally well. But when the participants were told that the task was a measure of "natural athletic ability," the whites' performance deteriorated. The very fact that whites felt they were being judged against a negative stereotype caused them to mess up. This is known as stereotype threat.

"In matters of race we often assume that when a situation is objectively the same for different groups, it is *experienced* in the same way by each group," Claude Steele, the psychologist who coined the term "stereotype threat," has written. "But [those burdened with negative stereotypes] know that they are especially likely to be seen as having limited ability. Groups not stereotyped in this way don't experience this extra intimidation. And it is a serious intimidation, implying as it does that they may not belong in walks of life where the tested abilities are important."

Stereotype threat is not seen just in the world of sports, but in almost every area of life. When, for example, Steele gave a group of undergraduates a standardized test and told them that it was a measure of their intellectual ability, white students did significantly better than their black counterparts. But when the same test was presented as a laboratory tool, with no relevance to intellectual ability, the scores of blacks and whites were pretty much identical.

It is all too easy to assume that racial patterns of success and failure are grounded in genetics, but the point of this chapter is to suggest that subtler and more elusive forces are at work. The tendency to see black and white as genetic types (which, to a large extent, underpins racial stereotyping) has long been contradicted by the findings of population genetics. If we could only ditch our race-tinted spectacles, the world would not only *look* very different, it would soon *become* very different, too.

Acknowledgments

I first came across the name Anders Ericsson in a roundtable discussion with sports scientists in 2008. One after another referred—sometimes in admiration, sometimes in defiance—to a psychologist in Florida who was turning the conventional wisdom on its head. The subversive idea at the center of Ericsson's work is that excellence is not reserved for the lucky few but can be achieved by almost all of us.

I was intrigued by Ericsson's ideas, not least because they chimed with a conviction that had been growing in my own mind as I pondered my own experiences as a sportsman and the evidence of interviews with dozens of the world's top athletes.

The first part of this book is based, in large measure, on Ericsson's revolutionary research. Although we disagree on the role of intuition in expert decision making, many of my conclusions are drawn from his ideas and those of his disciples. My debt to him is considerable, not least because he answered all my questions and queries with tireless enthusiasm, as well as offering comments on an early draft of the book.

I also owe a large debt to other writers who have sought

to popularize some of Ericsson's ideas in the months since I began writing the book, most particularly Geoff Colvin (*Talent Is Overrated*), Daniel Coyle (*The Talent Code*), and Malcolm Gladwell (*Outliers*). All are books of superlative quality that clarified and enhanced my understanding, and I have quoted from each of them.

Jonny Geller, my agent, demonstrated characteristic enthusiasm to get the book off the ground, and Claire Wachtel, my editor at HarperCollins, made countless perceptive suggestions. I am eternally grateful to both. I also owe a huge debt to *The Times* and my various editors for the support they have provided throughout my career. David Chappell, in particular, has been a constant friend and counselor, as has Tim Hallissey. *The Times* is a wonderful newspaper to work for.

Dilys, my mother, provided comments, suggestions, and impeccable advice throughout the writing of the book, and it is infinitely better as a result. This book is dedicated to her. Many friends and colleagues read early drafts, and I am indebted to each of them: Tim Hallissey, Mark Thomas, Owen Slot, Mark Williams, and Kathy Weeks.

Throughout the final two parts of the book, I draw on the work of many brilliant academics, thinkers, scientists, and philosophers. I have endeavored to credit each of them both in the text and endnotes. In particular, psychologist Richard Gregory inspired the core ideas of chapter 8, and John Harris the moral stance of chapter 9. Chapter 10 is written, in large part, as a response to the always thought-provoking Jon Entine.

Ben Goldacre's book *Bad Science* provided invaluable insight into the nature and significance of the placebo effect, and Dylan Evans's book *Emotion* brilliantly summarized the evolutionary theory of human emotion.

Notes

1. THE HIDDEN LOGIC OF SUCCESS

10 **"I propose to show":** The quotes from Francis Galton are taken from *Hereditary Genius: An Inquiry into Its Laws and Consequences* (New York: D. Appleton, 1884).

11 **In 1991 Anders Ericsson:** The study of violinists at the Music Academy of West Berlin is published in one of the most seminal papers in the study of expertise: K. Anders Ericsson, Ralf Th. Krampe, and Clemens Tesch-Romer, "The Role of Deliberate Practice in the Acquisition of Expert Performance," *Psychological Review* 100, no. 3 (1993): 363–406.

14 **"There is absolutely no evidence of a 'fast track'":** This view was based on a wide-ranging study of musical achievement: John A. Sloboda, Jane W. Davidson, Michael J. Howe, and Derek G. Moore, "The Role of Practice in the Development of Performing Musicians," *British Journal of Psychology* 87 (1996): 287–309.

14 **"Nobody—but *nobody*":** Jack Nicklaus with Ken Bowden, *Golf My Way: The Instructional Classic, Revised and Updated* (New York: Simon and Schuster, 2005), 204.

14 **The same conclusion—about the primacy of practice—is ar-**

rived at by widening the perspective: The observation that standards are rising in music, sports, and academia—and that this cannot be the consequence of humans getting more talented—is contained in K. Anders Ericsson, "The Influence of Experience and Deliberate Practice on the Development of Superior Expert Performance," in *The Cambridge Handbook of Expertise and Expert Performance*, ed. K. Anders Ericsson, Neil Charness, Paul J. Feltovich, and Robert R. Hoffman (Cambridge, England: Cambridge University Press, 2006).

16 **"with less than a decade's intense preparation with the game":** The ten-year rule for chess is demonstrated by H. A. Simon and W. G. Chase in "Skill in Chess," *American Scientist* 61 (1973): 394–403. In golf it is detailed in Al Barkow and David Barrett, *Golf Legends of All Time* (Lincolnwood, Ill.: Publications International, 1998). For nineteenth-century scientists, poets, and authors it is detailed in E. Raskin, "Comparison of Scientific and Literary Ability: A Biographical Study of Eminent Scientists and Letters of the Nineteenth Century," *Journal of Abnormal and Social Psychology* 31 (1936): 20–35.

17 **To conclude this section:** Malcolm Gladwell, *Outliers: The Story of Success* (New York: Little, Brown, 2008), 21–25.

21 **Now consider the following feat of memory:** K. A. Ericsson, W. G. Chase, and S. Faloon, "Acquisition of Memory Skill," *Science* 208 (1980): 1181–82; Geoff Colvin, *Talent Is Overrated: What Really Separates World-Class Performers from Everybody Else* (New York: Penguin, 2008), 36–37.

24 **"[W]hen he heard the digits":** Colvin, *Talent Is Overrated*, 46.

25 **a devastatingly simple experiment:** W. G. Chase and H. A. Simon "Perception in Chess," *Cognitive Psychology* 4 (1973): 55–81; Chase and Simon, "The Mind's Eye in Chess," in *Visual Information Processing*, ed. Chase, 215–81. Chase and Simon were building on the pioneering work of A. D. de Groot.

29 **I am standing in a room at Liverpool John Moores University:** Much of Mark Williams's work at Liverpool John Moores University on perceptual expertise in sport is contained in A. Mark Williams and Paul Ward, "Perceptual Expertise: Development in Sport," in *Expert Performance in Sports: Advances in Research*

on Sport Expertise, ed. Janet L. Starkes and K. Anders Ericsson, 219–50 (Champaign, Ill.: Human Kinetics, 2003). Further excellent analysis is contained in David A. Rosenbaum, Jason S. Augustyn, Rajal G. Cohen, and Steven A. Jax, "Perceptual-Motor Expertise," in Ericsson et al., *Cambridge Handbook of Expertise.*

33 **visual function of elite and non-elite soccer players was tested:** P. Ward, A. M. Williams, and D. F. C. Loran, "The Development of Visual Function in Elite and Sub-elite Soccer Players," *International Journal of Sports Vision* 6 (2000): 1–11.

37 **"The most important differences are not at the lowest levels of cells or muscle groups":** K. Anders Ericsson, "Development of Elite Performance and Deliberate Practice: An Update from the Perspective of the Expert Performance Approach," in Starkes and Ericsson, *Expert Performance in Sports.*

40 **There is a simple house fire:** Gary Klein's research on the firefighters and nurses is contained in his book *Sources of Power: How People Make Decisions* (Cambridge, Mass.: MIT Press, 1999)

44 **"One key trait the study found":** Colvin, *Talent Is Overrated,* 97.

44 **General Problem Solver:** The program was developed by Herbert Simon, J. C. Shaw, and Allen Newell.

44 **"The most important ingredient":** Bruce G. Buchanan, Randall Davis, and Edward A. Feigenbaum, "Expert Systems: A Perspective from Computer Science," in Ericsson et al., *Cambridge Handbook of Expertise.*

46 **"Although it is tempting":** Paul J. Feltovich, Michael J. Prietula, and K. Anders Ericsson, "Studies of Expertise from Psychological Perspectives," in Ericsson et al., *Cambridge Handbook of Expertise.*

47 **"Had I been playing the same game":** Garry Kasparov's quote about how he would have drawn had he been playing against a very strong human is taken from a match commentary written for *USA Today.*

49 **In robot soccer, for example, positions on the pitch:** The complexity of robot soccer can be gleaned from Jeffrey Johnson and Blaine A. Price, *Complexity Science and Representation in Robot Soccer,* Lecture Notes in Computer Science 3020 (Berlin: Springer, 2004).

49 **"Gretzky doesn't look like a hockey player":** Charles McGrath, "Elders on Ice," *New York Times Magazine,* March 23, 1997.

50 **circumventing combinatorial explosion via advanced pattern recognition:** This idea does not imply that humans do not rely on sophisticated processing. It is just that the processing takes a different form from that of computers. This has been well articulated by Daniel C. Dennett, "Higher Games," *Technology Review*, September/October 1997.

53 **"Deep Blue's general knowledge of chess":** American Physical Society, "This Month in Physics History: February 1996: Deep Blue vs. Gary Kasparov," *APS News* 11, no. 2 (2002): 2.

2. MIRACULOUS CHILDREN?

56 **"Mozart's father":** Geoff Colvin, *Talent Is Overrated: What Really Separates World-Class Performers from Everybody Else* (New York: Penguin, 2008). Colvin also uses the experiences of Tiger Woods to demonstrate the myth of the child prodigy.

58 **Earl Woods was a former baseball player:** The lengthy description of the early life of Tiger Woods is condensed from Earl Woods with Pete McDaniel, *Training a Tiger: A Father's Guide to Raising a Winner* (New York: William Morrow, 1997).

60 **Two years before Venus Williams was born:** The description of the Williams sisters is condensed from various interviews involving Richard, Serena, and Venus, along with numerous books on the Williams sisters.

64 **On April 19, 1967, Laszlo Polgar:** In addition to my personal interviews of Laszlo Polgar and his three daughters, extra information was gained from Cathy Forbes, *The Polgar Sisters: Training or Genius?* (New York: Henry Holt, 1992), as well as Susan Polgar, *Breaking Through: How the Polgar Sisters Changed the Game of Chess* (London: Everyman Chess, 2005).

71 **How good are you at mental arithmetic?:** The current evidence on the nature of calculating ability is brilliantly summarized in Brian Butterworth, "Mathematical Expertise," in Ericsson et al., *Cambridge Handbook of Expertise*.

74 **"There is a blackboard in our kitchen":** Sarah Flannery with

David Flannery, *In Code: A Mathematical Journey* (Chapel Hill, N.C.: Algonquin Books, 2001), 3.

74 **"Calculators from an early age":** Butterworth, "Mathematical Expertise," 561.

3. THE PATH TO EXCELLENCE

77 **How many hours have you spent driving your car?:** Excellent surveys of the principles of purposeful practice can be found in K. Anders Ericsson and N. Charness, "Expert Performance: Its Structure and Acquisition," *American Psychologist* 49, no. 8 (1994): 725–47; and Ericsson, Krampe, and Tesch-Romer, "Role of Deliberate Practice."

78 **This is why (as dozens of studies have shown) length of time in many occupations:** Studies showing that mere experience does not lead to improved performance (unless guided by the principles of purposeful practice) include Robyn M. Dawes, *House of Cards: Psychology and Psychotherapy Built on a Myth* (New York: Free Press, 1994); S. M. Doane, J. W. Pelligrino, and R. L. Klatzky, "Expertise in a Computer Operating System," *Human-Computer Interaction* 5 (1990): 267–304; and J. Shanteau and T. R. Stewart, "Why Study Expert Decision Making? Some Historical Perspectives and Comments," in *Organizational Behavior and Human Decision Processes* 53, no. 1 (1992): 95–106.

87 **"One reason [for the success of futsal] lies in the math":** Daniel Coyle's absorbing account of his examination of futsal is in his fascinating book *The Talent Code* (New York: Bantam, 2009), 24–29.

89 **"phenomenal"** (footnote): Kuper and Szymanski's research into the factors underpinning success in international soccer is in their excellent *Soccernomics: Why England Loses, Why Germany and Brazil Win, and Why the U.S., Japan, Australia, Turkey—and Even Iraq—Are Destined to Become the Kings of the World's Most Popular Sport* (New York: Nation Books, 2009).

92 **how the body and mind can be radically altered:** An excellent summary of the research on the plasticity of the brain can be found in Nicole M. Hill and Walter Schneider, "Brain Changes in the De-

velopment of Expertise: Neuroanatomical and Neurophysiological Evidence about Skill-Based Adaptations," in Ericsson et al., *Cambridge Handbook of Expertise*. The most accessible and readable account of the importance of myelin is in Coyle, *Talent Code*.

98 **But careful study has shown that creative innovation follows a very precise pattern:** The finding that creativity emerges from rigorous practice can be found in K. Anders Ericsson, "Creative Expertise as Superior Reproducible Performance: Innovative and Flexible Aspects of Expert Performance," *Psychological Inquiry* 10 (1999): 329–33.

98 **Take Pablo Picasso:** For a great summary of the research, including detail on the life and works of Picasso, see Robert W. Weisberg, "Modes of Expertise in Creative Thinking," in Ericsson et al., *Cambridge Handbook of Expertise*.

101 *provided the perfect conditions for feedback:* The importance of feedback can be seen across the essays in Ericsson et al., *Cambridge Handbook of Expertise*. For excellent studies relating to the application of feedback to medicine, see Dawes, *House of Cards*; and K. Anders Ericsson, "Deliberate Practice and the Acquisition and Maintenance of Expert Performance in Medicine and Related Domains," *Academic Medicine* 79 (2004): S70–S81.

103 **Think about an amateur golfer:** The application of the principles of purposeful practice in golf can be found in K. Anders Ericsson, "The Path to Expert Golf Performance: Insights from the Masters on How to Improve Performance by Deliberate Practice," in *Optimizing Performance in Golf*, ed. P. R. Thomas, 1–57 (Brisbane, Australia: Australian Academic Press, 2001).

105 **"I never hit a shot":** Jack Nicklaus with Ken Bowden, *Golf My Way*, 79.

109 **Sport is, to use the jargon of economics, a *zero-sum game*:** For an introduction to zero-sum games and other aspects of game theory see Robert Gibbons, *Game Theory for Applied Economists* (Princeton, N.J.: Princeton University Press, 1992).

4. MYSTERIOUS SPARKS AND LIFE-CHANGING MIND-SETS

113 **"Camp was real competitive":** This is one of a series of fascinating interviews Marlo Thomas conducted for her book *The Right Words*

at the Right Time (New York: Atria, 2002), which shows how chance events can have a huge influence on personal development.

115 **what psychologist Michael Rousell calls a spontaneous influence event:** See Michael A. Rousell, *Sudden Influence: How Spontaneous Events Shape Our Lives* (Westport, Conn.: Praeger, 2007).

117 **In 2003, Greg Walton and Geoffrey Cohen:** Walton and Cohen, "Mere Belonging," unpublished manuscript, 2006.

119 **The rapid escalation in numbers over time:** On how single sparks ignited such powerful motivational responses among Russian tennis players and South Korean golfers, see chapter 5 of Coyle, *Talent Code.*

120 **"Se Ri Pak fulfilled all the bright promise":** Joe Concannon, "Major Accomplishment for Pak in LPGA Event," *Boston Globe*, May 18, 1998.

121 **"Note that in each case the bloom grew":** Coyle, *Talent Code*, 99–100.

123 **the groundbreaking research of Carol Dweck:** Carol S. Dweck, *Self-Theories: Their Role in Motivation, Personality, and Development* (Philadelphia: Taylor and Francis/Psychology Press, 2000). For a very readable introduction, see Dweck, *Mindset: The New Psychology of Success* (New York: Random House, 2006).

124 **"Maybe the most striking thing":** Dweck, *Self-Theories*, 7–9.

125 **"We saw that the students":** Ibid., 9–10.

129 **In 1998, Carol Dweck and a colleague took four hundred fifth-graders:** This research is in Andrei Cimpian et al., "Subtle Linguistic Cues Impact Children's Motivation," *Psychological Science* 18 (2007): 314–16.

140 **"Enron was the ultimate 'talent' company":** Malcolm Gladwell, "The Talent Myth," *New Yorker*, July 22, 2002. See also the documentary film *The Smartest Guys in the Room.*

5. THE PLACEBO EFFECT

156 **But Beecher was not the first doctor to have been astonished by the placebo effect:** For a brilliantly written introduction to the placebo effect, see Ben Goldacre, *Bad Science* (London: Fourth Estate, 2008). Henry Beecher's research on the subject is in "The Powerful Placebo," *Journal of the American Medical Association* 159, no. 17 (1955):

1602–06. See also P. Skrabanek and J. McCormick, "Peter Parker," in *Fads and Fallacies in Medicine* (Amherst, N.Y.: Prometheus, 1990).

156 **In 1972 an experiment was conducted:** Barry Blackwell, Saul S. Bloomfield, and C. Ralph Buncher, "Demonstration to Medical Students of Placebo Responses and Non-drug Factors," *Lancet* 1, no. 763 (June 1972): 1279–82.

159 **the actively religious have significantly better health outcomes:** For a superb introduction to the relationship between religious beliefs and medical outcomes, see Anne Harrington, "Uneasy Alliances: The Faith Factor in Medicine; the Health Factor in Religion," in *Science, Religion, and the Human Experience*, ed. James D. Proctor (New York: Oxford University Press, 2005). The survey on kibbutzim (footnote) is in J. D. Kark et al., "Psychosocial Factors among Members of Religious and Secular Kibbutzim," *Israeli Journal of Medical Science* 32, nos. 3–4 (1996): 185–94.

162 **formally studying whether and how religious belief impacts performance:** I am indebted to Nick J. Watson and Daniel R. Czech for their excellent summary of the current research on religious beliefs and sports, "The Use of Prayer in Sport: Implications for Sports Psychology Consulting," *Athletic Insight* 7, no. 4 (2005). See also D. R. Czech and K. L. Burke, "An Exploratory Investigation of Athletes' Perceptions of Christian Prayer in Sport," *International Journal of Sport* (in press); as well as D. R. Czech et al., "The Experience of Christian Prayer in Sport—An Existential Phenomenological Investigation," *Journal of Psychology and Christianity* 2 (2004): 1–19.

162 **Jeong-Keun Park of Hoseo University:** J. Park, "Coping Strategies Used by Korean National Athletes," *Sport Psychologist* 14, no. 1 (2000): 63–80.

165 **"Doubt is the fundamental cause of error in sports":** For the elimination of doubt in golf, see W. Timothy Gallwey, *The Inner Game of Golf* (New York: Random House, 1998).

169 **To win, one must surgically remove doubt:** For a survey of the often benign effects of irrational optimism, see David A. Armor and Shelley E. Taylor, "When Predictions Fail: The Dilemma of Unrealistic Optimism," in *Heuristics and Biases: The Psychology of Intuitive Judge-*

ment, ed. Thomas Gilovich, Dale Griffin, and Daniel Kahneman (Cambridge, England: Cambridge University Press, 2002), 334–47.

173 **"To discover a new placebo":** Quote from Nicholas Humphrey, "Great Expectations: The Evolutionary Psychology of Faith Healing and the Placebo Effect," chap. 19 in *The Mind Made Flesh: Essays from the Frontiers of Evolution and Psychology* (New York: Oxford University Press, 2003).

176 **the term *doublethink*:** George Orwell, *1984* (New York: Signet Classic, 1950), 214. The malleability of human beliefs is a central theme of *1984*. It is also described in graphic and often gripping detail in *When Prophecy Fails*, a classic book in social psychology by Leon Festinger, Henry Riecken, and Stanley Schachter (New York: Harper, 1956).

177 **Psychologists took one hundred participants and divided them randomly into two groups:** R. Buehler and D. Griffin, "Getting Things Done: The Impact of Predictions on Task Completion," paper presented at the annual meeting of the American Psychological Association, Toronto, Canada, August 1996.

6. THE CURSE OF CHOKING AND HOW TO AVOID IT

191 **Russell Poldrack, a neuroscientist at UCLA:** Poldrack et al., "The Neural Correlates of Motor Skill Automaticity," *Journal of Neuroscience* 25, no. 22 (June 2005): 5356–64.

192 **This situation has been re-created by Robert Gray:** Gray, "Attending to the Execution of a Complex Sensorimotor Skill: Expertise Differences, Choking, and Slumps," *Journal of Experimental Psychology: Applied* 10, no. 1 (March 2004): 42–54.

195 **"Once [a motor skill] is de-chunked"** (footnote): Quoted from Gershon Tenenbaum and Robert C. Eklund, eds., "Why Do Athletes Choke under Pressure?" chap. 19 in *Handbook of Sport Psychology* (Hoboken, N.J.: John Wiley and Sons, 2007). Beilock's chapter is a superb introduction to the whole subject of choking in sports and the explicit monitoring theory.

196 **This outcome has been demonstrated by Charles Kimble:** C. E. Kimble and J. S. Rezabek, "Playing Games before an Audience:

Social Facilitation or Choking?" *Social Behavior and Personality* 20, no. 2 (1992): 115–20.

7. BASEBALL RITUALS, PIGEONS, AND WHY GREAT SPORTSMEN FEEL MISERABLE AFTER WINNING

203 **"If we want to understand the basis of superstition in humans":** Skinner, "'Superstition' in the Pigeon," first published in *Journal of Experimental Psychology* 38 (1947): 168–72. See also B. F. Skinner, *Behavior of Organisms: An Experimental Analysis* (New York: D. Appleton-Century, 1938); and Skinner, *Science and Human Behavior* (New York: Macmillan, 1953).

204 **"Most rituals grow out of exceptionally good performances":** George Gmelch, "Superstition and Ritual in American Baseball," *Elysian Fields Quarterly* 11, no. 3 (1992): 25–36.

207 **according to some devilishly complicated game theory:** For more on game theory and the rationality of superstition, see Drew Fudenberg and David K. Levine, "Superstition and Rational Learning," Harvard Institute of Economic Research Discussion Paper no. 2114. See also Stuart A. Vyse, *Believing in Magic: The Psychology of Superstition* (New York: Oxford University Press, 1997).

211 **In the late 1960s, Paul Ekman, an American psychologist, took a trip to Papua New Guinea:** Ekman, "An Argument for Basic Emotions," *Cognition and Emotion* 6, no. 3 (1992): 169–200.

212 **"Our common emotional heritage":** Dylan Evans, *Emotion: A Very Short Introduction* (New York: Oxford University Press, 2001).

8. OPTICAL ILLUSIONS AND X-RAY VISION

217 **Take a look at the Charlie Chaplin mask:** Richard Gregory, "Knowledge and Perception in Illusion," *Philosophical Transactions of the Royal Society of London Series B* 352 (1997): 1121–28. See also Gregory's analyses of perception in "Perceptual Illusions and Brain Models," *Proceedings of the Royal Society of London Series B* 171 (1968): 179–296; and *Concepts and Mechanisms of Perception* (London: Duckworth, 1974).

219 **just how much work the brain does in perception:** For a brilliant introduction to various quirky phenomena and what they say about perception and much else, see Graham Lawton, "Mind Tricks: Six Ways to Explore Your Brain," *New Scientist*, September 19, 2007.

219 **"Do you understand what I'm trying to say?":** Makio Kashino, "Phonemic Restoration: The Brain Creates Missing Speech Sounds," *Acoustical Science and Technology* 27, no. 6 (2006): 318–21.

220 **"He heard a voice":** For a fascinating and detailed description of Bradford's case, see R. L. Gregory and J. G. Wallace, "Recovery from Early Blindness: A Case Study," in *Experimental Psychology Society Monograph No. 2* (London: Heffer, 1963).

221 **a series of distinct words separated by tiny gaps of silence:** For more on the mechanics of perception and what it says about consciousness, see Daniel C. Dennett, *Consciousness Explained* (Boston: Little, Brown, 1991). For an alternative view, see M. R. Bennett and P. M. S. Hacker, *Philosophical Foundations of Neuroscience* (Oxford, England: Blackwell, 2003).

221 **"Perception is thoroughly permeated by our concepts":** P. F. Strawson, "Perception and Its Objects," in *Perception and Identity: Essays Presented to A. J. Ayer*, ed. G. F. Macdonald (London: Macmillan, 1979).

222 **Clinicians with long experience are able to make better diagnoses:** The superior perceptual abilities of medical experts is described in Michelene T. H. Chi, "Laboratory Methods for Assessing Experts' and Novices' Knowledge," and Geoff Norman et al., "Expertise in Medicine and Surgery," both in Ericsson et al., *Cambridge Handbook of Expertise*.

223 **chick spotters:** See Richard Horsey, "The Art of Chicken Sexing" University College London Working Papers in Linguistics 14 (2002), www.phon.ucl.ac.uk/home/PUB/WPL/02papers/horsey.pdf.

226 **more than half the participants failed to spot the guy in the ape costume:** D. J. Simons and C. Chabris, "Gorillas in Our Midst: Sustained Inattentional Blindness for Dynamic Events," *Perception* 28, no. 9 (1999): 1059–74.

227 **a student walking through campus is asked for directions by a passerby:** D. J. Simons and D. T. Levin, "Failure to Detect Changes

to People during a Real-World Interaction," *Psychonomic Bulletin and Review* 5 (1998): 644–49.

228 **Eastern Air Lines Flight 401 has just taken off:** See "Crash of Eastern Airlines Flight 401," http://freshgasflow.com/flight401 .htm. See also Rob and Sarah Elder, *Crash* (New York: Atheneum, 1977). There is an excellent documentary about the crash called *Fatal Attraction* in the Air Crash Investigation series.

229 **"Well ah, tower, this is Eastern, ah, 401":** For the full cockpit voice recorder transcript, see http://aviation-safety.net/investiga tion/cvr/transcripts/cvr_ea401.php.

9. DRUGS IN SPORT, SCHWARZENEGGER MICE, AND THE FUTURE OF MANKIND

236 **doped with Oral-Turinabol over a twenty-year period:** For accounts of doping in East Germany, see Werner W. Franke and Brigitte Berendonk, "Hormonal Doping and Androgenization of Athletes: A Secret Program of the German Democratic Republic Government," Doping in Sport Symposium, www.clinchem.org/ cgi/content/full/43/7/1262. See also Steven Ungerleider, *Faust's Gold: Inside the East Germany Doping Machine* (New York: Thomas Dunne Books, 2001).

240 **"It is as easy to evade the testers":** Mark Fainaru-Wada and Lance Williams, *Game of Shadows: Barry Bonds, BALCO, and the Steroids Scandal That Rocked Professional Sports* (New York: Gotham, 2007).

241 **According to Julian Savulescu:** Savulescu's views are contained in a series of papers, including "Why We Should Allow Performance Enhancing Drugs in Sport," *British Journal of Sports Medicine* 38 (December 2004): 666–70; J. Savulescu and B. Foddy, "Performance Enhancement and the Spirit of Sport: Is There Good Reason to Allow Doping?" in *Principles of Healthcare Ethics*, ed. Ashcroft et al. (Chichester, England: Wiley, 2007); and J. Savulescu and B. Foddy, "Good Sport, Bad Sport: Why We Should Legalise Drugs in the Olympics," in *The Best Australian Sportswriting 2004* (Melbourne, Australia: Black, 2005).

247 **genetically modified athletes are already among us:** For more on gene transfer technology and sport, see Andy Miah, *Genetically Modified Athletes* (London: Routledge, 2004).

247 **These are deep ethical waters:** For an exemplary account of the morality of enhancement with regard to sport and much more, see John Harris, *Enhancing Evolution* (Princeton, N.J.: Princeton University Press, 2007). For an alternative view, see Michael J. Sandel, *The Case Against Perfection* (Cambridge, Mass.: Harvard University Press, 2007). See also John Broome, *Weighing Lives* (New York: Oxford University Press, 2004).

250 **the morality of enhancement:** For a discussion of the ethical difference between enhancements for positional and for inherent reasons, see Harris, *Enhancing Evolution*.

10. ARE BLACKS SUPERIOR RUNNERS?

257 **"no white, Asian or *East African* runner":** Jon Entine, "The Story Behind the Amazing Success of Black Athletes," Run-Down, http://run-down.com/guests/je_black_athletes_p1.php. See also Jon Entine, *Taboo: Why Black Athletes Dominate Sports and Why We're Afraid to Talk About It* (New York: Public Affairs, 2000).

261 **Some scientists have resorted to smuggling:** For an excellent survey of epidemiological and other issues surrounding race, see Kenan Malik, *Strange Fruit: Why Both Sides Are Wrong in the Race Debate* (Oxford, England: Oneworld, 2008).

263 **In 1972 Richard Lewontin:** Lewontin, "The Apportionment of Human Diversity," *Evolutionary Biology* 6 (1972): 391–98.

265 **This does not quite imply** (footnote): A. W. Edwards, "Human Genetic Diversity: Lewontin's Fallacy," *BioEssays* 25, no. 88 (August 2003): 798–801.

266 **The question we are left with:** An important—but rather technical—point of logic should be made here. We have assumed from the beginning of this chapter that one of the reasons that *individuals* have different ability levels in a simple sport such as running is because of genetics. But if this is true, must we not—as a matter of logical necessity—accept that the differences

in ability levels between *population groups* are also genetically determined?

The surprising answer is: No. To understand why, imagine a sack of genetically diverse seed that is randomly divided into two bunches. Bunch A is grown in a field with good lighting and Bunch B in a field with poor lighting. The differences in height between the seedlings in Bunch A will be exclusively genetic, since they have all been subjected to the same environmental conditions. The same is true of Bunch B. But the difference in the average height between Bunch A and Bunch B is exclusively environmental—caused by the different lighting conditions.

This tells us that the variation *within* populations has no logical connection with the variation *between* populations. Or, to put it another way, even if we know that the differences in athletic ability between individuals is driven by genetics, there is no reason to infer from this that the difference in ability levels between population groups is also driven by genetics. The question remains an open one.

266 **John Manners, an expert:** Manners's theory is presented in "Raiders from the Rift Valley," in *East African Running: Towards a Cross-Disciplinary Perspective*, ed. Yanni Pitsiladis et al. (New York: Routledge, 2007).

276 **This explanation becomes compelling:** Marianne Bertrand and Sendhil Mullainathan, "Are Emily and Greg More Employable Than Lakisha and Jamal?: A Field Experiment on Labor Market Discrimination," *American Economic Review* 94 (September 2004): 991–1013.

277 **"[Obama] has a debt to great American athletes":** Simon Barnes, "From Jesse Owens to Barack Obama, via Muhammad Ali and Tiger Woods," *Times* (London), November 7, 2008.

282 **Between 2001 and 2005 Jeff Stone:** Links to much of the superb research of Jeff Stone and his colleagues can be found at the University of Arizona's Social Psychology of Sport Web site, www.u.arizona.edu/~jeffs/sportlab.html.

285 **"In matters of race":** Claude Steele, "Thin Icc: Stereotype Threat and Black College Students," *Atlantic Monthly*, August 1999.

Index

Abrahams, Harold, 210
Agassi, Andre, 134
Alekhine, Alexander, 24, 69
Ali, Muhammad, 151, 154, 163, 179, 277, 280–81
Alser, Hans, 121
Amaechi, John, 89–90
amnesia, expert-induced, 36, 190
Anand, Viswanathan, 70
Andrews, Paul, 7
anticipation, 31
anticlimax, of winning, 209–10, 213
Arakawa, Shizuka, 85–86, 127
Ariely, Dan, 158
arithmetic, 71–75
artificial intelligence, 44, 52
Ashburn, Richie, 203
Ashison, Gideon, 143–44
Atherton, Mike, 205–6
attention:
  capacity for, 227
  and choking, 191, 192–93, 196–99
  inattentional blindness, 226–32
attitude, 133–36
automaticity, 95
autopilot, mindless practice on, 78–79

Bale, John, 259
Barnes, John, 281
Barnes, Simon, 277
Barnsley, Roger, 17–18
baseball:
  age-based selection in, 18
  superstition in, 202–5
basketball, and height, 52n

Bawden, Mark, 199
Beatles, 9, 99–100
Beckett, Samuel, 128n
Beckham, David, 61–62, 154
Beecher, Henry, 155–56
Beilock, Sian, 195n
beliefs:
  aimed at whatever works, 178
  changing, 173–74, 199
  health benefits of, 159
  as placebo, 151, 158–60, 173–74
  potency of, 151, 153, 154
  taking the positives, 175
Bengtsson, Stellan, 121
Benjamin, Joel, 53
Benson, Herbert, 159
Berrigan, Daniel, 114
Bertrand, Marianne, 276
Billington, Bradley, 8
Binet, Alfred, 72
birth dates, skewed, 17–19, 20
birthdays, shared, 118, 122
Biwott, Amos, 268
Bjorkman, Jonas, 174
black athletes, 255–86
  African American, 260, 266, 274–77
  altitude training of, 272–73
  genetic variation in, 263–66
  Jamaicans, 260, 266, 274–77
  Kenyan, 257, 258–60, 267–74
  and racial stereotypes, 282–86
  sporting success of, 277–82
Boggs, Wade, 203, 205
Bollettieri, Nick, 133–36
Bolt, Usain, 255–56

Boston Marathon, 15
Bradford, Sidney, 220–21
brain:
  basal ganglia, 191
  and choking, 188–93, 194, 196
  neural connections in, 93
  and perception, 218–21
  plasticity of, 93
  prefrontal cortex, 191
  psychological reversion, 195, 199
Brazil, soccer players in, 86–89
Breuer, Grit, 246
Britain, governance of, 51–52
British Cycling Team, 91, 136–37, 208–9
British Olympic movement, 136–37
Brunza, Jay, 172
Buchanan, Bruce, 44
Buckner, Bill, 184
Butterworth, Brian, 74, 75
Butterworth, Jeffrey, 108–9

Campese, David, 202
Capriati, Jennifer, 61
Carre, Matt, 62
Cavalli-Sforza, Luigi Luca, 265
cell regeneration, 247
central nervous system, 36
Chambers, Dwain, 240
Chaplin, Charlie, mask, 217–18, 219
Chariots of Fire (film), 210
Charters, Peter, 5–6, 10, 92
Chase, William, 15–16, 21, 25
chess:
  chunking information in, 30, 48, 49
  decision making in, 47–48, 49, 51
  ELO ratings, 38
  escalating variables in, 45, 47
  feedback loops in, 102–3
  Kasparov vs. Deep Blue, 37–39,
    46–47, 52–53
  memory in, 24–26, 46–47
  midgame theory, 103
  Polgar family, 66–71
  and practice, 48, 66–71
  studying historic games, 103
  ten years' practice in, 15–16

chick spotters, 223–24
child prodigies, 55–71
  hours of practice, 14, 63, 64
  internal motivation of, 63–64, 67
  mental math, 71–75
  Mozart, 55–58, 63
  Polgar theories, 64–71
  Williams sisters, 59–61
  Woods, 58–59
China, table tennis in, 82, 91, 136
choking:
  author's experience, 181–84,
    199–200
  brain systems in, 188–93, 194, 196
  capacity for, 196
  as common phenomenon, 185
  in complex tasks, 195–96
  and focus, 191, 192–93, 196–99
  in golf, 185–88, 193–94
  names for, 184
  overcoming, 198–99
  psychological reversion in, 195
  in tennis, 194–95
  under pressure, 184-85, 200n
chunking, 24, 30, 191
  and de-chunking, 195n
  and decision patterns, 48, 49
  and kinesiology, 31–32
Clifford, Simon, 87, 88
Cohen, Geoffrey, 117–18, 119
Collier, Sue, 7
Colvin, Geoff, 56, 85–86
  Talent Is Overrated, 21–22, 44
combinatorial explosion, 45, 47, 49–50
complexity, 50, 97–100
concentration, 78, 83, 92
Conte, Victor, 240
Courier, Jim, 134
Coyle, Daniel, 118, 121
  The Talent Code, 87–88, 119
creativity:
  lightning bolt theory of, 98–99
  and purposeful practice, 98
  in technical innovation, 100
cricket, 31, 205–6
Cromwell, Dean, 279

cultural theory of emotion, 212–13
cycling, 91, 136–37, 208–9
Czech, D. R., 163

Darwin, Charles, 10, 278
Davis, Randall, 44
Davis, Steve, 200
Dawkins, Richard, 151
decision making:
  in chess, 47–48, 49, 51
  by chunking patterns, 48, 49
  combinatorial explosion, 47, 50
  by computer, 44
  and experience, 51
  by firefighters, 40–43, 44–45, 47, 51
  by hospital nurses, 41, 43, 78
  independent, 63
  and intuition, 47
  knowledge in, 43, 51
  pattern-recognition theory, 48
  on perceptual cues, 43
  research in, 40–43, 51–52
  in sports, 45, 47
  talent in, 43–44
Deep Blue (chess), 37–39, 46–47, 52–53
Devi, Shakuntala, 71
doctors, diagnostic accuracy of, 109
doublethink, 176–77
doubt, 164–66, 168–69, 184
Douglas, Desmond, 28–29, 32–34
  decisions made by, 41–42
  practice hours of, 33–34
  "sixth sense" of, 42
Dweck, Carol:
  on Enron, 142
  talent studies of, 123–29
  on words of praise, 129–32, 135,
    137–38, 145

East Germany, steroid use in,
    233–40, 243
economics, author's study of, 115–16
education, lowering standards in, 132
Edwards, A. W., 265n
Edwards, Jonathan, 149–51, 152–53,
    154, 163, 179

effort-based praise, 130–32, 135, 138,
    144–46
Ekman, Paul, 211–12
Elbert, Thomas, 93
Enron, 138–43
Entine, Jon, 257–61, 275–76
Ericsson, Anders, 92–93, 108, 127
  on deliberate practice, 80
  and iceberg illusion, 22
  memory studies of, 21, 23, 31
  performance studies of, 11–14, 16,
    23, 36–37
eureka moments, 98
Evans, Dylan, *Emotion*, 212
evolution, 15
  of emotions, 212–13
  mutations in, 106
  and race, 278
  and superstition, 207
Ewald, Manfred, 238, 239, 251
excellence:
  capacity for, 111
  citadels of, 133–38
  combinatorial explosion in attain-
    ment of, 45
  in competition, 154
  in complex tasks, 94
  and experience, 45–46
  long-term process to, 15–16, 122,
    129
  and practice, 13, 15, 17, 45–46,
    65–71, 77
  and talent, 17, 111–12
  ten years' minimum to, 15–16
experience:
  in decision making, 51
  and deep concentration, 78
  and excellence, 45–46
  ten-year rule, 16, 63
expert-induced amnesia, 36
expertise, science of, 32
extrasensory perception (ESP), 41, 42

failure:
  embracing, 128
  fear of, 142

Faldo, Nick, 177, 179, 186, 187, 193
Fard, W. D., 151–52
Federer, Roger, 10, 11, 31–32, 35, 36, 50, 222
feedback loops, 101–3
Feigenbaum, Edward, 44
Feltovich, Paul, 46
Ferguson, Sir Alex, 213–14
Ferguson, George, 263
figure skating, 83–86, 127
firefighters:
  concentration needed by, 78
  decisions made by, 40–43, 44–45, 47, 51
  knowledge of, 222
Fischer, Bobby, 38, 63, 69
Flannery, Susan, 73–74, 75
focus:
  and choking, 191, 192–93, 196–99
  misplaced, 194
Foreman, George, 151
Fore tribe, 211–12
Fosbury, Dick, 97
Franke, Werner, 246
Franz, Peter, 181
futsal (*futebol de salão*), 86–89

Galileo, 249
Gallas, William, 208
Gallwey, Timothy, *The Inner Game of Golf,* 165, 176
Galton, Francis, *Hereditary Genius,* 10
Gamm, Rüdiger, 71–72, 73, 94
Garrett, Henry Edward, 278–79
Gates, Bill, 9
Gebrselassie, Haile, 269, 270
General Electric (GE), 44
General Problem Solver, 44
genetic enhancement, 245–49
Gibson, Althea, 278
Gladwell, Malcolm:
  on Enron, 140, 143
  Outliers, 9, 16, 17–18
Gmelch, George, 204–5
Goldacre, Ben, 156, 178

golf:
  choking in, 185–88, 193–94
  feedback in, 103–6
  motivational spark in, 119–21
  practice in, 14, 58–59
  ten years to excellence in, 16
  U.S. Open (2008), 169–71, 177
Gordon, Alison, 7
gorilla test, 226–28
Graff, Steffi, 194
Gray, Robert, 192
Gregory, Richard, 219
Gretzky, Wayne, 49–50, 53, 224

Hamm, Mia, 91, 114–15
hand-eye coordination, 36
Hansen, Steen, 145
Hardy, Fred, 260
Hargrove, Mike, 203
Harpending, Henry, 264–65
Harrington, Anne, 160, 161, 165
Harris, John, 247, 249
Harvard, John, 205
Hayes, John, *The Complete Problem Solver,* 16
Heaps, Simon, 121–22
Henman, Tim, 174–75
high jump, 97
Hines, Jim, 256
Hingis, Martina, 134
Hoch, Scott, 193–94
Hodder, Keith, 7
Honecker, Erich, 238
Höppner, Manfred, 237, 238, 239, 251
Howe, Michael, *Genius Explained,* 57
Hsu, Feng-Hsuing, 37–39
human limitations, 96–100
Humphrey, Nicholas, 173–74
Hussain, Nasser, 206

IBM, and Deep Blue, 37–39, 52–53
iceberg illusion, 22
ice hockey:
  birthdays of players, 17–18, 20

combinatorial explosion in, 49, 50
Gretzky's genius in, 49–50, 224
Immelt, Jeff, 44, 53
innovation, 96–100
instinct, for sports, 27–28, 31
intelligence:
  and praise, 130–32, 138
  and talent myth, 123–29
intuition, 47
irrational optimism, 168–74
Ivanisevic, Goran, 202

Jackson, Nathan (fict.), 117–18
James (table tennis), 190–91, 192
Jankovic, Jelena, 134
Jeffries, Jim, 280
Johnson, Ben, 238
Johnson, Jack, 280
Johnson, Zach, 172–73
Jordan, Michael, 128
Juninho (soccer), 86

Kark, Jeremy, 159n
Karpov, Anatoly, 38, 69, 70
Kashino, Makio, 219
Kasparov, Garry, 37–39, 46–47, 50, 52–53, 69, 70, 224
Keen, Peter, 63, 136–37
Keen, Trinko, 167
Keino, Kip, 273, 282
Kenny G, 97
Kenya, runners from, 257, 258–60, 267–74
Kimble, Charles, 196–97
kinesiology, 31–32
Kirsty (figure skater), 83–84
Klein, Gary:
  on chess decisions, 47–48
  on decision making, 39–43
  Sources of Power, 40–41, 53
Knight, Darius, 143–46
knowledge:
  building, 94
  in complex tasks, 94
  in decision making, 43, 51
  development of, 46

and memory retrieval, 47
and perception, 221
power of, 37–39, 53
top-down, 219–21, 225–26
Kocher, Theodor, 156
Korea, golfers from, 119–21
Kosashvili, Yona, 69
Kournikova, Anna, 120, 134
Krause, Ute, 251–53
Krieger, Heidi/Andreas, 233–39, 251–53
Kroen, Bill, 95
Kuper, Simon, 89n

language:
  learning, 48–49
  and perception, 219, 221
Lauren (table tennis player), 188–89, 190–91
Lewontin, Richard, 263–64
Lindsay, Sarah, 197–99
Linnaeus, Carolus, 278
Liszt, Franz, "Feux Follets," 14–15
long-distance runners, 93
Louis, Joe, 277, 280

MacArthur, Daniel, 275
Macci, Rick, 61
Mailer, Norman, 151
Maiyo, Cherono, 268
Manners, John, 266–67
Maradona, Diego, 11
Marks, Jonathan, 262
Martin, Todd, 188
Martinez, Dennis, 203, 204
Marx, Karl, 160
mathematics:
  mastery of, 15, 100
  prodigies of, 71–75
McKinsey consultants, The War for Talent, 140–41
McNabb, Donovan, 282
Mediate, Rocco, 169, 171
memory:
  episodic, 94
  iceberg illusion of, 22

memory *(cont.)*
  of letters, 20–21, 23–24
  of numbers, 21–22, 23, 24, 31, 73
  of patterns, 24
  and practice, 23
  and retrieval, 46–47
mental exercises:
  alphabet, 20–21
  anagrams, 79–80
  gorilla test, 226–28
  optical illusion, 224–25
  perception, 217–18
mental representations, acquired, 37
mental toughness, 128
mental vs. physical success, 36
meritocracy, myth of, 8–11, 19
Michelangelo, 100
Miller, George A., *The Magical Number Seven*, 21
mind-set, fixed vs. growth, 123–29, 134–35, 137, 141–42
mnemonics, 24
motivation:
  by association, 117–23
  internal, 63–64, 67, 115–16
  and mind-sets, 130–32
  mysterious sparks, 113–17, 129
  research into, 117–23
  sustained, 122–23
motor chunking, 191
motor system, control of, 35
Mozart, Wolfgang Amadeus, 55–58, 63, 99
Mullainathan, Sendhil, 276
Murray, Andy, 164
Murray, Jim, 282
muscle memory, 36
music:
  circular breathing in, 97
  finger dexterity in, 93
  practicing, 11–13, 16, 80–81
  rising standards in, 14–15
myelin, 93

Nadal, Rafael, 164, 173

Nandi distance runners, 269–71, 272, 273
Navratilova, Martina, 210
Newton, Isaac, 98
Nick Bollettieri Tennis Academy, 133–36
Nicklaus, Jack, 14, 105, 173
Norman, Greg, 185–88, 193, 194
Norwood, Scott, 188
Novotna, Jana, 194–95
nurses, decisions made by, 41, 43, 78

Obama, Barack, 154, 277
O'Brien, Parry, 97
obsessive-compulsive disorder, 207–8
O'Driscoll, Michael, 8
Ohms, Jim, 203
Olympic Games:
  (1896), 15
  (1900), 15
  (1924), 15
  (1936), 279–80
  (1968), 256, 282
  (2000), 149–51, 181–84
  (2002), 197–99
  (2004), 208–9
  (2008), 63, 136–37, 208, 255–56
  (2014), 83
Omega Club, 6–8, 10, 19
O'Neal, Shaquille, 113–14, 122
one thousand hour rule, 16
Oosterom, Joop van, 75
optical illusion, 224–25
Orwell, George, *1984*, 176–77
Osovnikar, Matic, 256
Owens, Jesse, 279–80

Pak, Se Ri, 119–21, 122
paradigm shifts, 97–100
Park, Inbee, 120
Park, Jeong-Keun, 162–63
pattern recognition, 24, 35, 48, 50
Paul, Saint, 151, 152
Peale, Norman Vincent, *The Power of Positive Thinking*, 161–62, 163–65

Pelé (soccer), 86, 88
Pendleton, Victoria, 208–9
perception:
  and the brain, 218–21
  Chaplin mask, 217–18, 219
  of experts vs. nonexperts, 222–26
  inattentional blindness, 226–32
  optical illusion, 224–25
  and vision, 33, 218–21, 222–26
perceptual cues, 43
performance:
  dignity of, 244
  and practice, 12–17, 80–81
  psychology of, 154
  and religious belief, 162
  research in, 11–14, 16, 23, 36–37
  transformation of, 111
  world-class, 82–83
performance placebo, 165, 177–79
performance psychology, 168
peripheral nervous system, 35
perseverance, 17, 122, 213
Peters, Steve, 209, 210
Phillips, Ken, 188–90
Picasso, Pablo, 98–99
Pickens, Morris, 172
Piérce, Mary, 61
pigeons, conditioning of, 203–4
pilots:
  decisions made by, 43
  inattentional blindness of, 228–32
Pitsiladis, Yannis, 267–72, 273, 275
placebo effect:
  and colors of pills, 156–57
  and doublethink, 172–77
  doubt vs., 164–66, 168–69
  and irrational optimism, 168–74
  mind over matter, 153–58
  packaging and price, 157–58
  positive thinking, 161–62
  and a quiet place, 166–68
  and religion, 151–53, 158–60,
    162–64, 173–74
  sardines, 149–51
  self-belief, 172–73
  in sports, 161–68

  of superstitions, 206
  in World War II, 155–56
poetry, studies of, 99
Poldrack, Russell, 191
Polgar, Judit, 67, 69–70
Polgar, Laszlo, 64–71, 75, 103, 111
Polgar, Sofia, 67, 68–69
Polgar, Susan, 66–68, 70, 75
positive affirmations, 168
positive thinking, 161–62, 163–65
  irrational optimism, 168–74
  research study of, 178–79
Pound, Dick, 243–44
practice:
  acquired mental representations
    in, 37
  on autopilot (mindless), 78–79
  and child prodigies, 57
  and creative innovation, 98
  deliberate, 80
  easy vs. challenging, 80
  end product of, 22
  and excellence, 15, 17, 45–46,
    65–71, 77
  and experience, 46
  one thousand hours per year, 16
  opportunities for, 19
  and performance, 12–17, 80–81
  potential for change via, 23
  and professionalism, 15
  purposeful, 80–81, 85–86, 91, 92,
    94, 96, 98, 110–11, 171–72
  quantity vs. quality of, 80
  ten-thousand-hour rule, 16, 22, 50,
    57, 92, 121, 129
  transformative, 96
praise, and mind-set, 130–32, 135,
  137–38
prayer, 163
President's Council on Bioethics, 244,
  248
Primorac, Zoran, 166
productivity, improving, 110
progress, practice toward, 80–83, 85

Ramanujan, Srinivasa, 73, 74

Ramprakash, Mark, 202
Reid, John, 51
Reisman, Marty, 95, 210
relaxation technique, 167–68
relentlessness, 213
religion, as placebo, 151–53, 158–60,
    162–64, 173–74
response times, 32, 33
retrieval structure, 24
Revlon, Charles, 223
Rivaldo (soccer), 86
Rivelino (soccer), 86
Robinson, Jackie, 277, 280
robots, 50
robot soccer, 49
Roe, Anne, 99
Ronaldinho (soccer), 88
Ronaldo (soccer), 86, 88
Rousell, Michael, 115
Rumelhart, David, 51
Russell, Jack, 205–6

Saltin, Bengt, 273
Sang, Joe, 259
Savins, Paul, 7
Savulescu, Julian, 241, 253
Schwarzenegger, Arnold, 218
Schwarzenegger mice, 245–49
Seirawan, Yasser, 37
Seles, Monica, 63
self-doubt, 164–66, 184
self-help movement, 163
SF, memory feats of, 21–22, 23, 24,
    25, 31
Sharapova, Maria, 134
Shearer, Alan, 164
Sheen, Martin, 114
Shwarzer, Mark, 202
sickle cell anemia, 261–62
Simon, Carly, 114, 122
Simon, Herbert, 15–16, 25, 49
skill building, plateaus in, 95
Skilling, Jeffrey, 138–41
skills, circumstantial, 20
Skinner, B. F., 203–4
Sloboda, John, 14

Smith, Gene, 282
Snead, Sam, 96
snooker, 188, 200
soccer:
    age-based selection in, 18
    expertise in, 34–35
    and futsal, 86–89
    practice, 61–62
    rising standards in, 100
    visual function in, 33
Southgate, Gareth, 196
sparks, motivational, 113–17, 129
Spartak club, Moscow, 7–8
speed, in sports, 32, 34
speed skating, 197–99
spontaneous influence events, 115
sports:
    age-based selection in, 18–19
    combinatorial explosion in, 49, 50
    decision making in, 45, 47
    gene doping in, 246–48
    genetic factors in, 52n
    instincts in, 27–28, 31
    as meritocracy, 9
    placebo effect in, 161–68
    practice in, see practice
    rising standards in, 14–15
    robots in, 50
    simple activities in, 50–51
    speed in, 32, 34
    steroids in, 239–45
    ten years to excellence in, 16
    variables in, 10, 45
    zero-sum games, 109–12
sports science, 29
Springstein, Thomas, 246
standards:
    lowering, 132
    rising, 100
Starkes, Janet, 31–32
Steele, Claude, 285
steroids:
    benefits and costs of, 242–43
    given to German teens, 233–39
Stevenson, Robert Louis, 210
Stewart, Alex, 206

Stich, Michael, 26–27, 30
Stokes, Jimmy, 7
Stone, Jeff, 282, 285
Strawson, Sir Peter, 221
stress management, 163
stroke execution, 35
success:
　hidden logic of, 22
　opportunity for, 10, 17
　and talent myth, 10–11
sumo wrestling, body size as factor
　in, 52n
superstition, 201–8
Sweden, table tennis in, 121
Swindell, Greg, 202–3
Syed, Andrew, 5, 6, 8, 19
Syed, Matthew, 3–8
　anticlimax of victory, 209
　and autobiographical bias, 8–9
　choking in Sydney, 181–84, 194,
　　199–200
　and his brother, 5, 8, 19
Szymanski, Stefan, 89n

table tennis:
　author's experiences in, 3–8, 19–20,
　　81–82, 101–2, 116
　Chinese excellence in, 82, 91, 136
　difficult practice conditions in,
　　143–46
　expertise in, 34–35
　feedback loops in, 101–2
　hours of practicing, 5
　motivational sparks in, 121–22
　multi-ball training in, 82, 92, 101
　number of players in, 3
　players' wrists, 93
　purposeful practice in, 81
　response times in, 28–29, 32
　rising standards in, 100
　service action in, 97
　trajectory of development in,
　　19–20
taking the positives, 174–79
talent:
　in corporate world, 138–43

in decision making, 43–44
and excellence, 17, 111–12
and giving up, 17
and motivational spark, 121
myth of, 10–11, 51, 123–29
as overrated, 20–26
physical, 35
and practice, 13–14
special gifts, 11
what it is, 11–20
talent-based praise, 144–46
taxi drivers, brains of, 93
tennis:
　author's game with Stich, 26–27
　on autopilot, 78–79
　choking in, 194–95
　expertise in, 34–35
　eye-tracking system in, 29–31
　motivational spark in, 120
　perfect timing in, 35–36
　practice in, 59–61
　real, 32
　superstition in, 201–2
　taking the positives, 174–75
　training systems, 133–38
ten-thousand-hour rule, 16, 22, 50,
　57, 92, 121, 129
ten-year rule, 16, 63
Terminator fallacy, 218
Tetris video game, 196–97
Thomas, Marlo, 113, 114
Thomas, Scott, 271
Toseland, James, 210
Tour de France, 241
Touré, Kolo, 208
training systems:
　access to, 92
　applying the lessons of, 106–9
　and attitude, 133–34
　design and construction of, 91
　high altitude, 272–73
　neural connections adapted in, 93
　and physical changes, 93
　rising standards in, 100
transformational moments, 115
Trott, Paul, 7

Tyler, S. W., 80
typists, speed plateaus of, 95, 96

variables, escalation in number of, 45, 47
Velzian, John, 274
Vernacchia, Ralph, 163
visual perception, 33, 218–21, 222–26

WADA (World Anti-Doping Authority), 240, 241-42, 247n
Waldner, Jan-Ove, 97
Walters, Guy, *Berlin Games,* 280
Walton, Greg, 117–18
Weisberg, Robert, 58, 98
Wellman, Andy, 7
Wenger, Arsène, 169, 175n, 179
White, Jimmy, 188
White, John, 204–5
Williams, Doug, 282
Williams, Mark, 30
Williams, Oracene, 60–61
Williams, Richard, 60–61, 81
Williams, Serena, 59–61, 63–64, 114, 202

Williams, Venus, 59–61, 63, 114
Wilson, Connie, 120
winning, anticlimax of, 209–10, 213
win-win games, 110
Wishbow, N., 99
Witt, Karen, 6–7
Woods, Earl, 58-59
Woods, Tiger, 11, 169–73, 176, 179
  early years of, 58-59, 62, 63, 64
  and excellence, 154
  and purposeful practice, 95, 105, 171-72
  and superstition, 202
  in U.S. Open (2008), 169-71
World Series (1986), 184
World War II, placebos in, 155–56
Wright, Ron, 204–5

Xinhua, Chen, 81–82, 92, 101–2, 105

zero-sum games, 109–12, 249–51
Zico (soccer), 86, 88